I0013937

"Advances and Prospect of Big Data Analytics, Artificial Intelligence, Machine Learning and Deep Learning"

By Ajit Kumar Roy

Copyright: akroy@2017

Dedication:

Dedicated to my granddaughter 'ANGANA'

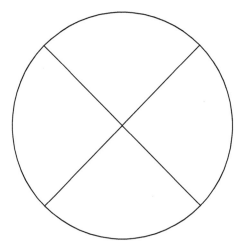

PREFACE

Now we live in a world of data. Big data has been the hottest buzzword across all industries. It's one of those things big companies and startups constantly talk about when people ask what "the next big thing" will be. Data is produced in greater quantities and by more sources than ever before and analyzed faster and with greater sophistication than was imaginable just a few years ago. Every day, new tools are created to turn raw data into information, and information into visual representations. The reach and applicability of big data seem limitless. With so many technology and internet enabled devices all around data is being produced at unprecedented levels globally. Many innovations have been made toward expanding the technological capacity to generate, store, and analyze data from multiple sources and for a multitude of purposes. Individuals, firms, machines, and government agencies produce data at unprecedented rates. Some 2.5 quintillion bytes of data are produced every day, and approximately 90 percent of existing data was produced in the last two years alone. The ever-increasing data footprint provides a range of possibilities for usage by government. "In the last five years, more scientific data has been generated than in the entire history of mankind," says Winston Hide, associate professor of bioinformatics at HSPH. "You can imagine what's going to happen in the next five." And this data isn't simply linear; genetics and proteomics, to name just two fields of study, generate high-dimensional data, which is fundamentally different in scale. In big data lies the potential for revolutionizing everything. Police employing seismology-like data models can predict where crimes will occur and prevent them from happening. Astronomers using the Kepler telescope snag information on 200,000 stars every 30 seconds, which has led to the discovery of the first Earth-like planets outside our solar system. Businesses sifting social networking and supply-chain data dynamically tailor their products to fulfill desires we don't even know we have. The same phenomena are at play in public health. For some time, DNA sequencing has held big data's starring role, after all, a single human genome consists of some 3 billion base pairs of DNA. Researchers at HSPH and across the campus at Harvard are sequencing and analyzing human genomes to ferret out clues to infections, cancer, and non-communicable diseases. Advanced analysis facilitates businesses more of an insight into any organization and production processes, customers and markets.

Artificial intelligence (AI) *is a hot topic right now.* AI is everywhere these days. It's simultaneously heralded as both the greatest thing from driving cars, diagnosing diseases better, and so on and the worst thing imaginable displacing millions of jobs, and a step towards the inevitable AI domination of humans.AI taking off Now because of availability **of** huge amount of data to learn, and the digitization of society is providing the available raw material to fuel its advances Machine learning is often used to build predictive models by extracting patterns from large datasets. These models are used in predictive data analytics applications including price prediction, risk assessment, predicting customer behavior, and document classification. Predictive analytics applications use machine learning to build predictive models for applications including price prediction, risk assessment, and predicting customer behavior. Machine learning is the subfield of computer science that gives computers the ability to learn without being explicitly programmed. Machine learning is using artificial intelligence to allow machines to "learn" without being explicitly programmed. Deep Learning will drive AI adoption into the enterprise. For those still living underneath a rock, it is a fact that Deep Learning is the primary driver and the most important approach to AI. Deep Learning is used as a function evaluation component in a much larger search algorithm.

According to Peter Fader "The real beauty of analytics isn't just collecting a lot of data, but it's figuring out ways to do it in a synergistic manner". According to the survey report, the jobs that are in the jeopardy of getting extinct are the ones that have become repetitive and are most likely to be taken over by Artificial Intelligence (AI) in next five years or so. *These include job profiles such as BPO, manual testing, system maintenance and infrastructure management* etc. In the United States alone, the demand for people with the deep analytical skills in big data including machine learning and advanced statistical analysis could outstrip current projections of supply by 50 to 60 percent. By 2018, as many as 140,000 to 190,000 additional specialists may be required. Also needed an additional 1.5 million managers and analysts with a sharp understanding of how big data can be applied. Companies must step up their recruitment and retention programs, while making substantial investments in the education and training of key data personnel. The greater access to personal information that big data often demands will place a spotlight on another tension, between privacy and convenience.

Against this backdrop, a book entitled *"Advances and Prospect of Big Data Analytics, Artificial Intelligence, Machine Learning and Deep Learning"* is compiled aiming to keep abreast with the latest technological trends for future generation of job seekers. The book with the following chapters is likely to give present scenario of technological advancement as well as outlook to be adopted by stakeholders.

Chapter 1:	*Big Data Trend*
Chapter2:	*Machine Learning*
Chapter-3:	*Artificial Intelligence*
Chapter-4:	*Deep Learning*
Chapter-5:	*Difference between Artificial Intelligence (AI), Machine Learning, and Deep Learning?*

The book will not only give awareness of future trends of the above modern technologies but also motivate readers to tale a right career path.

AJIT KUMAR ROY

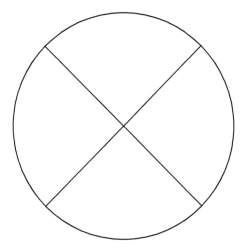

ABOUT THE BOOK

Our ability to generate data has moved light-years ahead of where it was only a few years ago, and the amount of digital information now available to us is simply unimaginable. Big data analytics is the heart of the digital transformation. It provides the ability to analyze data quickly and to transform it into an action plan, to get better insights, to take faster and more accurate decisions, and ultimately have a valuable competitive advantage. Technological advances in storage and computations have enabled cost-effective capture of the informational value of big data in a *timely* manner. Consequently, one observes a proliferation in real-world adoption of analytics that were not economically feasible for large-scale applications prior to the big data era. Petabytes of raw information could provide clues for everything from preventing TB to shrinking health care costs if we can figure out how to use them. Data has indeed become the new currency of the digital economy. According to a new report by digital transformation firm Atos, 40% of businesses are using data analytics in key functions such as sales or marketing, while 23% plan to implement it within the next year. By 2020, 90% of companies intend to do the same. Analytics skills are already in extremely high demand, largely outstripping supply. A study by McKinsey, for one, projects that 'by 2018, the US alone may face a 50% to 60% gap between supply and requisite demand of deep analytic talent.' And this is only going to deepen, with the Bureau of Labor Statistics (BLS) estimating that the number of roles for individuals with this skill set will grow by 30% over the next seven years. Eric Schmidt, executive chairman of Google's parent company Alphabet, for one, recently told CNBC, 'I think a basic understanding of data analytics is incredibly important for this next generation of young people.

In 2017, the term *"Big Data"* continues to gradually fade away, but the Big Data space itself is booming. We are seeing everywhere anecdotal evidence pointing to more mature products, more substantial adoption in

Fortune 1000 companies, and rapid revenue growth for many startups. In the meantime, the froth has indisputably moved to the machine learning and artificial intelligence side of the ecosystem. Machine learning is using artificial intelligence to allow machines to "learn" without being explicitly programmed. Technology giants such as **Google, Apple, and Face book** are already investing their money, effort, and time towards integrating Artificial Intelligence.

Mark Cuban has an even more surprising quote: "Artificial Intelligence, deep learning, machine learning, whatever you are doing if you don't understand it—learn it. Otherwise you are going to be a dinosaur within 3 years". Data analysis is complex and requires both human and machine's working together. IBM, who earned a reported $4billion from Big Data in 2013 and are investing significantly in their Watson Artificial Intelligence and Machine Learning system, recognize this.

According to the survey report, the jobs that are in the jeopardy of getting extinct are the ones that have become repetitive and are most likely to be taken over by Artificial Intelligence (AI) in next five years or so. These include job profiles such as BPO, manual testing, system maintenance and infrastructure management etc. ***A survey reveals that the future of IT lies in Cyber Security, Big Data and Data Science, Big Data Architect, Big Data Engineer, Artificial Intelligence and IoT Architect, and Cloud Architect as these job profiles will be high in demand in the near future.*** In the United States alone, the demand for people with the deep analytical skills in big data including machine learning and advanced statistical analysis could outstrip current projections of supply by 50 to 60 percent. By 2018, as many as 140,000 to 190,000 additional specialists may be required. Also needed an additional 1.5 million managers and analysts with a sharp understanding of how big data can be applied. Companies must step up their recruitment and retention programs, while making substantial investments in the education and training of key data personnel. The greater access to personal information that big data often demands will place a spotlight on another tension, between privacy and convenience.

Against this backdrop, a book entitled "*Advances and Prospect of Big Data Analytics, Artificial Intelligence, Machine Learning and Deep Learning*" is compiled aiming to keep abreast with the latest technological trends for future generation of job seekers. The book with the following chapters is likely to give present scenario technological advancement as well as outlook to be adopted by stakeholders.

Chapter 1: **Big Data Trend**
Chapter2: **Machine Learning**
Chapter-3: **Artificial Intelligence**
Chapter-4: **Deep Learning**
Chapter-5: **Difference between Artificial Intelligence, Machine Learning, and Deep Learning?**

With the above chapters, the book may clarify and answer many questions like

- ✓ *Why Is AI Taking off Now?*
- ✓ *What are the Deep Learning Tools that Drive AI Advancement?*
- ✓ *How deep learning is a new software model that needs a new computing model?*
- ✓ *Why AI researchers have adopted GPU-accelerated computing?*
- ✓ *How AI, Machine Learning and Deep Learning are close but not the same?*
- ✓ *How personalized medicine will soon become a reality?*
- ✓ *Why Data is abundant and cheap but knowledge is scarce and expensive?*
- ✓ *Why data is the sword of the 21st century?*
- ✓ *Why there is a high demand for Data scientists?*

A thorough reading of the book is expected to enrich understanding about AI, Machine, Deep learning and Big Data Analytics for skill development to equip oneself for 21st century jobs.

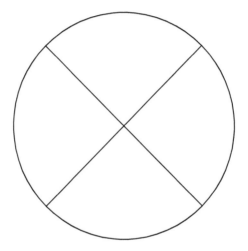

Contents

Chapter 1: Big Data Trend

1.1 Every Day Big Data Statistics – 2.5 quintillion bytes of data are created every day

Data is everywhere and its importance spans across industries. From big financial corporations to small restaurant chains, data files are the backbone of many businesses. Perhaps that's why the amount of data created daily is gargantuan. IBM reported that every single day, 2.5 quintillion bytes of data are created. The current number for daily data creation is so large that 90 percent of existing data in the world has just been created in the last two years.

With that amount of data being created every day, data loss incidents can be crippling to a company. While many cases of data destruction stem from natural disasters, such as high-power hurricanes or treacherous tornados, these are not the only catalysts for company data loss.

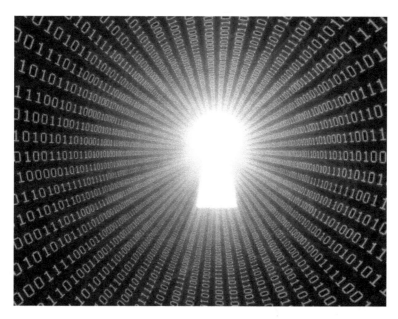

The financial harm of lost data is a very real threat for many companies.

Man-made disasters leading to data loss: A cloud services provider recently conducted a study that found 65 percent of IT professionals cited man-made disasters as the leading cause for lost data. Polled IT staffers were also asked what they saw as the most impactful consequences of this type of data loss. Profit loss, damage to the overall company reputation and reduced productivity were listed among the negative effects.

The study also found that in cases of considerable data loss, 81 percent of IT resources are needed to deal with the problem – a considerable amount of resources, considering the problem itself is preventable. IT professionals also did a bit of introspection on what exactly within a company is negatively impacted due to these incidents.

Participants noted that there tends to be an overall drop in office morale and an increased level of micro-management within IT departments. However, the most concerning side effect lies in the resulting firing that often follows these events.

Despite an increased job loss due to these incidents, the most daunting number in the survey dealt with IT confidence. Out of the surveyed professionals, 64 percent believed that if data disappeared and there was no recovery plan in place, their company would go out of business.

Clearly, data loss is a serious threat to the survival of even the most successful business. As such, companies should take a serious look at their current mechanisms for online backup.

"Most data servicers provide instant upgrades that are automatically programmed into your backup system."

<u>Companies can quickly bounce back with cloud backup services</u>: IT pros noted that when it comes to quick recovery, the general ballpark for an acceptable period is 24 hours or less. This may seem like a daunting request for something that requires 81 percent of IT resources on call. However, when companies invest in data backup systems and recovery solutions, this time frame is a walk in the park.

Leading data service companies can offer their clients options for both remote backup and online storage. This double-barreled protection assures that company data is securely stored in two trusted locations. Cloud backup services also allow companies to access their data from any location at any time.

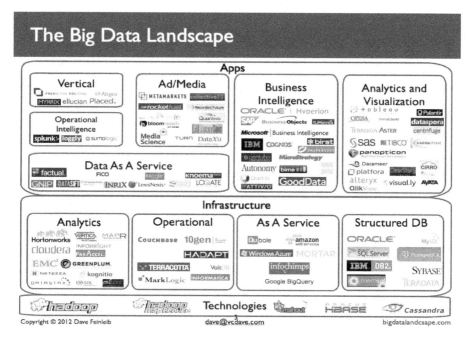

Most data servicers provide instant upgrades that are automatically programmed into your backup system. Businesses do not need to worry about remembering upgrades or even paying for the latest tweaks to the system. With automated tuning systems in place, data backup services provide companies with the best possible software in a convenient manner. For even more secure measures, data providers often offer options for recovery services. These mechanisms assure that your business has systems in place to access the backed-up data in times of crisis.

For companies looking to assure speedy recovery from a data disaster – man-made or otherwise – an investment in a reputable data backup service is a necessity.

http://www.livevault.com/2-5-quintillion-bytes-of-data-are-created-every-day/

1.2   10 things I wish people understood about data

Paul de Schacht, Data Scientist, Travel Intelligence, Amadeus IT Group

The analogy I like to use to describe what I do for some of my non-data scientists friends is the process of turning coal into diamonds. Fragmented, messy data, is the 'coal' and the 'diamonds' are the meaningful takeaways from data that can help businesses make informed decisions. After much time and pressure, we turn data, which is nothing more than facts and numbers, into information with relevance and purpose. But during this process, several steps must be followed before informed decisions can be made.

Here's a list of 10 things I wish most people understood about the process of extracting data.

1. Harvest: First, you should retrieve the data. If you are lucky, it can be as simple as synchronizing files or calling un-documented web APIs. In other cases, you need to develop a dedicated web scraper for every data source and maintain it to deal with the evolving website.

2. Storage: There is little guarantee that the remote service will stay available, so you need to store the downloaded data in a so-called 'data lake'. The data lake accepts all data formats, including the nasty ones and exposes an easy (but controlled) route to the raw data. It is important to store the raw data and not some derived form, since our understanding of the raw data grows over time.

3. Munging: This often forgotten but essential process unifies messy and disparate data sets into a common, clean format. It is often said that the cleaning of data takes up 80% of a data scientist's time. Errors will always creep into large datasets, especially when they are spread over a long-time span. Due to the nature of errors, the munging is a semi-automated process but will always require human intervention.

4. Data Quality: Due to the constant evolution of data and data sources, quality monitoring is a part of data processing and goes hand in hand with finding out the root causes of quality alerts. For example, if the capacity of an airport drops suddenly – there could be an error in the source data, or perhaps there was a major disruption at the airport? Continuous massaging of data, combined with a reality check is necessary.

5. Intuition: As a data scientist, you need to understand the datasets. Most likely, you will calculate some basic statistics (totals, averages, and spread) and plot many graphs (scatter, trend lines, etc.) to get a sense of what is interesting. During this exploration, the data scientist starts crafting a story and starts explaining the data in a business context. Interactive tools such as IPython, R and Excel are often used, but command line tools such as awk and gnu plot are equally effective as well.

6. Analysis & Modelling: This process ranges from simple KPI extraction to highly advanced data modeling and machine learning. The techniques require theoretical and mathematical skills, but they are only one aspect of the model lifecycle. How does an air traffic model react to correct but exceptional data, such as a sudden drop of passengers during the Eyjafjallajökull volcano eruption? Can the model be easily updated? Some models are real-time and demand a quick deployment, for which a tight integration with DevOps is indispensable.

7. Big Data: Do not automatically assume you need a Big Data cluster for your data job. Some small problems perfectly fit the map-reduce or the Spark paradigm, while some large volume problems would not work with a distributed approach. Clusters come with an overhead and the low prices for RAM and SSD drives enable data jobs to be executed on a single machine. Even Excel combined with PowerPivot goes a long way.

8. Domain Knowledge: Data without domain expertise remains nothing more than facts and numbers. You acquire domain knowledge by asking many questions, which is why curiosity and passion are often said to be necessary qualities in a data scientist. For example, you should not accept outliers as mere exceptions. In most cases, there is a story behind the outlier, which eventually contributes to your domain knowledge.

9. Communication: In the end, your findings need to be communicated into clear and non-technical terms so that everybody can grasp the insights. The results of the modelling are still a bunch of numbers that need to be translated in a graph. Visualization is a crucial step in data processing. Building compelling visualizations require a special set of soft skills that are hard to pin down; they sit between art, science and storytelling.

10. Human Context: There are some interesting resources that use data in service of humanity. DataKind organizes 'data dives' in which pro bono data scientists collaborate with NGO's to tackle humanitarian problems. The open knowledge foundation strives to free as much data as possible and they gather open source tools that help process data. These organizations strive to unlock information and create easy access to open data. This empowers everyone to help expose inequalities. In the same open data spirit, Amadeus data scientists maintain with great care a collection of travel and leisure related data.

Editor's note: It's been labeled the sexiest profession of the 21st Century, one where demand has raced ahead of supply, a hybrid of data hacker, analyst, communicator, and trusted advisor. Data scientists are people with the skill set (and the mind-set) to tame Big Data technologies and put them to good use. But what kind of person does this? Who has that powerful –and rare- combination of skills? In this series, Amadeus' team of Data Scientists seeks to unlock the answers to those questions and their impact on travel.

1.3   Are You Ready for The Era Of 'Big Data'?

By Brad Brown, Michael Chui, and James Manyika Article Actions

Radical customization, constant experimentation, and novel business models will be new hallmarks of competition as companies capture and analyze huge volumes of data. Here's what you should know.

The top marketing executive at a sizable US retailer recently found herself perplexed by the sales reports she was getting. A major competitor was steadily gaining market share across a range of profitable segments. Despite a counterpunch that combined online promotions with merchandizing improvements, her company kept losing ground.

When the executive convened a group of senior leaders to dig into the competitor's practices, they found that the challenge ran deeper than they had imagined. The competitor had made massive investments in its ability to collect, integrate, and analyze data from each store and every sales unit and had used this ability to run myriad real-world experiments. At the same time, it had linked this information to suppliers' databases, making it possible to adjust prices in real time, to reorder hot-selling items automatically, and to shift items from store to store easily. By constantly testing, bundling, synthesizing, and making information instantly available across the organization—from the store floor to the CFO's office—the rival company had become a different, far nimbler type of business.

What this executive team had witnessed first-hand was the game-changing effects of big data. Of course, data characterized the information age from the start. It underpins processes that manage employees; it helps to track purchases and sales; and it offers clues about how customers will behave.

But over the last few years, the volume of data has exploded. In 15 of the US economy's 17 sectors, companies with more than 1,000 employees store, on average, over 235 terabytes of data—more data than is contained in the US Library of Congress. Reams of data still flow from financial transactions and customer interactions but also cascade in at unparalleled rates from new devices and multiple points along the value chain. Just think about what could be happening at your own company right now: sensors embedded in process machinery may be collecting operations data, while marketers scan social media or use location data from smart phones to understand teens' buying quirks. Data exchanges may be networking your supply chain partners, and employees could be swapping best practices on corporate wikis.

All of this new information is laden with implications for leaders and their enterprises.1) Emerging academic research suggests that companies that use data and business analytics to guide decision making are more productive and experience higher returns on equity than competitors that don't. 2) That's consistent with research we've conducted showing that "networked organizations" can gain an edge by opening information conduits internally and by engaging customers and suppliers strategically through Web-based exchanges of information.

Over time, we believe big data may well become a new type of corporate asset that will cut across business units and function much as a powerful brand does, representing a key basis for competition. If that's right, companies need to start thinking in earnest about whether they are organized to exploit big data's potential and to manage the threats it can pose. Success will demand not only new skills but also new perspectives on how the era of big data could evolve—the widening circle of management practices it may affect and the foundation it represents for new, potentially disruptive business models.

1.4   Five big questions about big data

We outline important ways big data could change competition: by transforming processes, altering corporate ecosystems, and facilitating innovation. We've organized the discussion around five questions we think all senior executives should be asking themselves today.

At the outset, we'll acknowledge that these are still early days for big data, which is evolving as a business concept in tandem with the underlying technologies. Nonetheless, we can identify big data's key elements. First, companies can now collect data across business units and, increasingly, even from partners and customers (some of this is truly big, some more granular and complex). Second, a flexible infrastructure can integrate information and scale up effectively to meet the surge. Finally, experiments, algorithms, and analytics can make sense of all this information. We also can identify organizations that are making data a core element of strategy. In the discussion that follows, we have assembled case studies of early movers in the big data realm (see "Seizing the potential of 'big data'" and the accompanying sidebar, "AstraZeneca's 'big data' partnership.")

Sidebar - Parsing the benefits: Not all industries are created equal

In addition, we'd suggest that executives look to history for clues about what's coming next. Earlier waves of technology adoption, for example, show that productivity surges not only because companies adopt new technologies but also, more critically, because they can adapt their management practices and change their organizations to maximize the potential. We examined the possible impact of big data across many industries and found that while it will be important in every sector and function, some industries will realize benefits sooner because they are readier to capitalize on data or have strong market incentives to do so (see sidebar, "Parsing the benefits: Not all industries are created equal").

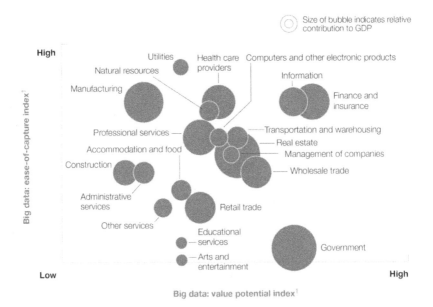

Size of bubble indicates relative contribution to GDP

Big data: value potential index[1]

[1]For detailed explication of metrics, see appendix in McKinsey Global Institute full report
Big data: The next frontier for innovation, competition, and productivity, available free of charge online at mckinsey.com/mgi.
Source: US Bureau of Labor Statistics; McKinsey Global Institute analysis

The era of big data also could yield new management principles. In the early days of professionalized corporate management, leaders discovered that minimum efficient scale was a key determinant of competitive success. Likewise, future competitive benefits may accrue to companies that can not only capture more and better data but also use that data effectively at scale. We hope that by reflecting on such issues and the five questions that follow, executives will be better able to recognize how big data could upend assumptions behind their strategies, as well as the speed and scope of the change that's now under way.

1. What happens in a world of radical transparency, with data widely available?

As information becomes more readily accessible across sectors, it can threaten companies that have relied on proprietary data as a competitive asset; the real-estate industry, for example, trades on information asymmetries such as privileged access to transaction data and tightly held knowledge of the bid and asks behavior of buyers. Both require significant expense and effort to acquire. In recent years, however, online specialists in real-estate data and analytics have started to bypass agents, permitting buyers and sellers to exchange perspectives on the value of properties and creating parallel sources for real-estate data.

Beyond real estate, cost and pricing data are becoming more accessible across a spectrum of industries. Another swipe at proprietary information is the assembly by some companies of readily available satellite imagery that, when processed and analyzed, contains clues about competitors' physical facilities. These satellite sleuths glean insights into expansion plans or business constraints as revealed by facility capacity, shipping movements, and the like.

One big challenge is the fact that the mountains of data many companies are amassing often lurk in departmental "silos," such as R&D, engineering, manufacturing, or service operations—impeding timely exploitation. Information hoarding within business units also can be a problem: many financial institutions, for example, suffer from their own failure to share data among diverse lines of business, such as financial markets, money management, and lending. Often, that prevents these companies from forming a coherent view of individual customers or understanding links among financial markets.

Some manufacturers are attempting to pry open these departmental enclaves: they are integrating data from multiple systems, inviting collaboration among formerly walled-off functional units, and even seeking information from external suppliers and customers to co-create products. In advanced-manufacturing sectors such as automotive, for example, suppliers from around the world make thousands of components. More integrated data platforms now allow companies and their supply chain partners to collaborate during the design phase—a crucial determinant of final manufacturing costs.

2. If you could test all your decisions, how would that change the way you compete?

Big data ushers in the possibility of a fundamentally different type of decision making. Using controlled experiments, companies can test hypotheses and analyze results to guide investment decisions and operational changes. In effect, experimentation can help managers distinguish causation from mere correlation, thus reducing the variability of outcomes while improving financial and product performance.

Robust experimentation can take many forms. Leading online companies, for example, are continuous testers. In some cases, they allocate a set portion of their Web page views to conduct experiments that reveal what factors drive higher user engagement or promote sales. Companies selling physical goods also use experiments to aid decisions, but big data can push this approach to a new level. McDonald's, for example, has equipped some stores with devices that gather operational data as they track customer interactions, traffic in stores, and ordering patterns. Researchers can model the impact of variations in menus, restaurant designs, and training, among other things, on productivity and sales.

Where such controlled experiments aren't feasible, companies can use "natural" experiments to identify the sources of variability in performance. One government organization, for instance, collected data on multiple groups of employees doing similar work at different sites. Simply making the data available spurred lagging workers to improve their performance.

Leading retailers, meanwhile, are monitoring the in-store movements of customers, as well as how they interact with products. These retailers combine such rich data feeds with transaction records and conduct experiments to guide choices about which products to carry, where to place them, and how and when to adjust prices. Methods such as these helped one leading retailer to reduce the number of items it stocked by 17 percent, while raising the mix of higher-margin private-label goods—with no loss of market share.

3. How would your business change if you used big data for widespread, real-time customization?

Customer-facing companies have long used data to segment and target customers. Big data permits a major step beyond what until recently was considered state of the art, by making real-time personalization possible. A next-generation retailer will be able to track the behavior of individual customers from Internet click streams, update their preferences, and model their likely behavior in real time. They will then be able to recognize when customers are nearing a purchase decision and nudge the transaction to completion by bundling preferred products, offered with reward program savings. This real-time targeting, which would also leverage data from the retailer's multitier membership rewards program, will increase purchases of higher-margin products by its most valuable customers.

Retailing is an obvious place for data-driven customization because the volume and quality of data available from Internet purchases, social-network conversations, and, more recently, location-specific smart phone interactions have mushroomed. But other sectors, too, can benefit from new applications of data, along with the growing sophistication of analytical tools for dividing customers into more revealing micro-segments.

One personal-line insurer, for example, tailor's insurance policies for each customer, using fine-grained, constantly updated profiles of customer risk, changes in wealth, home asset value, and other data inputs. Utilities that harvest and analyze data on customer segments can markedly change patterns of power usage. Finally, HR departments that more finely segment employees by task and performance are beginning to change work conditions and implement incentives that improve both satisfaction and productivity.[4]

4. How can big data augment or even replace management?

Big data expands the operational space for algorithms and machine-mediated analysis. At some manufacturers, for example, algorithms analyze sensor data from production lines, creating self-regulating processes that cut waste, avoid costly (and sometimes dangerous) human interventions, and ultimately lift output. In advanced, "digital" oil fields, instruments constantly read data on wellhead conditions, pipelines, and mechanical systems. That information is analyzed by clusters of computers, which feed their results to real-time operations centers that adjust oil flows to optimize production and minimize downtimes. One major oil company has cut operating and staffing costs by 10 to 25 percent while increasing production by 5 percent.

Products ranging from copiers to jet engines can now generate data streams that track their usage. Manufacturers can analyze the incoming data and, in some cases, automatically remedy software glitches or dispatch service representatives for repairs. Some enterprise computer hardware vendors are gathering and analyzing such data to schedule preemptive repairs before failures disrupt customers' operations. The data can also be used to implement product changes that prevent future problems or to provide customer use inputs that inform next-generation offerings.

Some retailers are also at the forefront of using automated big data analysis: they use "sentiment analysis" techniques to mine the huge streams of data now generated by consumers using various types of social media, gauge responses to new marketing campaigns in real time, and adjust strategies accordingly. Sometimes these methods cut weeks from the normal feedback and modification cycle.

But retailers aren't alone. One global beverage company integrates daily weather forecast data from an outside partner into its demand and inventory-planning processes. By analyzing three data points—temperatures, rainfall levels, and the number of hours of sunshine on a given day—the company cut its inventory levels while improving its forecasting accuracy by about 5 percent in a key European market.

The bottom line is improved performance, better risk management, and the ability to unearth insights that would otherwise remain hidden. As the price of sensors, communications devices, and analytic software continues to fall, more and more companies will be joining this managerial revolution.

5. Could you create a new business model based on data?

Big data is spawning new categories of companies that embrace information-driven business models. Many of these businesses play intermediary roles in value chains where they find themselves generating valuable "exhaust data" produced by business transactions. One transport company, for example, recognized that while doing business, it was collecting vast amounts of information on global product shipments. Sensing opportunity, it created a unit that sells the data to supplement business and economic forecasts.

Another global company learned so much from analyzing its own data as part of a manufacturing turnaround that it decided to create a business to do similar work for other firms. Now the company aggregates shop floor and supply chain data for many manufacturing customers and sells software tools to improve their performance. This service business now outperforms the company's manufacturing one.

Big data also is turbo charging the ranks of data aggregators, which combine and analyze information from multiple sources to generate insights for clients. In health care, for example, several new entrants are integrating clinical, payment, public-health, and behavioral data to develop more robust illness profiles that help clients manage costs and improve treatments.

And with pricing data proliferating on the Web and elsewhere, entrepreneurs are offering price comparison services that automatically compile information across millions of products. Such comparisons can be a disruptive force from a retailer's perspective but have created substantial value for consumers. Studies show that those who use the services save an average of 10 percent—a sizable shift in value.

Confronting complications

Up to this point, we have emphasized the strategic opportunities big data presents, but leaders must also consider a set of complications. Talent is one of them. In the United States alone, our research shows, the demand for people with the deep analytical skills in big data (including machine learning and advanced statistical analysis) could outstrip current projections of supply by 50 to 60 percent. By 2018, as many as 140,000 to 190,000 additional specialists may be required. Also needed an additional 1.5 million managers and analysts with a sharp understanding of how big data can be applied. Companies must step up their recruitment and retention programs, while making substantial investments in the education and training of key data personnel.

The greater access to personal information that big data often demands will place a spotlight on another tension, between privacy and convenience. Our research, for example, shows that consumers capture a large part of the economic surplus that big data generates: lower prices, a better alignment of products with consumer needs, and lifestyle improvements that range from better health to more fluid social interactions.[5] As a larger amount of data on the buying preferences, health, and finances of individuals is collected, however, privacy concerns will grow.

That's true for data security as well. The trends we've described often go hand in hand with more open access to information, new devices for gathering it, and cloud computing to support big data's weighty storage and analytical needs. The implication is that IT architectures will become more integrated and outward facing and will pose greater risks to data security and intellectual property. For some ideas on how leaders should respond, see "Meeting the cyber security challenge."

Although corporate leaders will focus most of their attention on big data's implications for their own organizations, the mosaic of company-level opportunities we have surveyed also has broader economic implications. In health care, government services, retailing, and manufacturing, our research suggests, big data could improve productivity by 0.5 to 1 percent annually. In these sectors globally, it could produce hundreds of billions of dollars and euros in new value. In fact, big data may ultimately be a key factor in how nations, not just companies, compete and prosper. Certainly, these techniques offer glimmers of hope to a global economy struggling to find a path toward more rapid growth. Through investments and forward-looking policies, company leaders and their counterparts in government can capitalize on big data instead of being blindsided by it.

About the author(s)

Brad Brown is a director in McKinsey's New York office; **Michael Chui** is a senior fellow with the McKinsey Global Institute (MGI) and is based in the San Francisco office; **James Manyika** is a director of MGI and a director in the San Francisco office.

http://www.mckinsey.com/business-functions/strategy-and-corporate-finance/our-insights/are-you-ready-for-the-era-of-big-data

1.5 Why Companies Must Scale Up Their Data-Analytics Skills to Reap the Gains

Ramakrishnan K, is AVP and Data Analytics Practice Head for Retail, CPG & Logistics, Infosys: June 2016

Evolution and the Need: The evolution of data warehousing and business intelligence DWBI industry has been somewhat steady but real stark. The fundamental tenet or reason for business intelligence (BI) was the need to analyze data and derive insights for driving business. The DWBI industry has completed one full cycle. From the initial days and start of the cycle, when the production and transaction processing systems could not be loaded further for analyses, management information system (MIS) paved the need for a separate database. Then data warehouses, data marts and data stores along with lucid processing techniques (SCD) came into existence from Kimball. As time went by, the latency started to shrink and real-time/near-real-time processing and multi-processor processing got prominence. Then with online channels coming in search, many such techniques/vendors came into prominence. Subsequently, the era of Big Data started and today, the latency has shrunk further - we are talking about processing at the end-points as the key enabler for business. The environment we operate in is becoming boundary-less and organizations should be nimble to accommodate this evolution.

Current Trends: The industry is moving at a trailblazing speed to cater to this phenomenon or evolution of processing at end- points. There are quite a few startups/products that offer to make this Data to Insights a reality. These products are talking about reduced implementation time and time to insights. Some of the new breed of players likes Waterline, Trifacta, Beyond Core, to name a few, provide a strong capability for data wrangling-cum-visualization that makes processing at end-points a reality. These cut across any kind of source data - structured, un-structured, social, etc., and provide the ability to pull/wrangle this data to provide insights for driving business. It is not just the new breed of tools, the existing players like SAS, Tableau, Teradata, Micro-strategy, Microsoft, and the like are providing features to cut across sources and also have the capability to link with the Big Data environment which serves as a bridge for seamless integration.

Here are a few examples from various industry segments to elucidate the point. With the plethora of data channels and mediums, it is imperative for retailers to have a 360-degree view of their customers. This will aid in tracking them closely and offering them campaigns that are relevant to an individual's buying patterns and habits. It is important for retailers to have a seamless view of their online channel and brick-and-mortar stores to drive optimum inventory and growth. Using the traditional BI approach, retailers typically spend 5-6 working days for completing one complete campaign cycle. Leveraging the virtualization or augmented architecture, we can do the same within a few hours today and with very less data hops. Similarly, with sensors coming into existence, a whole lot of business imperatives are met seamlessly across industry segments and mainly in the logistics and manufacturing segments. Some of the critical business cases are remote monitoring of equipment, Parcel tracking, and real-time monitoring.

The Change

Accommodating the changes mentioned above, using the traditional BI approach will mean a whole lot of cycle time in getting such types of data into the DW for consumption and insights generation. One cannot wait for the traditional methods and timelines of BI to run business today. To keep up with this evolution or business dynamics, all industry segments are already or will certainly have to modernize their landscape, i.e., move into technology platforms that provide for quick and seamless integration of various types of data for insights generation. Adoption of new technology platforms does not mean moving from one platform to another; it is about creating an augmented architecture that leverages the data wherever it is with minimal hops to provide insights.

To manage and execute this change, apart from the Big Data stalwarts, other roles that are gaining even more prominence and significance within organizations are the data wranglers, data blenders, data scientists, and their clan. A lot has been said about the job description of these roles and hence we will not preach any further on the same. It is imperative for organizations/businesses to groom this clan that has the flair for looking at data and arriving on patterns, insights that will contribute to business growth. It is not enough to just adapt to the technology or platform, it is important to have the right set of folks that will provide or execute on processing at end-points paradigm. Also, the bucketing of analytics into predictive, preventive, etc., is eroding and is becoming pervasive and boundary-less. Analytics or insights at the point of data delivery are the need of the hour.

As DWBI became main stream to business from just serving MIS, data analytics and the need for processing at end-points is becoming mainstream today and organizations must be abreast to ride the wave. In today's world of data from everywhere and anything, this is a key measurement. How quickly are organizations able to integrate and leverage this data in deriving insights without much redundancy is the measure of success? While lot has been said and done about the evolution of DWBI to data and analytics and the need for organizations to keep up with the pace to be relevant, I observe that more has been said than done. So, pilots are not bad after all - ideal way to get started will be to identify a line of business that is mature enough and create the augmented platform for them to be self-sufficient. Augment this team with the data analysts and measure the additional insights that are being delivered to business.

The IT industry is already into the next generation and every organization must plan their strategy for modernizing. As the management cliché goes, we must be doing things better to do better things - modernize to monetize.

http://www.communicationstoday.co.in/index.php/enterprise-network/enterprise-network-industry/2632-why-companies-must-scale-up-their-data-analytics-skills-to-reap-the-gains

1.6   Our devices are talking… but are we listening?

We could be wasting some of the invaluable information hiding in our smart device's data

Big Data Business Intelligence Cloud

Social sharing

More and more, the devices we buy are talking to one another. Consumer and industrial original electronics manufacturers (OEMs) alike are building 'smart' devices that are connected to the internet. From devices that we wear, to those in the cars that we drive, in our homes and the buildings we work in, all the way to smart cities. They are all talking. It's predicted there will be 50 billion connected devices worldwide in 2020, so that's a lot of talk!

Our devices are already communicating with each other to share information on our movements, our preferences and our habits all the time. The Internet of Things (IoT) isn't something futuristic from a science fiction film, it is here and now – our 'things' can connect with each other and affect one another's behaviours with very little input from us. Think of each of those 50 billion devices collecting information as they talk with one another. That's a lot of data. And yet, recent research from Forrester shows that although more than half of companies making IoT devices are collecting this data, only a third are making use of it.

So why is this information going to waste? Every time our devices connect, they produce extremely valuable data that can not only give insight into the immediate sensor environment and operational status of a device, but will actually lead to determinable actions, automated or otherwise, based on human and device behavior. Take car manufacturers for instance. With smart device technology, the data they can capture around our driving habits could be invaluable not just to them but to a few companies as well. They have data on where we typically travel from, how long it takes us to get there, the time we leave our house in the morning and maybe even what we listen to enroot. Even our coffee machines and fridges are part of the IoT ecosystem. Your coffee machine knows exactly how many times a day you enjoy a brew and when your coffee beans need replenishing. Put that information in the hands of digital marketers and they know exactly when you're running low on caffeine and so when to show you relevant adverts and offers from coffee suppliers.

These insights can be even more basic. For instance, a leading pest control agency is using IoT inspired sensor technology to detect mice in industrial buildings, using wireless data connectivity to communicate with technicians as well as with the customer about an infestation. For example, how big is the problem, what areas of the building are vulnerable and exposed to mice and, therefore, what action needs to be taken? The possibilities are endless. So why aren't more companies taking advantage; why is there still such a data disconnect?

Unfortunately, the barrier comes down to the analysis process. Analyzing data can be an overwhelming prospect at the best of times – and that's just when it's data which relates to your company. We've already shown how much data smart devices are producing, but where do you start on analyzing it? If companies are collecting all that data, they need to be data-driven in order to turn it into insights – and that means finding a way to make it as accessible, visual and understandable to as many people as possible, whether in a business context or otherwise.

The key to seeing the whole story in IoT data is to approach it with an open mind, rather than searching for a specific answer. It needs to be explored and interacted with for hidden insights and gems that you might not have thought about looking for – and that's going to require investment and skill.

That said it's an investment that needs to be made. Companies cannot afford to neglect the massive opportunity for getting their approach to data analysis around IoT devices right. There are business platforms out there that have been built to support the analysis of large amounts of data in an easy-to-understand, visual way, whether the user has experience in the field of data analysis or not.

While some investment is required up front, organizations embracing IoT should not be afraid to 'fail-fast', which means thinking small initially, experimenting and analyzing in order to learn what works as efficiently as possible. In addition, while the skill sets of data scientists are indeed important, especially at the operations layer and in the long term, we encourage organizations to harness existing talent in the first instance to gain valuable insight immediately.

Ultimately, however, to make the most of IoT, users will have to go on exploratory journeys for insights, where they can collaborate and experiment with data analysis with partners outside their organization – combining several internal and external data sets for 'out of the box' insights on human (or indeed mouse) behaviours.

The future is here, and those companies that embrace it now and make the data they have accessible and understandable will be the ones turning data into gold dust. With the right attitude and investment in analyzing IoT data, they're in the best position to understand what makes us tick and either make internal business changes for the better or even turn data into revenue by selling insights on.

https://channels.theinnovationenterprise.com/articles/our-devices-are-talking-but-are-we-listening?utm_campaign=weekly_mail&utm_content=ie_Friday_2017-03-31&utm_medium=email&utm_source=ie_weekly_email&mkt_tok=

eyJpIjoiTldJMFlUSTBNemM0Wm1WbSIsInQiOiJZRFhLbzVvdWlDQ0pnbHk0Q2xKR
0ZkejhYSFFnSHhxS3diZ0ljVGthWGhQRUhXWDVKd25Nb1orZmNcL01FUklpalFLay
tJZlJ0R21XVnR2UmpqWGFXTkJaUsrRVZUUQyttTEV6dlI4SGhjVZkczV4b2ZjWUt
pd2t2eG8wVUslODEifQ%3D%3D

1.7   Data Analytics Top Trends for Retail In 2017
Maria Maguire; 27Mar, 2017

4 things retailers should be aware of this year

Social sharing

Retailers are in the midst of difficult times, with ongoing economic uncertainty, the rising power of the consumer, and an ever-growing influx of competitors meaning that they are having to constantly adapt. In the battle for survival, data is proving one of the most effective weapons in their arsenal. By using data properly, retailers can improve operating margins by in excess of 60%. The majority of retailers have realized this. In a survey of retail executives by JDA Software Group and PricewaterhouseCoopers (PwC), 86% of retail executives polled said they plan to increase investment in big data tools over the coming year.

The benefits that can be achieved from data in retail come in many forms. In a recent Forbes Insights report, 'Data Elevates the Customer Experience: New Ways of Discovering and Applying Customer insights,' respondents cited the most useful of these as improved revenue generation and lower cost reduction, better understanding of customer buying patterns and behaviors, and accelerated process efficiencies and quality improvements. Another recent study by FICCI, in association with PWC, found that analytics could generate in-depth insights in everything from procurement and supply chain through to sales and marketing.

In 2017, we are set to see retailers again increase their focus and investment in data analytics as they bid to stay ahead of the competition.

Here, we've looked at some of the trends that data practitioners working in the retail space should be aware of this year.

Location analytics becomes vital

Forrester estimates that the adoption of location analytics will increase to more than two-thirds of data and analytics decision-makers by the end of 2017, up from less than 50% last year. It can benefit businesses in a variety of ways, but retailers in particular stand to benefit. They can, for example, send geo-targeted push notifications to mobiles, which research has found to be 6-8 times more effective than other notifications. It can also be used in-store to help better understand people's purchasing behavior. US fashion retailer Nordstrom, for example, has spent millions introducing technologies like sensors and Wi-Fi signals into its stores that enable them to track such information, and as IoT explodes the number of data points is only going to increase. One customer could generate more than 10,000 unique data in a single visit from various sensors placed throughout a store, indicating where they will go; at what point they make the decision to pick up an item, and so forth. This information could be used by the retailer to get an idea of where products and promotions can be placed to maximum effect.

There are a number of firms making this easier. Foursquare, for example, has recently released Foursquare Analytics, which CEO Jeff Glueck claims is 'kind of the Google Analytics of the world'. It is a dashboard designed to provide retailers and restaurants with greater visibility into location intelligence, changing store visit patterns among demographics, and their share of consumer visits in relation to competitors. Another making wave is Euclid Analytics. Euclid Analytics is a US-based company that uses location analytics to monitor consumer traffic in shops and malls, using Wi-Fi signals from smart phones to track and analyze everything from how many enter a store to how long they stay, and the number of times they return.

Data from in-store tech grows

The key to enabling a better customer experience in-store is to incorporate as many technologies as possible to collect data, essentially by re-creating the online shopping experience. This is being greatly aided by two emerging technologies set for mass adoption in the coming years - Augmented Reality and IoT.

Augmented reality has been used in store for a number of years. IKEA, for one, introduced augmented reality to their catalogs in 2013 for customers to 'virtually' place furniture in their houses before purchase. Japanese beauty retailer Shiseido's Tokyo stores also has 'cosmetic mirrors' installed that allow customers to scan product barcodes and see a virtual image of their faces with the product applied to it to get a better idea of how it looks. Such products improve the shopping experience for the customer while also helping the retailer collect more information so they can improve the experience again in the future. As Dream Sail VR game developer Cindy Mallory noted in an interview with us, 'The way a user interacts with VR allows for extremely pervasive information collection,' and the potential here is truly limitless.

Another technology set to explode in-store is the IoT. Almost 70% of retail decision-makers are ready to make the necessary changes for adoption, according to the 2017 Retail Vision Study from Zebra Technologies. Meanwhile, according to a 2015 report from Juniper Research, retailers will spend $2.5 billion on connected devices by 2020. Aside from the ability to monitor customer movements in store, this will provide particularly in the supply chain, where efficient data collection and analysis can provide real-time analysis of supply and demand and help organizations retain an appropriate stock level. Tom Moore, Industry Lead of Retail and Hospitality at Zebra Technologies, told Retail Touch Points that, 'Retailers' number one business challenge to compete in this dynamic marketplace is inventory visibility. Best case, most retailers are 50% to 60% accurate from that perspective, so if they're going to have any kind of e-Commerce strategy and leverage them in-store resources and inventory, they need to make sure that product is there.'

Cross-platform analytics helps track and improve consumers' entire experience

Customers now engage with a range of touch points before purchase. They may view a product on several social media platforms, on the company website, and in-store before they make a purchase. However, in the earlier-mentioned PWC's survey, only 12% of CEOs surveyed said they provide a seamless shopping experience across channels.

One of the main problem analysts having with tracking data as it moves across platforms is that the data gets trapped in silos. Analysts need to break down these silos to track audiences across platforms so they can understand where products are being purchased and to understand the purpose of online visits before purchase in store, which will then help them to better target offers. Retailers can also take this real-time data to help sales teams to communicate with customers at any stage during the customer journey, whether before, during, or after the store visit, and on any medium, from text to email.

Shift from Predictive Analytics to Explanatory Analytics

Investing in predictive and software analytics for loss prevention and price optimization is still on the up. Predictive analytics makes informed guesses about what customers will want in the future and it is incredibly useful. It is, however, an incomplete approach because it only gives you a likely outcome if nothing changes. It can only tell you what the future will probably be like, it does not tell you why outcomes are likely, the correlations driving those outcomes, or how to intervene to affect them. In order to alter an outcome, you have to be looking to explain why it will happen.

This can only be done with explanatory modeling. So, for example, in retail, predictive modeling is useful in that it would be able to give you an accurate estimate of, say, which shop requires certain stock. It doesn't offer an explanation of why the shop will require it, and would subsequently do little to address root causes and leave the retailer vulnerable in terms of inventory management. Explanatory modeling, on the other hand, will identify things that are having an impact. For instance, it would identify that the weather is driving an uptick in coats, people buy more coats in the cold, and that the weather will get better next week so you will need to change stock levels.

https://channels.theinnovationenterprise.com/articles/data-analytics-top-trends-for-retail-in-2017?utm_campaign=weekly_mail&utm_content=ie_Friday_2017-03-31&utm_medium=email&utm_source=ie_weekly_email&mkt_tok=eyJpIjoiTldJMFlUSTBNemM0Wm1WbSIsInQiOiJZRFhLbzVvdWlDQ0pnbnbHk0Q2xKR0ZkejhYSFFnSHhxS3diZ0ljVGthWGhQRUhXWDVKd25Nb1orZmNcL01FUklpalFLaytJZlJ0R21XVnR2UmpwWGFXTkNaUsrRVZUQyttTEV6dll4NGSGhjcVZkczV4b2ZjWUtpd2t2t2eG8wVUs1ODEifQ%3D%3D

1.8   The Promise of Big Data

Petabytes of raw information could provide clues for everything from preventing TB to shrinking health care costs—if we can figure out how to use them.

Harvard School of Public Health microbiologist Sarah Fortune went to Camden, Maine in late 2010 to attend a small but widely revered conference on innovation called PopTech. Fortune had for more than a decade been trying to crack one of the tuberculosis bacterium's most infuriating characteristics: its rising resistance to antibiotic drugs.

Standing on the Camden Opera House stage, backlit by mammoth close-ups of fluorescent cells, Fortune shared with her fellow PopTech attendees TB's grim annual statistics: 2 billion people—nearly one-third of the world's population—are latent carriers. Every year, 15 million become sick and 1.4 million die.

Unlike most bacteria, TB cells do not replicate as carbon copies but in random patterns, she told the audience. TB cells behave more like snowflakes than Xeroxes. Fortune believes it is this variety that gives TB its extraordinary ability to defy conventional antibiotics.

Using silicon chips and a special camera, Fortune, the Melvin J. and Geraldine L. Glimcher Assistant Professor of Immunology and Infectious Diseases, and her fellow researchers had developed a way to capture 10,000 still images of this telltale growth every few days— exponentially more data than they had only a few years ago.

The images are combined like old-fashioned flip books into what Fortune calls "movies." But only the human eye can assess the moving pictures, one by one—a method so laborious that it inhibits scientific progress.

The question troubling Fortune, and what had brought her to the conference, was the following: How could her lab swiftly analyze this unprecedented treasure trove? The new data could be a gold mine—one that could yield fundamental insights about potential diagnostic tools, treatments, even a vaccine—but not without ways to speed up analysis. Fortune needed help.

The dilemma of big data

Winston Hide, Associate Professor of Biostatistics

What was happening in Sarah Fortune's lab is playing out in laboratories, businesses, and government agencies everywhere. Our ability to generate data has moved light-years ahead of where it was only a few years ago, and the amount of digital information now available to us is essentially unimaginable.

"In the last five years, more scientific data has been generated than in the entire history of mankind," says Winston Hide, associate professor of bioinformatics at HSPH. "You can imagine what's going to happen in the next five." And this data isn't simply linear; genetics and proteomics, to name just two fields of study, generate high-dimensional data, which is fundamentally different in scale.

"Imagine a city made out of stacks of paper, each stack printed with sets of data," says Hide. He flings his arms in the air, drawing mega space. "Imagine a whole planet that size. Imagine a million planets! Imagine a galaxy full of those, and we haven't even got there yet! That's high-dimensional data."

Revolutionary applications

Sarah Fortune, Melvin J. and Geraldine L. Glimcher Assistant Professor of Immunology and Infectious Diseases

In big data lies the potential for revolutionizing, well, everything. Police employing seismology-like data models can predict where crimes will occur and prevent them from happening. Astronomers using the Kepler telescope snag information on 200,000 stars every 30 seconds, which has led to the discovery of the first Earth-like planets outside our solar system. Businesses sifting social networking and supply-chain data dynamically tailor their products to fulfill desires we don't even know we have.

The same phenomena are at play in public health. For some time, DNA sequencing has held big data's starring role—after all, a single human genome consists of some 3 billion base pairs of DNA. Researchers at HSPH and across the campus at Harvard are sequencing and analyzing human genomes to ferret out clues to infections, cancer, andnon-communicable diseases.

The Scale

On a computer, data is translated into 0s and 1s called bits. Eight bits make up one byte—enough information to represent one letter, number, or symbol.

2.5 petabytes

Memory capacity of the human brain

13 petabytes

Amount that could be downloaded from the Internet in two minutes if every American got on a computer at the same time

98 petabytes

Websites indexed by Google

4.75 Exabytes

Total genome sequences of all people on Earth

422 Exabytes

Total digital data created in 2008

1 Zettabyte

World's current digital storage capacity

1.8 Zettabytes

Total digital data created in 2011

Source: Popular Science and Katie Peek

But the potential public health uses of big data extend well beyond genomics. Environmental scientists are capturing huge quantities of air quality data from polluted areas and attempting to match it with equally bulky health care datasets for insights into respiratory disease. Epidemiologists are gathering information on social and sexual networks to better pinpoint the spread of disease and even create early warning systems. Comparative-effectiveness researchers are combing government and clinical databases for proof of the best, most cost-effective treatments for hundreds of conditions—information that could transform health care policy. And disease researchers now have access to human genetic data and genomic databases of millions of bacteria—data they can combine to study treatment outcomes.

According to McKinsey & Company, with the right tools, big data could be worth $9 billion to U.S. public health surveillance alone and $300 billion to American health care in general, the former by improving detection of and response to infectious disease outbreaks, and the latter largely through reductions in expenditures.

A critical bottleneck

It's hardly a given, though, that we'll get to this nirvana any time soon. Our ability to generate data far outstrips our ability to analyze it. "If we really start trying to exploit all these databases, we will need more trained staff and more resources to do it," says Victor De Gruttola, who chairs HSPH's biostatistics department.

Most researchers agree that lives are lost every day that data sit in storage, untouched. The problems are vast and urgent. Consider just one example—recent news that a dozen Indian patients had contracted totally drug-resistant tuberculosis. "Even just a few people in Mumbai is a terrible danger sign," says Fortune, because it could portend the rapid spread of a highly transmissible and untreatable infection.

To counter these trends, some scientists are venturing into crowd sourcing. Others are developing sophisticated algorithms to parse data in a keystroke. And still more are inventing ways to share massive, disparate datasets to yield surprising insights.

Wisdom of the crowd

At PopTech, frustrated with the slow pace of her research, Sarah Fortune took a risk that most scientists wouldn't. She asked the audience for advice on how to analyze her images. "We would like to engage lots of eyes in that process," she said.

When Fortune walked off the stage, Josh Nesbit, a young entrepreneur in the audience, resolved to meet her. Nesbit had launched a company, Medic Mobile that had built an emergency response system after the Haiti earthquake, calling on 2,500 Creole speakers to translate text messages. When the system was overwhelmed by victims, texting for help, Nesbit turned to a Silicon Valley crowd sourcing company called Crowd Flower. This has signed up more than 2 million people to perform micro-tasks, often for pennies a task. The volunteers used Crowd Flower's website to translate, map, and organize nearly 100,000 messages, imploring rescuers for food, water, and help escaping from fallen buildings.

The evening after Fortune's talk, at a glitzy reception, Nesbit shared his story. Fortune instantly saw the possibilities: She could crowd source the image processing of her growing TB cultures. In May 2011, Crowd Flower put one of Fortune's laboratory "movies" online. Some 1,000 interested people, with no scientific expertise, signed on to help. They measured and labeled the distance between cells as one cell split into two and two splits into four, shooting off in patterns too random for computer programs to track. In two days, they'd measured cell growth in a 5,300-image movie. Without their collective eyes, it would have taken three months.

More important, their analysis generated new, fundamental findings about TB cells, which are shaped like cough drops. "We discovered that mycobacterial cell growth is not even," Fortune says. "One end of the cell is different from the other end, and in fact, it only grows from one end." She calls the non growing ends "privileged"—that is, not terribly vulnerable to antibiotics. That crowd-enabled insight, she says, may yield clues to pathogenesis and drug treatment.

Finding all the needles in a haystack

The Scale, continued

1 petabyte = 1 quadrillion bytes enough to store approximately: 2.8 million copies of the full text of the Encyclopedia Britannica; or1,903 years of music recorded at standard quality for an Apple iPod; oras much data as a stack of DVDs, each containing a two-hour standard definition video, roughly 1.8 times as high as the Empire State Building.

1 terabyte= 1 trillion bytes enough to store approximately: 2,767 copies of the full text of the Encyclopedia Britannica; or16,667 hours of music recorded at standard quality for an Apple iPod; or1,333 hours of standard definition video

1 gigabyte= 1 billion bytes enough to store approximately: 212 copies of War and Peace or almost three copies of the full text (all 32 volumes) of the Encyclopedia Britannica; or 250 songs recorded at Apple iTunes standard quality; or 80 minutes of standard definition video

1 megabyte= 1 million bytes enough to store a 500-page book in plain text

1 kilobyte= 1 thousand bytes enough to store a short paragraph's worth of plain text

1 byte enough to store one letter of the alphabet

Sources: Apple Computer, New York Times, Amazon.com, >Perma-bound.com, the Official Website of the Empire State Building

Around the time that Fortune was wondering how to quickly analyze thousands of images, David Reshef was pondering an even larger problem: He wanted to parse millions of relationships buried in big data. An MD/PhD candidate at the Harvard-MIT Division of Health Sciences and Technology, Reshef and his brother, Yakir, spent their childhoods in Kenya with their physician parents, planting in David a lifelong fascination with global health.

In 2007, Reshef met PardisSabeti, an assistant professor in HSPH's Department of Immunology and Infectious Diseases and a computational biologist at the Broad Institute. Reshef talked excitedly about his desire to apply computational methods to public health problems. Sabeti, a geneticist who has made discoveries about malaria and the lethal African Lassa virus by mining big data, found Reshef remarkably like-minded. "You should come at work with me," she told him.

They began developing tools for visualizing relationships in huge databases (including a World Health Organization database containing more than 60,000 relationships among data from 200 countries). But visualization tools work best when scientists have an idea of what to visualize in a pile of data. Reshef wasn't seeking the proverbial needle in a haystack; he wanted to find all the needles.

To discover hidden relationships in the data, he needed a treasure-seeking tool, the computational equivalent of a metal detector. Reshef and his brother, Yakir, who was just graduating from Harvard with a math degree, started to spend every spare minute together, scribbling equation on the glass walls of the Broad and consulting with Sabeti and Michael Mitzenmacher, professor of computer science at Harvard. One hot night, running the latest version of their algorithm on a PC, they realized their program finally worked—and fast. (The algorithm now produces results in minutes or hours, depending on the size of the dataset. Without it, the data could take months to analyze.) "We were so excited, we called Pardis," Reshef says. It was 3 a.m.

Over the next year, they tested the tool, called MINE, on several giant datasets, including the WHO data and a 6,700-variable database of the human gut microbiome that generated 22 million possible paired relationships. Last December, the Reshef brothers were the lead authors of a paper in Science that showed the tool's range. The algorithm has helped pinpoint interesting associations between gut bacteria, demonstrating that both diet and gender influence gut bacteria. The tool also identified non-intuitive associations between female obesity and income. In just a few weeks, more than 50,000 visitors tapped the MINEwebsite, including, says Sabeti, visitors from "every imaginable field: genomics to finance to pharma to education and beyond."

Harmonizing incompatible data

To analyze data, whether through crowd sourcing or algorithms, you have to start with a decent database—or several. Sharing massive datasets offers huge potential for improving public health. Biostatistics chair Victor De Gruttola is working on an Institute of Medicine project identifying indicators and methods for monitoring HIV care in the U.S. "There are many tremendous sources of information, but none are sufficient in themselves to gauge the prevalence of HIV care, as well as access to mental health and substance abuse treatment and support services," he says. For example, the U.S. Centers for Disease Control and Prevention captures diagnostic, demographic, and medical information, but no data on the use of antiretroviral drugs. Medicaid and Medicare track service use through claims data, but not clinical measurements such as immune function at diagnosis. De Gruttola posits that if researchers could join these datasets, they'd learn which vulnerable groups of patients aren't getting the treatments they need.

Easier said than done - That's in part because scientists employ a mélange of incompatible structures to create their data. Winston Hide, the biostatistics associate professor, has taken a step toward fixing that problem. He and researchers at 30 organizations, including Oxford University, have invented a common language and tools for sharing data across disciplines, called Investigation-Study-Assay (ISA). (For information, visit isacommons.org.) The technology is intended to be simple for researchers to use—a sort of scientific lingua franca.

In just two weeks, Hide joined a cancer database with a stem cell dataset—and got a big payoff. "We discovered a single gene that we think is responsible for the initiation of a whole class of leukemia," he says. "Not until we could combine the information coherently could we discover things about the underlying molecular biology."

A new way of doing science

These innovative methods for mining big data are transforming the way science is done. Sabeti and Reshef are excited by the potential of hypothesis-generating (rather than hypothesis-driven) science, providing researchers with important new questions to answer. Analyzing genetic data for natural selection, for example, Sabeti had stumbled on clues to the virulence of Lassa fever, a deadly infection endemic in West Africa. She and Reshef believe that the hypothesis-generating power of big data will ultimately help researchers gain insights into the most pressing public health problems, such as the emergence and spread of resistant strains of malaria.

Meanwhile, Winston Hide believes younger scientists—raised in an era of social networking—will embrace an idea that previous generations of researchers have not: sharing data freely. It's an option that makes intuitive sense, he says, to generations raised with social networking.

Crowd sourcing is also breaking down the walls between the academy and the rest of the world. For many scientists, though, it's a tough transition: Academics have typically held their data close, because tenure, promotions, and reputation rest on being the first to publish. Sharing research takes a leap of faith in a cutthroat academic world that has yet to embrace the notion of a public commons of data. The change also comes with ethical questions, including privacy dilemmas. And employing crowds to analyze one's data begs the question of quality: How can you trust the results?

Surprisingly, Fortune says she trusts the results more than those that would have come from her lab. "I think the power of crowd sourcing is that they're going to give us better data than we can generate ourselves." That's because Crowd Flower uses redundancy to ensure quality (five people may analyze the same image). Indeed, she's become a huge fan of speeding scientific progress through crowd sourcing. "I love the idea of citizen science," she says. "We're asking people to do some not very sophisticated tasks. You could stand in line at the bank and measure bacteria for me."

To a single citizen scientist labeling a batch of images, the work may feel tedious. In fact, it's transformative—a small contribution to what may be public health's data-driven revolution. "It's just the beginning," says Winston Hide. "You should watch this space."

Elaine Grant is the former assistant director of development communications and marketing at HSPH.

https://www.hsph.harvard.edu/news/magazine/spr12-big-data-tb-health-costs/

1.9   5 big data trends that will shape AI in 2017
By Hope Reese | January 3, 2017, 6:40 AM PST

AI and machine learning are dependent on large amounts of data. But big data is hard to organize and analyze. Here's what experts are looking out for in the coming year, when it comes to data.

While "big data" can be a misunderstood buzzword in tech, there's no denying that the recent AI and machine learning push is dependent on the labeling and synthesis of huge amounts of training data. A new trend report by advisory firm Ovum predicts that the big data market—currently at $1.7 billion—will swell to $9.4 billion by 2020.

So, what do data insiders see happening in the coming year? Tech Republic spoke to several leaders in this field to find out.

Here are five big data trends to watch in 2017, from the experts.

1. AI and machine learning will increase the need for big data analytics

There's no question that the AI boom depends on data labeling and analysis. "Machine learning has really come along," said Carla Gentry, a data scientist in Louisville, KY. "2017 will be the year we see more expertise, but still it will struggle, with understanding, proper usage and talent."

"IoT on the other hand, will surge with toys, car accessories, home and security uses but it will also set up nasty hackers with lots more access to our private lives," Gentry said.

Monte Zweben, co-founder and CEO of Splice Machine, has a background in AI. "AI applications powered by machine learning depend on data to develop more predictive models," said Zweben. "The more data, and, even more importantly, more data that represents the concepts you need to learn, makes AI applications better.

For example, said Zweben, "the more electronic medical records a system sees that reflect dangerous sepsis events in hospitals, the better a system can predict them before they happen."

Big data, according to Tony Baer, principal analyst for information management at Ovum, "has emerged from its infancy to transition from buzzword to urgency for enterprises across all major sectors."

"The growing pains are being abetted by machine learning, which will lower barriers to adoption of big data-enabled analytics and solutions," said Baer, "and the growing dominance of the cloud, which will ease deployment hurdles."

2. Self-service big data tools hitting the web

With advances in data processing and cloud applications, there is a plethora of free data platforms online that make organizing and synthesizing data easy—even for beginners.

"Every platform is becoming cloud-available," said Zweben. "Even big data platforms like Splice Machine are available now as a self-service platform. You specify how much storage and compute you need and databases appear in the cloud for both your apps and data warehouses to use in minutes. There are no wires, racks, networks, or servers to configure," he said.

There are also a number of machine learning platforms, from tech giants like Baidu, Amazon, Microsoft, IBM, Google, and others. Here's more on how to choose a good data platform.

Michael Cavaretta, director of analytics infrastructure at Ford Motor Company, said he also sees this as a trend that will continue in 2017.

"Cloud implementations of big data are increasing in popularity as it drives down the entry cost for these technologies," Cavaretta said. "For many, building a big data stack just isn't cost effective—particularly for startups—and works best when the majority of the data can be hosted on a single instance."

3. Analytics are still struggling to keep up

But even with all the great tools and data warehouses, analytics remain complicated. "Even with giant data warehouses now available on Big Data like Hadoop and Spark, companies still struggle to transfer data from operational systems to analytical systems," said Zweben. "That gap and enable the seamless combination of both workloads."

"Analytics will always struggle to keep up," said Cavaretta. "As more data and better algorithms become available, more automation is possible along with better predictions. As the methods disseminate, they become the cost of doing business, driving more analytic innovation."

4. Data cleansing becoming an industry

In order to get training data into machine learning systems, it must first be cleansed, which means making sure that the information in a database has been checked for errors in format, duplications, etcetera. "Machine learning systems are only as good as the data they train on", said Zweben, "and the secret is transforming raw operational data into learnable features". The fact that someone visited an online shoe retailer, for instance is useful", he said. "But knowing they went there today is invaluable".

5. Democratization of data

Jim Adler, head of data at the Toyota Research Institute, has previously talked to Tech Republic about how data doesn't live in lakes. Rather, "it lives in silos where accountability, focus, and mission are clear," said Adler. "Server-less, micro-service architectures are making it increasingly easy for these silo-owners to access, analyze, and manage their data without racking servers, configuring virtual machines, or even paying by the hour. Going server less allows data owners to focus on their data application and pay just for what they use—by the minute."

1.10 Could Big Data Solve the Global Water Crisis?

Elliot Pannaman – 24 March, 2017

Innovative startups are looking to solve a global problem

Social sharing

Big data has already become part and parcel of the business world, a necessity to get ahead rather than a luxury extra. Such has been the focus on data's effect in business or sports that its potential importance elsewhere has been somewhat overlooked. Uptake has been slightly slower outside of the corporate environment, but many believe that big data has the power and potential to solve some of the world's biggest issues.

One such issue is that only 59% of the world's population has access to clean water. In certain areas, the problem is far worse - according to the Guardian, in sub-Saharan Africa 'only 16% (pdf) of the population have access to a personal water source like a tap, or a pump in a neighbour's yard.' Across the world, some 663 million people have no reliable access at all to clean water all year round. Climate change issues are only likely to intensify the problem, and finding solutions for less economically developed countries is a priority.

It's important to remember, though, when talking about water shortage, that the problem isn't confined to these less economically developed countries. Flint, Michigan's recent water crisis is an example of a poor water supply brought about by corporate incompetence in an economically powerful country, rather than a lack of supply. According to TechCrunch, in 2016, 'only nine US states reported safe lead levels in their schools' water supply.' This lead content almost invariably comes from irresponsible industry, and without significant investment it's difficult to see the problem improving.

Raising awareness of and combating, poor water supplies isn't easy, but there are a number of companies looking to exploit the power of big data to bring about significant change. Water shortage is as often economic or political as it is geographical, and the use of data in more effectively distributing water could help to solve the less the positive news is that Silicon Valley's role in providing water solutions is growing, and that the commercial market for these companies is far more lucrative than many might think, with TechCrunch claiming that 'venture-stage companies in water perform better than many investors and entrepreneurs realize.'

Companies like Water Smart are looking to address issues like drought through smarter, data-driven solutions and 'personalized customer engagement solutions.' To help suppliers reach water conservation goals, the company plans to educate residents on the need for conservation, reduce water use by an average of 5%, detect and alert residents to possible leaks, and detect and notify irrigation violators. Water Smart recently raised $7 million for a $21 million valuation, a figure that should be persuasive for potential future investors.

Another startup, Pluto AI, is developing a deep learning solution for water management. The company promises to 'enable water facilities to prevent water wastage, predict asset health, and minimize operating costs.' Pluto offers time stamped water data taken from sensors and meters, and uses a cutting-edge deep learning algorithm to analyze it. Its mission is to make deep learning the norm in the water industry, and its recent raise of $2.1 million from Silicon Valley VC firms may see that it does so.

India is doing some interesting work with water data, too. In a country which struggles with water distribution, the Bangalore Water Supply and Sewerage Board (BWSSB) uses data to manage, monitor, support, and administer the city's water supply. The hope is that it can address the mounting issue of equitable drinking water distribution, whilst keeping on top of the city's increasingly complex distribution systems. Already, BWSSB has made considerable savings and has cut down the city's wastage significantly.

Data alone won't solve the global water crisis, but the work of innovative new companies is as welcome as the investment they are receiving. Technology has the potential to solve some of the world's biggest problems, and water shortage is one in which data could have a real impact, given its ability to reduce waste and improve efficiency.

https://channels.theinnovationenterprise.com/articles/could-big-data-solve-the-global-water-crisis?utm_campaign=weekly_mail&utm_content=ie_Friday_2017-03-31&utm_medium=email&utm_source=ie_weekly_email&mkt_tok=eyJpIjoiTldJMFlUSTBNemM0Wm1WbSIsInQiOiJZRFhLbzVvdWlDQ0pnbHk0Q2xKR0ZkejhYSFFnSHhxS3diZ0ljVGthWGhQRUhXWDVKd25Nb1orZmNcL01FUklpalFLaytJZlJ0R21XVnR2UmpqWGFFXTkNJaUsrRVZZUQyttTEV6dlI4SGhjVZkczV4b2ZjWUtpd2t2eG8wVUs1ODEifQ%3D%3D

1.11 Why big data analytics is at the heart of digital transformation

By: MARCO POZZONI 14 Mar 2017

Digital transformation is reshaping the way the channel does business across all industries. Already today, organizations are focusing on delivering new classes of applications, such as Internet of Things (IoT), Virtual Reality or Artificial Intelligence.

All of these applications have one thing in common: they require big data analytics. By 2020, IDC is predicting that 50% of the G2000 companies will see the majority of their business depend on their ability to create digitally enhanced products, services and experiences.

The channel is no different, and requires a data-first approach to manage the means in which distributers draw from consumer behaviour and sell products.

From analytics to action plan

Big data analytics is the heart of the digital transformation. It provides the ability to analyze data quickly and to transform it into an action plan, in order to get better insights, to take faster and more accurate decisions, and ultimately have a valuable competitive advantage. Advanced analysis grants businesses more of an insight into any organization and production processes, customers and markets.

For a successful digital transformation journey, channel partners need to establish new ways of leveraging and monetizing on data. For that, data analytics need to be embedded in all new apps. It is therefore not surprising that by 2019, 40% of IT projects will create new digital services and revenue streams that monetize on data. Data has indeed become the new currency of the digital economy.

What is analytics without storage?

While data analytics is the heart of the digital transformation, storage is the heart of any data analytics solution and here is why: high-performance storage ensures that analysis tools can access data quickly. A solid storage foundation is necessary for the success of any data analytics project.

If the foundation is shaky, the entire performance, security and, ultimately, the success of the project, will be affected. For this reason, it is worth paying special attention to storage - right from the start.

In order to exploit data fully, users need the ability to leverage data wherever it resides and apply analytics to it. Analytics tools such as Splunk provide an open platform that can access other data stores, including Hadoop and make data in Splunk available for accessing and sharing across the organization. In order to realize top performance from Splunk – especially for ingesting and searching data quickly - you require a corresponding fast, available, scalable storage platform.

Data in no time - So, what's the problem?

Big Data Business Planning Chief Data Officer

Social sharing

Hating your data isn't going to solve anything or help anyone. If it's not working well for you then change it up. Detect the problem, solve it and you'll be most appreciative of your data in no time. So, what's the problem?

Victoria Wilson

Data is fragmented

We live in a world where everything happens quickly. Phone calls are fast, deals are done quickly and you can microwave a decent dinner in under two minutes. It's great when you want to get lots done but let's focus in on phone calls and communications – quick contact often means that a lot of detail is missed and is either left blank in the database or filled in retrospectively with errors.

What if employees then gain more information later on and write it down in their notebook or in a spreadsheet they have created? That's already two more data stores which are not connected to the original database. Sure, that person might know the customer inside out but if they decided to migrate to Hawaii, how would their replacement know what's going on?

That's the point. They wouldn't.

So if a small company of 30 employees had one database and then various spreadsheets and notebooks containing other information – that's a ridiculous amount of 'databases' for one company.

How can marketing send a targeted campaign to companies in Manchester if that field in the address is either blank, missed, or in someone's notebook somewhere? It'd be a tiresome job to root around for all the information so it's either sent out to a few contacts, or the whole database is just blasted – leaving a bad taste in the recipients' mouths.

What would be easier is to send the data in for cleansing – there it can be appended, formatted and corrected meaning all the details are there in the database which can be accessed by all employees – no more silos, notebooks (except for doodling) or spreadsheets. Plus, you can get some technology too which for B2B companies is super helpful – it auto-populates company information just from an email address which is useful in this world where everyone wants things done this very minute.

Data isn't the real deal

Not the data's fault. You update your phone software, otherwise, you won't trust it is safe from viruses (and you can't Snapchat without the latest updates). You update your own appearance; otherwise, you don't trust you can look the best you can. So why won't you update your data to ensure it provides the best information for communications?

Data goes out of data super quickly – it' decays at a rate of roughly 20-24% each year and with people changing addresses, moving jobs, passing away etc. it really does pay to have a database which has been screened and corrected regularly. I bet you didn't know that every month 500,000 people in the UK move to a new house, 50,000 people pass away, 40,000 addresses are changed by the Royal Mail, 20,000 people sign up to The Mailing Preference Service and 475,000 company and individual details change. So, an un-cleaned database isn't the real deal, but a clean one is – not only will communications blossom, you'll be compliant too and then, and only then, can you trust your database.

Data is dull

Data is only ever dull if you don't do anything with it. Even then it's more of a diamond in the rough and just needs polishing up to be wonderful. If you think data is dull then I'm quite surprised as there's nothing boring about opportunity. Reports might be a bit well... dreary but what you can do with a rich database is exciting – think of the profiling, shared access, targeted campaigns and how awesome the level of communication will be if every detail of every contact/company is right there in the CRM. Trust me when I say that once you start reaping the benefits, good quality data will be paramount in your day to day operations. Just three short points really regarding why people don't enjoy their data and three short solutions to these problems. Just remember, there's never any 'bad data' just out of date or incomplete data. Make data work for you.

https://channels.theinnovationenterprise.com/articles/don-t-be-a-hater-of-your-data?utm_campaign=weekly_mail&utm_content=ie_Friday_2017-04-07&utm_medium=email&utm_source=ie_weekly_email&mkt_tok=eyJpIjoiTnp BNU1UQmhOelJqTkdaaiIsInQiOiJieThzcnUrMEVvemEzU0ZaSUlpWG45NG1 aYzM3TVF3K2NneGZMQ05WU0Q3U2ZqTkQ1Ulp2RTZrdnJ0aUVRZk9FY3 ZVOHlvbVVvR0tWR0pKQVZnYmh4djNENWJRYUczYVM0ZElNTDRCdVd aeDZvR2tld1ltMk9DNkVUU09mNGJnVCJ9

1.12 Data Analytics Must Be Compulsory in MBA Programs

Why business schools that leave it off their programs are failing their students

Social sharing

According to a new report by digital transformation firm Atos, 40% of businesses are using data analytics in key functions such as sales or marketing, while 23% plan to implement it within the next year. By 2020, 90% of companies intend to do the same. This comes with a number of challenges, the most pressing of which is finding the requisite talent to implement data initiatives. But, with the talent gap well publicized, are universities doing everything they can to help ensure there is a pipeline there for companies to recruit from?

Analytics skills are already in extremely high demand, largely outstripping supply. A study by McKinsey, for one, projects that 'by 2018, the US alone may face a 50% to 60% gap between supply and requisite demand of deep analytic talent.' And this is only going to deepen, with the Bureau of Labor Statistics (BLS) estimating that the number of roles for individuals with this skill set will grow by 30% over the next seven years. Many believe that data analytics is no longer just a useful addition to a CV, it is now essential. Eric Schmidt, executive chairman of Google's parent company Alphabet, for one, recently told CNBC, 'I think a basic understanding of data analytics is incredibly important for this next generation of young people. That's the world you're going into.' Jonathan Rosenberg, adviser to CEO Larry Page, agreed, adding that, 'My favorite statement that echoes Eric's is 'Data is the sword of the 21st century, those who wield it well, the samurai.''

Asking Google if data is important is a bit like asking Ford if cars are the future of transport, but they are not alone. In Alteryx's 'The Business Grammar Report', 26% of business leaders in the UK said they believe that data and analytics are the most important skills for potential employees, while 60% consider them to be one of the top two skills. Alteryx VP EMEA Stuart Wilson added further that it had found that business leaders would be willing to offer a 30% higher salary to someone that has data skills over someone who doesn't.

Universities are already catering for this demand to an extent. Business schools have been criticized in the past for not being innovative enough and failing to keep pace with change. David Sproul, chief executive of Deloitte UK, is among those to call on business schools to do more to make technology a more central part of the curriculum, citing the ever-evolving threat of cyber-attacks and the risk of disruptive innovation. But, in fairness, universities have been quick to develop data analytics courses, with almost 100 schools now offering data-related undergraduate and graduate degrees, as well as certificates for working professional or graduate students wanting to augment other degrees. MIT's Sloan School of Management, for example, will this year take 30 graduates in their new one-year course, which will only be the prelude to a spell in a Big Data finishing school. This first cohort of students will pay $75,000 in tuition fees for their Master of Business Analytics degree, with classes ranging from 'Data mining: Finding the Data and Models that Create Value' to 'Applied Probability'. In the UK, Imperial College's one-year M.Sc. in business analytics will run you close to £26,000 ($32,000) and is in only its first year of operation.

In many people's eyes, though, they have not gone far enough. In Alteryx's survey, 79% of respondents said that the skill should be made a compulsory part of MBA programmes, and given that it is now essential in more or less every job it is hard to disagree. Indeed, you could probably make an argument for it being present in some form on courses in every discipline, not just business but humanities and other social sciences. Conspiracy theorists might argue that universities have a vested interest in restricting data analytics skills to certain courses because they can charge more for them. This additional cost is easily justified because they are compensated for by the high wages and employability. Melissa Bowers, director of the business analytics master's program at the University of Tennessee's Haslam College of Business, says her business analytics master's program has placed 100% of its graduates within three months of graduation since its first class graduated in 2011. According to the University of Tennessee—Knoxville website, the average base salary of 2015 graduates from its business analytics master's program was $80,800, and the average total salary of 2015 graduates, including signing bonuses and stock options, was $86,800. These theories are unlikely to be true, with backward-thinking and a failure to keep up the far more likely option. However, by failing to include data analytics on MBAs, universities are doing their students a huge disservice, whether through design or mere backward-thinking. In order to meet the needs of organizations in the future, and young people entering employment, data analytics skills alongside business knowledge will be necessary to fill the data talent gap, and it must be made a compulsory component of MBAs.

1.13 Is Data Set to Become the Next Electricity?

Will it become so ubiquitous that we'll forget it's there?

Social sharing

It has now been over 260 years since Benjamin Franklin managed to trap electricity in a jar, bringing the world into a new era. It is safe to say that electricity has had a bigger impact on the world than almost anything else in the last 500 year1s. It has allowed for new manufacturing techniques, huge jumps forward in technological capabilities, and has vastly improved the lives of practically every person around the world.

Talking to a few people at the Big Data Innovation Summit in London, one of the most interesting things I heard was that people expect data to become like electricity in the next decade. It is unlikely to have the same kind of impact, changing the way that people live in a profound way, but in that we will be excited not by the electricity that allows technology to run, but by the technology itself.

To some extent we have begun to see this already, with the use of personal assistants from Google and Amazon. People are thinking more about how cool it is that they can simply say something and a box in the corner of the room will answer. There is little talk about the background data that allows this to happen, the millions of voices they can understand, the ways that they can retrieve the data, how they record certain phrases and not others, etc. It is a well packaged technology and few people would really think about how it actually works.

However, because of the nature of what data is - information about people and things - it naturally has more of a value as an entity in itself. This makes it more likely to be stolen. Where you may occasionally have electricity stolen by a neighbor, you aren't going to find one person stealing millions of people's electricity. It is this that makes it more difficult to see data becoming the next electricity, you can't resell electricity after stealing it. You can't even easily store electricity, which makes it infinitely more difficult to steal. Even if you do steal it, the danger is to the person trying to steal it, not the person whose electricity has been stolen.

As we make our data more and more useable and the technology that utilizes it becomes increasingly intuitive with better user interfaces, the actual understanding of the data that underpins it is being lost. This is certainly no bad thing and shows the real power that it has and will continue to have moving forward. We need to make sure we are protecting our data in an effective and robust manner, which is the biggest challenge we currently face in seeing data spread wider than it already has.

1.14   How Is Big Data Changing Digital Marketing?

How has the use of big data impacted digital marketing?

According to one survey, almost 86% of its subjects claim that their organizations either already use big data for their digital marketing, or are considering using it. This trend is quite effective in digital marketing since it a) gives a better understanding of customers, b) improves the supply chain, and, c) powers the campaigns and deals with promotions. Still, this is just the tip of the iceberg of what big data must offer to digital marketers. Here are a few more things you should know about it.

Big data sources

The first thing you need to know is that all the information that you manage to gather from big data comes in six categories.

- 1. Web Mining: This is a simple process of extracting data from the open web, such as server logs, browser activity, but also documents and page content.

- 2. Search Information: The next part deals with search information, which does nothing else but studies the behavior of a specific target demographic.

- 3. Social Media: There is an interesting statistic which claims that 79% of all internet users are on Face book. By studying the pages, they like, the interests they list, and even the comments they are leaving, one can stumble upon an invaluable piece of information.

- 4. Crowd Sourcing: This source is a bit more direct since it works through already formed specific communities, such as forum users, survey participants, etc.

- 5. Transactional: Of course, not all data that interests you is textual. You also want to know logistic about the transactions of your clients and any relevant information about these activities. We are talking about things like flight reservations, credit card purchases, and even insurance claims.

- 6. Mobile: Finally, you need to keep in mind that in 2017, mobile users make up most online users. Therefore, it is vital for any business to dig into these user patterns. Naturally, the data is created by apps, seeing how average mobile users spend 89 percent of their time on mobile devices using them. This is also because most of them run silently in the background even when not used.

Business intelligence software

While having all this data is great on its own, it does not reveal much. Raw data is like clay that needs to be put into a mold to assume a meaningful shape. In other words, you need adequate business analytics software to interpret this data. Ideally, the information you get is displayed in the form of a dashboard, which allows you to fully assess its usefulness for your digital marketing efforts.

Real-time response

Finally, if you choose a platform that allows you to look at this data in real-time you can react to changes instantaneously. This will provide you with a unique chance to get ready for their next visit, perhaps even plan a better approach that will drastically improve your website. This can be things like email retargeting, avoiding sign-in barriers, or a 'save for later' button.

Conclusion

Over a century ago, John Wanamaker said that although one-half of all the money he spends on marketing goes to waste he can never know which part. Luckily, we have come a long way since then. Today, with modern BI software paired with big data fuels our digital marketing. We can then make sure that every dollar we invest gives us the best possible return. Because of this, it would be safe to say that big data is revolutionizing digital marketing.

https://channels.theinnovationenterprise.com/articles/how-is-big-data-changing-digital-marketing?utm_campaign=weekly_mail&utm_content=ie_Friday_2017-04-07&utm_medium=email&utm_source=ie_weekly_email&mkt_tok=eyJpIjoiTnpBNU1UQmhOelJqTkdaaiIsInQiOiJieThzcnUrMEVvemEzU0ZaSUlpWG45NG1aYzM3TVF3K2NneGZMQ05WU0Q3U2ZqTkQ1Ulp2RTZrdnJ0aUVRZk9FY3ZVOHlvbVVvR0tWR0pKQVZnYmh4djNENWJRUUczYVM0ZElNTDRCdVddaeDZvR2tld1ltMk9DNkVUU09mNGJnVCJ9

1.15 Out of the world: NASA's space probes and how Big Data is driving space explorations.

Posted by Manu Jeevan **on 11/04/2017**

Big data is everywhere today. Right from the shopping websites we use to buy our daily household necessities, to the programs used to track sales of an enterprise organization. But the penetration of big data is far and wide reaching. It wouldn't be wrong to say, it's out of this world, quite literally! NASA is using Big Data in space probes and more to help them solve other worldly problems. Here are some examples of how NASA is implementing Big Data technology:

Real Time Analytics through Elastic search

The team in control of NASA's Mars Rover spacecraft now has Big Data driven analytical engines at their fingertips. The open source **Elastic search** technology used by companies like Netflix and Goldman Sachs is used to plan the actions of the Rover, which was landed on Mars in 2012. NASA's Jet Propulsion Lab's mission planning, which runs the day-to-day mission planning, has now rebuilt its analytics systems around an Elastic search that processes all the data transmitted from the Rover during its four daily scheduled uploads.

Elastic search, which has achieved its 50 millionth download, means that anomalies and patterns in the datasets can be identified instantly. The rate of malfunction and failure can be greatly reduced, as correlations can provide mission-critical insights that can lead to a greater rate of scientific discovery. Anomaly resolutions are an application of this.

When a problem with the spacecraft has been identified, accurate details of its operations can be analyzed immediately to find out the last time this situation occurred, and what other elements were involved at that time.

The **Soil Moisture Active Passive (SMAP)** project, which was launched in 2015, also uses Elastic search. It is said, that the most interesting aspect of the Mars exploration is the possibility of identifying whether the planet has life. It is assumed that this question will be answered quickly using Elastic search. By 2020, the mission is to take life-detecting machines to Mars. The process needs to be fast, and hence technologies like Elastic search would indeed be a boon in such scenarios.

The SKA Project

Square Kilometers Array (SKA) is one of the biggest projects that have been currently planned. The construction will commence in 2018 and will be finished in the mid of 2020. The SKA will be the world's largest radio telescope, essentially a grouping of thousands of satellites that work together and peer deep into the farthest reaches of space.

It can detect even the weakest of signals from up to 50 light years away. The concept behind the project is to study more about the unknowns of our universe, right from black holes to the darkest of matter to the undiscovered planets. The potential of this project is just as huge as the construction itself, if not bigger.

So how is SKA related to Big Data? In reality, the SKA project is rather the very definition of big data. It is predicted that the SKA will generate up to 700 terabytes of data per second. To put that in another viewpoint, that is almost the same chunk of data transmitted through the whole internet every two days. Needless to mention, that is a huge amount of data, and it is launching some unique challenges for astronomers and data scientists. Most of these issues are related to storing and processing these large data chunks.

NASA identifies this as a hindrance not only with SKA but also with space as a whole. Hence, they are in the process of developing tools to handle storing and transmitting of this data. Data transmission through space has proven to be a big challenge. Transmitting data from deep space satellites and other spacecraft using radio frequencies is a very slow process. Therefore, scientists have invented better ways of doing the same, using optical communications, which will help increase download speeds, as well as the amount of data that can be transferred.

How NASA used big data to know more about Pluto:

In 2015, the **New Horizon** spacecraft had very few hours to fill its memory banks with as much data as possible from the dwarf planetary system. Finally, on October 25th, the last few hundred bits of that data finally arrived in one of NASA's profound space radio dishes.

Imagine for a moment that before the flyby, the dwarf planet was a pixilated blur. Scientists had faint ideas about Pluto's atmosphere, geology, and satellite system, and, *'pixilated'* worked as the perfect analogy for the clarity of those concepts. Now, New Horizons did not just deliver a picture of Pluto's massive heart, the survey flyby exposed the dwarf planet as one of the most dynamic and complex worlds in the solar system. Together, New Horizons collected 6.25 gigabytes of data. The spacecraft is equipped with seven different instruments like the multi-spectral imagers, particle sniffers, and dust collectors. When New Horizons was 3 billion miles away, the ground team collected the flyby data bit by bit, in 469 days.

Source: Mirror.co.uk

Every bit of data on New Horizons' drives is indexed according to when it was collected. Its engineers had to calculate exactly how many seconds it would take the probe to reach Pluto and then instruct the computer with things like, "At 299,791,044 seconds after New Horizons has left Earth, roll 32 degrees, pitch 15 degrees, yaw 256 degrees, and activate the Ralph imager for .25 seconds."

New Horizons was sending data every week for a year and a half. The images showed plains of frozen nitrogen, atmospheric haze layers, cryogenic volcanoes, vast glaciers, mountains made of water ice and geologic evidence that Pluto has been tectonically active for 4.5 billion years. The images also showed surprises like Chiron's 600-mile minimum equatorial canyon—from each of Pluto's five satellites.

Conclusion

These instances are only a few scenarios to explain the impact big data is having on space exploration. Though they seem rather conceptual, this progress could have a major impact on our routine activities. Sometimes, the farthest-reaching discoveries can have an enduring impact close to home. Whatever the case, big data is enabling scientists to get a clear picture of the universe. This indeed is just the beginning. Can you visualize what the future has in store?

<u>Manu Jeevan</u>

Manu Jeevan is a professional blogger, content marketer, and big data enthusiast. You can connect with him on LinkedIn, or email him at manu@bigdataexaminer.com.

http://www.edvancer.in/out-of-the-world-nasas-space-probes-and-how-big-data-is-driving-space-explorations/

1.16 Firing on All Cylinders: The 2017 Big Data Landscape

Matt Turck Managing Director at First Mark CapitalPublished on April 6, 2017**

It feels good to be a data geek in 2017.

Last year, we asked "Is Big Data Still a Thing?" observing that since Big Data is largely "plumbing", it has been subject to enterprise adoption cycles that are much slower than the hype cycle. As a result, it took several years for Big Data to evolve from cool new technologies to core enterprise systems deployed in production.

In 2017, we're now **well into this deployment phase**. The term "Big Data" continues to gradually fade away, but the Big Data space itself is booming. We're seeing everywhere anecdotal evidence pointing to more mature products, more substantial adoption in Fortune 1000 companies, and rapid revenue growth for many startups.

Meanwhile, the froth has indisputably moved to the machine learning and artificial intelligence side of the ecosystem. **AI** experienced in the last few months a **"Big Bang" in collective consciousness** not entirely dissimilar to the excitement around Big Data a few years ago, except with even more velocity.

2017 is also shaping up to be an exciting year from another perspective: **long-awaited IPOs**. The first few months of this year have seen a burst of activity for Big Data startups on that front, with warm reception from the public markets.

All in all, in 2017 the data ecosystem is firing on all cylinders. As every year, we'll use the annual revision of our Big Data Landscape to do a long-form, "State of the Union" **roundup of the key trends** we're seeing in the industry.

Let's dig in.

High level trends

Big Data + AI = The New Stack

As any VC privileged to see many pitches will attest, 2016 was the year when **every startup became a "machine learning company"**, ".ai" became the must-have domain name, and the "wait, but we do this with machine learning" slide became ubiquitous in fundraising decks.

Faced with an enormous avalanche of AI press, panels, newsletters and tweets, many people who had a long-standing interest in machine learning reacted the way one does when your local band suddenly becomes huge: on the one hand, pride; on the other hand, a distinct distaste for all the poseurs who show up late to the party, with ensuing predictions of impending gloom.

While it's easy to poke gentle fun at the trend, the evolution is both undeniable and major: machine learning is quickly becoming a key building block for many applications.

We're witnessing the **emergence of a new stack**, where Big Data technologies are used to handle core data engineering challenges, and machine learning is used to extract value from the data (in the form of analytical insights, or actions).

In other words: **Big Data provides the pipes, and AI provides the smarts.**

Of course, this symbiotic relationship has existed for years, but its implementation was only available to a privileged few.

The democratization of those technologies has now started in earnest. "Big Data + AI" is becoming the default stack upon which many modern applications (whether targeting consumers or enterprise) are being built. Both startups and some Fortune 1000 companies are leveraging this new stack (see for example, JP Morgan's "Contract Intelligence" application here).

Often, but not always, the cloud is the third leg of the stool. This trend is precipitated by all the efforts of the cloud giants, who are now in an open war to provide access to a machine learning cloud (more on this below).

Does democratization of AI mean commoditization in the short term? The reality is that AI remains technically very hard. While many engineers are scrambling to build AI skills, deep domain experts are, as of now, still in very rare supply around the world.

However, there is no reversing this democratization trend, and machine learning is going to evolve from competitive advantage to table stakes sooner or later.

This has consequences both for startups and large companies. For startups: unless you're building AI software as your final product, it's quickly going to become meaningless to present yourself as a "machine learning company". For large organizations: if you're not actively building a Big Data + AI strategy at this point (either homegrown or by partnering with vendors), you're exposing yourself to obsolescence. People have been saying this for years about Big Data, but with AI now running on top of it, things are accelerating in earnest.

Enterprise Budgets: Follow the Money

In our conversations with both buyers and vendors of Big Data technologies over the last year, we're seeing a **strong increase in budgets** allocated to upgrading core infrastructure and analytics in Fortune 1000 companies, with a key focus on Big Data technologies. Analyst firms seem to concur - IDC expects the Big Data and Analytics market to grow from $130 billion in 2016 to more than $203 billion in 2020.

Many buyers in Fortune 1000 companies are increasingly **sophisticated and discerning** when it comes to Big Data technologies. They have done a lot of homework over the last few years, and are now in full deployment mode. This is now true across many industries, not just the more technology-oriented ones.

This acceleration is further propelled by the **natural cycle of replacement** of older technologies, which happens every few years in large enterprises. What was previously a headwind for Big Data technologies (hard to rip and replace existing infrastructure) is now gradually turning into a tailwind ("we need to replace aging technologies, what's best in class out there?").

Certainly, many large companies ("late majority") are still early in their Big Data efforts, but things now seem to be evolving quickly.

Enterprise Data moving to the Cloud

As recently as a couple of years ago, suggestions that enterprise data could be moving to the public cloud were met with "over my dead body" reactions from large enterprise CIOs, except perhaps as a development environment or to host the odd non-critical, external-facing application.

The tone seems to have started to change, most noticeably in the last year or so. We're hearing **a lot more openness** - a gradual acknowledgement that "our customer data is already in the cloud in Sales force anyway" or that "we'll never have the same type of cyber-security budget as AWS does" - somewhat ironic considering that **security** was for many years the major strike against the cloud, but a testament to all the hard work that cloud vendors have put into security and compliance (HIPAA).

Undoubtedly, we're still far from a situation where most enterprise data goes to the public cloud, in part because of legacy systems and regulation.

However, the evolution is noticeable, and will keep accelerating. Cloud vendors will do anything to facilitate it, including sending a truck to get your data.

The 2017 Big Data Landscape

Without further ado, here's our 2017 landscape.

https://www.linkedin.com/pulse/firing-all-cylinders-2017-big-data-landscape-matt-turck

1.17 Leveraging Customer Analytics for Business Success

In collaboration with WNS, Sep 28, 2016

In the era of Big Data, businesses must be smart about how they deploy analytics tools to derive deeply valuable insights about their customers. In this transcript, Knowledge Wharton spoke with Wharton professor and analytics expert Peter Fader, Raj SivaKumar, head of the travel, technology and strategy unit at WNS, a global business process management company, and Mike Nemeth, head of the insurance practice in North America for WNS, to talk about best practices in analytics for business.

An edited transcript of the conversation follows.

Knowledge Wharton: People are talking a lot about big data and customer analytics. What is customer analytics and why should companies pay attention to that?

Peter Fader: Customer analytics has been around forever, from the time that marketing as we know it today, was born. Let's think about the 1950s or so, when we started realizing that customers are different from each other and that there's different ways that we can meet their wants and needs and anticipate what it is they might want next — and get smarter about how we'll deliver it.

We started collecting a lot of data. We started with demographics, sprinkled in a little bit of behavior, started asking questions about attitudes and started getting physiological measurements as well. Then let's mix in a little bit of social too. So, a lot of it is being smart about the kinds of data that we should be collecting to make better decisions. But then the analytics part is getting beyond the data, or more specifically, below the data. It's telling stories about the true underlying, unobservable processes that are driving that data and driving business success.

If you think about analytics, one of the ways that we like to break it down is into three broad buckets. We have descriptive analytics; we have predictive analytics and prescriptive analytics. The names are reasonably self-explanatory but it's interesting to see where the boundaries and the synergies are among them.

With descriptive analytics, that's just all about the data. Let's collect data. Let's come up with suitable summaries of it. Let's do some data visualization. Let's do some data science to really take the raw data and best frame what's going on.

"The real beauty of analytics isn't just collecting a lot of data, but it's figuring out ways to do it in a synergistic manner"–Peter Fader.

Then when we get to predictive analytics, the word predictive is a little bit misleading. It's not only about prediction, but it is this idea of drawing insights that aren't directly observable in the data. That's where we want to pull out people's true, underlying propensities, which is going to help us make predictions and it's going to help us make better decisions. Predictive analytics — that's the heart of analytics – it's the models that we build, the stories that we tell to really understand what's going on.

And then we layer on the prescriptive part. So now that we know what's really going on, now that we can project what's going to happen next, what do we do about it? How are we going to optimize? If we have a pile of money to spend, how are we going to allocate it across different kinds of activities or different customer segments or different geographic areas? It's all about this notion of descriptive, predictive and prescriptive. And that of course leads to decision-making, which is what my colleagues here can talk about with much more expertise.

Knowledge Wharton: What are some of the data sources companies are using in customer analytics?

Fader: There are a lot of generic data sources, some of which are becoming super-hot, some of which are tried and true. It all starts with demographics. Not to suggest that's necessarily the best, but it certainly is the oldest and the most common and there are a lot of companies that, even when they find better data sources, they care so much about just simple observable characteristics of the customer.

It's things like age and gender and geography, and moving a little bit into media habits, what kind of car you own. Tell me more about the characteristics of the zip code that you live in. So, demographics will kind of spread it out and will sometimes get into things, like I said, media habits, that wouldn't be a demographic, that would really be more of a behavior. But it's still something that we often use to label people.

"The first mistake that people make ... is that they assume the way they have the data organized and the data they're storing are going to be useful in an analytics project"–Mike Nemeth.

And then as we move from who people are, we move to what is it that they're thinking about. That's going into attitudes — things like wants and needs, your frustrations. One of the common attitudinal metrics that we focus on today would be the Net Promoter Score. Would you recommend this service to someone else? That's just one of a myriad of different attitudinal metrics. And there would be different kinds of behavioral metrics. We might say, 'It doesn't matter what people look like, it doesn't matter what they say, it's all about what they do.' That's going to be the transactions that people make, it's going to be their interactions with a website and it's going to be their interactions with each other. It's going to be their responses to inbound and outbound marketing activities.

And then that gives us a segue to the next one, which would be social. We care a lot about who someone relates to. How many people do you have in your social graph? How many of those links are inbound — people looking at you — versus outbound — you looking at other people? How central are you to the overall social network?

And then a real big one that's taking off today would be different kinds of physiological measures. If we think about it in terms of the whole wearable revolution, let's measure heart rate. Let's track people's eyes. Let's look at their movements — not just where they're going, but how fast they're moving and so on. The real beauty of analytics isn't just collecting a lot of data, but it's figuring out ways to do it in a really synergistic manner — that we can draw insights from these different kinds of metrics collectively that we couldn't draw from any one of these types by itself.

Knowledge Wharton: What are some of the common mistakes that companies make when they collect and use big data, as well as when they deploy analytics tools? What should they be doing?

Mike Nemeth: The first mistake that people make, in the insurance industry in particular, is that they assume the way they have the data organized and the data they're storing are going to be useful in an analytics project. And it isn't always. One of the first barriers is, 'How can I reorganize information from the various places that I have connections to, internally and externally? How can I organize that data and how can I transform the information to make it usable in an analytics project?'

"Asking the right question is so much more important in the end because if we ask the wrong question ... we can really quickly get to the wrong answer"–Raj SivaKumar.

It comes as a surprise sometimes to people. They tend to hire a bunch of expert analytics people. They buy tools. They put them all in a room and they say, 'We have a lot of data.' Insurance companies do have massive amounts of data. And they say, 'Tell us some insights.' And it's just really not that simple. The very first step is what data are we going to use? Where are we going to create a new data store that's used specifically for analytics purposes? How we manage that data, replicate that data over time, is really the first challenge that people tend to face.

Raj SivaKumar: In the travel industry, with data collection and storing data becoming so much cheaper, [the result is that,] unfortunately, the emphasis on data collection has overshadowed the emphasis on analytics. A lot of companies and a lot of people collect data - but for what purpose? And the key is to be able to ask the right question to get to the right answer. Asking the right question is so much more important in the end because if we ask the wrong question with the technology that we have, we can really quickly get to the wrong answer. So, the emphasis on analytics, the emphasis on interpreting the data, the emphasis on realizing that it's all about tradeoffs is so much more important in the current environment.

Fader: I surely agree. And I think about the old days. Again, I'm a historian of marketing and business; there's so much that we can learn. When we didn't have all of this data, when there really was more focus on decision-making than on data collection and data management, companies were pretty good at taking just a limited amount of data and squeezing as much value out of it as possible.

Unfortunately, today a lot of companies are saying, 'Well, we have all of this data that we didn't have 40 years ago so therefore whatever we knew back then is irrelevant.' It's important to think about what kind of data you need in order to address the specific questions and hypotheses that you have in mind, rather than this idea of, 'If we build it — a data warehouse — amazing things are going to happen.' So, we're all on the same page about that.

Knowledge Wharton: Some companies, particularly ones in the banking and insurance industries, sit on a lot of data. But they don't mine it to great effect. Can you tell us about the barriers that stop companies from mining data more effectively?

Nemeth: It begins with the fact that the data that's been traditionally collected in the insurance industry is not about the customer. We have elementary information like Peter mentioned earlier: gender, age, location, things of that nature. But really most of the data that is being set upon by insurance companies is information about the risk, not about the customer. So, it's about the house, it's about the car, it's about the business as opposed to about the customer. And we can intuit a certain amount of customer information from information about the risk, but most of it is not about the customer.

"Collecting information specific to the customer is a relatively new thing in the insurance industry"–Mike Nemeth

Collecting information specific to the customer is a relatively new thing in the insurance industry. These doors are suddenly wide open. And like Peter mentioned just a moment ago, all of a sudden, we have this influx of information that insurance companies have not had a lot of experience with. And so, they don't really know how to interpret the meaning of some of that information, how to combine it with information they do have experience with, to come up with good analytics results.

One of the keys to making that work is to add domain expertise to the analytics project teams. And this is sometimes overlooked, unfortunately. We hire analysts, we buy tools, we have data — we think those are the three components to produce these fantastic results. And they forget about the domain expertise that needs to go into the mix. And Raj hit the nail on the head when he said, 'I think we have more questions about this, so I won't go too deeply into it at the moment, but analytics is all about asking the right questions.' And the people who know what the right questions are the domain experts.

Fader: Everything that Mike just said, take out the word insurance and financial services and plug in pretty much any other industry and the same applies. In fact, in many ways insurance might be a step ahead of many other sectors because traditionally they have looked at, say, risks differently for different kinds of customers, as opposed to a lot of other sectors that have looked at the customer in some kind of singular way.

But indeed, the idea that our data collection has been much more focused on the products that we develop and the activities that we do to develop and serve those products, as opposed to those previously faceless,

nameless customers out there that were creating the demand for them —
that is a change. And I like to believe that a lot of the activities that I'm
doing and that happen at, say, academia in general are trying to get
companies to wake up and realize that it's not just a matter of collecting
more data about your products, it's about changing the kind of data, the
kinds of questions that you're asking, in a very transformational way.

SivaKumar: In the travel industry, and particularly with airlines,
the issue is tradeoffs. Let me give you a very simple example. Let's say
the marketing department would like to ensure that the customer with the
highest [value] year gets the preference in terms of seat assignment and
travel, whereas the revenue management department would like to make
sure that every single passenger pays the highest price. This tradeoff
between what you charge a customer versus you allocating a high value
customer who may not be paying a high value on that flight — it becomes
a classic tradeoff. The companies that … leverage the data to understand
the tradeoffs better, are going to be well served.

Fader: We've made it very clear, and I hope that people resonate
with the idea, that it's not just a matter of collecting more data. Let's go
back to the basic rubric of the descriptive, the predictive and the
prescriptive. There's so much attention these days on the descriptive part,
which is, 'let's collect lots of data, let's make lots of pretty pictures, let's
do a lot of what we call data science.' The problem is when we talk about
data science there's been too much emphasis on the data and not enough
emphasis on the science.

I think the next generation — as we start seeing that there are
limits not only to how much data we can collect, but the quality of data
that we collect — is going to start saying, 'Let's not collect anymore.
Let's think more carefully about that data. Let's understand the processes
that are driving it in the first place, and let's get smarter about the ways

that we can layer on top different kinds of prescriptive or optimal elements.'

We're going to see — I don't want to say a shift, I'm not saying we're moving away from data by any means — a broadening of our horizons. A little bit more of the science to balance out the focus that we've had on data so far.

http://knowledge.wharton.upenn.edu/article/leveraging-customer-analytics-for-business-success/

1.18 Use of Big Data in Government's Overarching Policies and Reforms

January 17, 2017 ;Divya Bharathi G, Prasanth Reddy Burramukku

Introduction

It is by now no surprise that we live in a world of data. Of late, big data has been the hottest buzzword across all industries. It's one of those things big companies and startups constantly talk about when people ask what "the next big thing" will be. Data is produced in greater quantities and by more sources than ever before and analyzed faster and with greater sophistication than was imaginable just a few years ago. Every day, new tools are created to turn raw data into information, and information into visual representations. The reach and applicability of big data seem limitless.

Around 40% of the world population has an internet connection today. In 1995, it was less than 1%. The number of internet users has increased tenfold from 1999 to 2013. The first billion was reached in 2005.Currently 3.6 billion people use internet and more than 4.9 billion use mobile phones to communicate. With so many technology and internet enabled devices all around data is being produced at unprecedented levels globally. Many innovations have been made toward expanding the technological capacity to generate, store, and analyze data from multiple sources and for a multitude of purposes. Individuals, firms, machines, and government agencies produce data at unprecedented rates. Some 2.5 quintillion bytes of data are produced every day, and approximately 90 percent of existing data was produced in the last two years alone. The ever-increasing data footprint provides a range of possibilities for usage by government.

Researches are being carried out to determine whether big data could help governments improve policy design and service delivery. Strengthening policy and promoting investments in big data and cloud computing areas offer potential tools for "changing production patterns, generating quality employment, creating local value-added, and enhancing the region's competitiveness and integration into global markets.

Methodology

Earlier much effort was put in by the government to gather, store and analyze large amounts of information. Many governments and firms have been collecting large amounts of data about their citizens or customers to better understand their preferences and provide better services and products. Big Data can significantly change the way public services reach citizens.

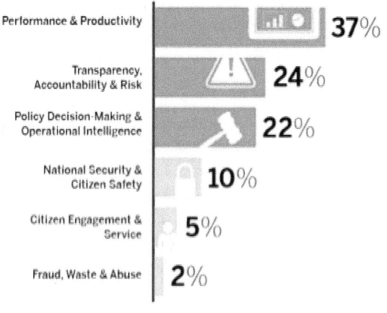

Performance & Productivity	37%
Transparency, Accountability & Risk	24%
Policy Decision-Making & Operational Intelligence	22%
National Security & Citizen Safety	10%
Citizen Engagement & Service	5%
Fraud, Waste & Abuse	2%

Source: SAP Performance Benchmarking (https://valuemanagement.sap.com)

For instance, when a 5.9 earthquake hit near Richmond, Virginia on August, 2011, residents in New York City read about the quake on Twitter feeds 30 seconds before they experienced the quake themselves. People are more connected than ever and increasingly empowered. Citizens expect to get the information they want, when they want it, and in whatever way they want to access it. In the past few years, digital technology i.e. online portals, mobile apps, self – service kiosks etc. has unleashed a tsunami of information on the government and changed the dynamic of its relationship with citizens. New expectations require governments to be ready to receive process, share and deliver information and services anytime, anywhere and on any device. Enter Big Data. Big Data provides the opportunity to transform the business of government by providing greater insight at the point of impact and ultimately better serving citizenry.

For Public sector organizations that are ahead of the curve on Big Data adoption, the greatest benefits lie in improved performance and productivity, transparency and risk assessment and policy decision making and operational intelligence.

So, the next time an earthquake strikes a city, its citizens might have already been forewarned and evacuated to shelters. That's the promise of Big Data for government.

Government collects all sorts of data from the public; it has access to birth data, death data, area of country, security data. In real time, Big Data can be of great use to the government in formulating and altering the policies of the country. Important role of big data is transforming the face of various sectors in the following way.

Taxation:

Many developing economies today face taxation challenges which include tax evasion, low collection rates, and weak tax administration. Tax evasion and income tax fraud are the main problems that are to be identified and addressed. Tax data includes business transactions, invoices, property details etc. Countries like Brazil, China, and the United States have used big data to formulate, improve, and manage tax policy and administration in diverse environments. Tax authorities have been using innovative technical solutions to implement sophisticated fraud detection strategies using socio-demographic data and taxpayers' behavior predictive analytics using big data. Tax administration system makes extensive use of big data solutions that use multi- and cross-referencing to verify business information which makes it very difficult for people to find the loopholes in the system. All these data analytics can help in prevent people from evading tax, which results in more national income thereby higher growth.

Climate Change:

With many of the countries ratifying the Paris Agreement in October, 2016, it is the duty of the country to ambitiously fight against the climate change. Big Data can adversely help our country in achieving the climate change goals. By getting data on a continuous basis from all the factories and industries in the country, the government can impose stricter rules and taxes on the factories which are polluting the most. This data can also help government in devising barriers to entry for companies implementing the technologies which are not complying with the ambitious pollution standards.

Big Data can also help government predict the weather conditions and thereby drought or famine in advance and can accordingly ease the regulations on import of food and other groceries to prevent inflation.

Smart Cities:

Smart Cities Awas Yojna Mission was launched by Prime Minister Narendra Modi in June 2015. A total of ₹980 billion has been approved by the Indian Cabinet for development of 100 smart cities and rejuvenation of 500 others. Smart cities can fundamentally change our lives at many levels such as less pollution, garbage, parking problems and more energy savings. Despite the path to implementation is full of the challenges, big data and the Internet of Things (IoT) have the power to drive the implementation. Big data and the IoT are going to work with other software and hardware to lead the vision of smart city to fruition.

How can big data contribute to smart cities?

- The traffic will be measured and regulated with the help of RFID tags on the cars. The RFID tags will send the geo location data to a central monitoring unit that will identify the congested areas. Also, the citizens will always know via their smart phones and mobile devices the exact status of public transportation and its availability.

- Even garbage collection will generate data. Residents who dispose of garbage will need to use a chip card in the containers. Garbage trucks will not collect and dispose garbage anymore. Each house will have garbage disposal units and garbage will be sucked from them to the garbage treatment centers which will dispose it in an environment friendly way. The garbage will be used to generate power for the city.

- The smart energy grid can measure the presence of people in a particular area in a particular moment and can accordingly adjust the street lights. For example, the smart grids will ensure that areas that are scantly populated will automatically have some of the street lights turned off. This will result in a lot of energy savings.

- Big data can help reduce emissions and bring down pollution. Sensors fitted in the roads will measure the total traffic at different times of a day and the total emissions. The data can be sent to a central unit which will coordinate with the traffic police. Traffic can be managed or diverted along other less congested areas to reduce carbon emissions in a particular area.

- Parking problems can be better managed. Cars will have sensors attached which can guide the car to the nearest available parking lots.

Big data can also help government in understanding the requirement of infrastructure in various parts of the country and thus can help it plan the usage of resources efficiently.

Defense Sector:

When the government has access to security data like how many soldiers are present in the border areas, coastal areas and hilly regions, it also knows the number of penetrations from terrorists in different regions, it can see in real time, the current assigned soldiers and assigned equipment and their use. Through all this information collected through drones, sensors etc., the government can formulate a plan for research and development of particular weapons, and same for training soldiers for desired tactics. The Military generals can update the strategy in real time and device policies which can make the defense sector function efficiently. With the real-time tracking of military activities of the neighboring countries, government can effectively allocate its resources to counter the strategies devised by the opponents.

Citizen Security:

Big data helps in reducing crime and achieving other citizen security goals. Data will make life more secured for the citizens. For example, children playing in the parks will wear bracelets with sensors which will allow the children to get tracked in case they go missing.

Conclusion:

For a developing nation like India, investing in big data can be very instrumental in helping it reach the growth targets. With the help of predictive analytics, big data can help the nation to plan and use its resources efficiently. It can help the government in better governance and track its growth effectively. Big data analysis will give the country a boost in its development plans and a step closer to its strategic goal.

References:

1. http://www.opengovasia.com/articles/big-data-helps-indian-government-collect-more-tax

2. http://www.businessinsider.in/Big-Data-Is-One-Of-The-Biggest-Buzzwords-In-Tech-That-No-One-Has-Figured-Out-Yet/articleshow/40554353.cms

3. https://publications.iadb.org/bitstream/handle/11319/7884/Big-Data-in-the-Public-Sector-Selected-Applications-and-Lessons-Learned.pdf

4. http://www.mondaq.com/x/475484/tax+authorities/Big+Data+And+The+Seismic+Shift+Happening+In+The+Tax+Sector

5. https://www.google.co.in/search?q=big+data+in+public+sector&esp
v=2&biw=1366&bih=662&source=lnms&tbm=isch&sa=X&ved=0ahUKEw
ij6LXd-LTRAhXBL48KHZOSD70Q_AUIBygC#imgrc=_

Authors Name: Divya Bharathi G, NMIMS, Mumbai and Prasanth Reddy Burramukku, NMIMS, Mumbai

1.19 The Return on the Data Asset in the Era of Big Data: Capturing the $1.6 trillion Data Dividend

April 15, 2014 by stbblogger

Several prior research studies have looked at the benefits of *any* point investment in big data and business analytics over no investment at all. Recognizing that a growing number of organizations have already invested in a base level of business analytics technology and capabilities, IDC set out to identify the difference between those organization and others that have invested in using more diverse data types and source, more diverse analytical tools and methods, and in distributing information to more diverse audience of end user types – at the right time. In short, our goal was to identify and quantify the additional value or the *data dividend* to be gained from investing in a more comprehensive and diverse set of big data and analytics capabilities.

As part of IDC's research study, underwritten by Microsoft, we surveyed 2,020 large and mid-sized organizations in 20 countries across a range of public and public-sector industries, including financial services, retail, manufacturing, health care, government, communications and professional services. 73% of survey respondents were from line of business or executive functions and 27% from the IT function; 62% of respondents had the title of manager or above. In addition, IDC relied on its 50 years of experience in tracking IT markets to assess and develop an economic net benefits model based on GDP, IDC forecasts for IT spending, labor and operational costs as a percentage of revenue, and spending by country on Big Data and Business Analytics hardware, software, and services.

First, our research showed a correlation between better outcomes from Big Data and Business Analytics projects and greater competitiveness of an organization in its industry or a better ability to fulfill its mission in public sector. Although correlation does not equate to causation, a growing body of case-based research shows financial and productivity benefits directly linked to better data-driven decision making enabled by Big Data and Business Analytics solutions.[1, 2]

Second, our research showed that the improved project outcomes accrue to the more innovative organizations that have embraced a data-driven culture, which has resulted in the introduction of:

- More new data types and sources
- More new analytics and new metrics
- More new users with access to big data and analytics solutions

All this, while investing in technology that enables right time access to the freshest available data. (For a more details on the IDC research methodology and results look for an upcoming white paper). Finally, we quantified the difference in benefits between organizations at the High and Low ends of the big data and analytics innovation spectrum and called it the *data dividend*. IDC research points to a worldwide *data dividend* of $1.6 trillion over a 4-year period.

We evaluated the *data dividend* across four business processes: (1) customer facing, (2) operations, (3) product or service innovation, and (4) support functions; and quantified the benefits into three categories: revenue increase, cost reduction, productivity improvement.

As the notion of data as an asset takes root throughout the world economy, there is a greater need to quantify the potential return on the data asset. IDC's newest research pegs that return or the data dividend to $1.6 trillion over the next four years. At an individual organization level the opportunity, for those who invest in the technologies, data, people, and practices at levels characteristic of the more innovative organizations, is the potential for a 60% improvement on the return on their data assets – a significant increase for any organization – private or public.

To put it simply: (Diverse Data Types and Connections + New Analytics + New Users and Insights) @ the right time = 60% greater data dividend

Stay tuned for a whitepaper and more IDC research in this area.

Dan Vesset, Program Vice President, IDC - Business Analytics and Big Data research

References:

[1]Strength in Numbers: How Does Data-Driven Decision-making Affect Firm Performance? Massachusetts Institute of Technology Sloan School of Management and University of Pennsylvania, 2011, by Erik Brynjolfsson, Lorin M. Hitt, Heekyung Hellen Kim.

[2] Competing on Analytics: The New Science of Winning. Harvard Business School Publication Corporation, 2007, by Thomas H. Davenport, Jeane G. Harris.

https://blogs.technet.microsoft.com/stbnewsbytes/2014/04/15/the-return-on-the-data-asset-in-the-era-of-big-data-capturing-the-1-6-trillion-data-dividend/

1.20 Beyond the hype: Big data concepts, methods, and analytics

Amir Gandomi and Murtaza Haider.

Ted Rogers School of Management, Ryerson University, Toronto, Ontario M5B 2K3, Canada

https://doi.org/10.1016/j.ijinfomgt.2014.10.007Get rights and content

Under a Creative Commons license

Open access

Highlights

- We define what is meant by big data.

- We review analytics techniques for text, audio, video, and social media data.

- We make the case for new statistical techniques for big data.

- We highlight the expected future developments in big data analytics.

Abstract

Size is the first, and at times, the only dimension that leaps out at the mention of big data. This paper attempts to offer a broader definition of big data that captures its other unique and defining characteristics. The rapid evolution and adoption of big data by industry has leapfrogged the discourse to popular outlets, forcing the academic press to catch up.

Academic journals in numerous disciplines, which will benefit from a relevant discussion of big data, have yet to cover the topic. This paper presents a consolidated description of big data by integrating definitions from practitioners and academics. The paper's primary focus is on the analytic methods used for big data. A particular distinguishing feature of this paper is its focus on analytics related to unstructured data, which constitute 95% of big data. This paper highlights the need to develop appropriate and efficient analytical methods to leverage massive volumes of heterogeneous data in unstructured text, audio, and video formats. This paper also reinforces the need to devise new tools for predictive analytics for structured big data. The statistical methods in practice were devised to infer from sample data. The heterogeneity, noise, and the massive size of structured big data call for developing computationally efficient algorithms that may avoid big data pitfalls, such as spurious correlation.

Keywords

- Big data analytics
- Big data definition
- Unstructured data analytics
- Predictive analytics

1. Introduction

This paper documents the basic concepts relating to big data. It attempts to consolidate the hitherto fragmented discourse on what constitutes big data, what metrics define the size and other characteristics of big data, and what tools and technologies exist to harness the potential of big data.

From corporate leaders to municipal planners and academics, big data are the subject of attention, and to some extent, fear. The sudden rise of big data has left many unprepared. In the past, new technological developments first appeared in technical and academic publications. The knowledge and synthesis later seeped into other avenues of knowledge mobilization, including books. The fast evolution of big data technologies and the ready acceptance of the concept by public and private sectors left little time for the discourse to develop and mature in the academic domain. Authors and practitioners leapfrogged to books and other electronic media for immediate and wide circulation of their work on big data. Thus, one finds several books on big data, including *Big Data for Dummies*, but not enough fundamental discourse in academic publications.

The leapfrogging of the discourse on big data to more popular outlets implies that a coherent understanding of the concept and its nomenclature is yet to develop. For instance, there is little consensus around the fundamental question of how big the data has to be to qualify as 'big data'. Thus, there exists the need to document in the academic press the evolution of big data concepts and technologies.

A key contribution of this paper is to bring forth the oft-neglected dimensions of big data. The popular discourse on big data, which is dominated and influenced by the marketing efforts of large software and hardware developers, focuses on predictive analytics and structured data. It ignores the largest component of big data, which is unstructured and is available as audio, images, video, and unstructured text. It is estimated that the analytics-ready structured data forms only a small subset of big data. The unstructured data, especially data in video format, is the largest component of big data that is only partially archived.

This paper is organized as follows. We begin the paper by defining big data. We highlight the fact that size is only one of several dimensions of big data. Other characteristics, such as the frequency with which data are generated, are equally important in defining big data. We then expand the discussion on various types of big data, namely text, audio, video, and social media. We apply the analytics lens to the discussion on big data.

Hence, when we discuss data in video format, we focus on methods and tools to analyze data in video format.

Given that the discourse on big data is contextualized in predictive analytics frameworks, we discuss how analytics have captured the imaginations of business and government leaders and describe the state-of-practice of a rapidly evolving industry. We also highlight the perils of big data, such as spurious correlation, which have hitherto escaped serious inquiry. The discussion has remained focused on correlation, ignoring the more nuanced and involved discussion on causation. We conclude by highlighting the expected developments to realize in the near future in big data analytics.

2. Defining big data

While it is ubiquitous today, however, 'big data' as a concept is nascent and has uncertain origins. Diebold (2012) argues that the term "big data ... probably originated in lunch-table conversations at Silicon Graphics Inc. (SGI) in the mid-1990s, in which John Mashey figured prominently". Despite the references to the mid-nineties, Fig. 1 shows that the term became widespread as recently as in 2011. The current hype can be attributed to the promotional initiatives by IBM and other leading technology companies who invested in building the niche analytics market.

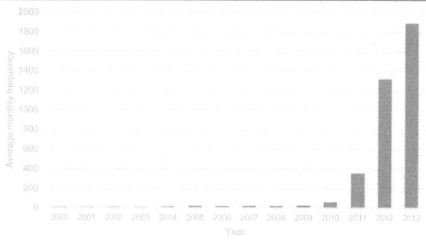

Figure 1: Frequency distribution of documents containing the term "big data" in ProQuest Research Library.

Big data definitions have evolved rapidly, which has raised some confusion. This is evident from an online survey of 154 C-suite global executives conducted by Harris Interactive on behalf of SAP in April 2012("Small and midsize companies look to make big gains with big data," 2012). Fig. 2 shows how executives differed in their understanding of big data, where some definitions focused on what it is, while others tried to answer what it does.

Clearly, size is the first characteristic that comes to mind considering the question "what is big data?" However, other characteristics of big data have emerged recently. For instance, Laney (2001) suggested that *Volume*, *Variety*, and *Velocity* (or the *Three V's*) are the three dimensions of challenges in data management. The Three V's have emerged as a common framework to describe big data (Chen, Chiang &Storey, 2012; Kwon, Lee, & Shin, 2014). For example, Gartner, Inc. defines big data in similar terms:

"Big data is high-volume, high-velocity and high-variety information assets that demand cost-effective, innovative forms of

information processing for enhanced insight and decision making." (Gartner IT Glossary, n.d.)

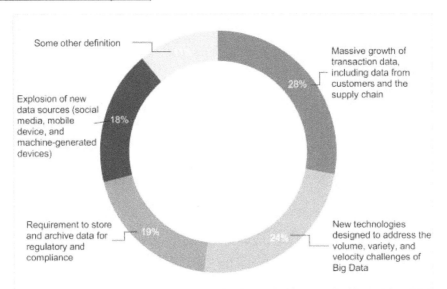

Figure 2: Definitions of big data based on an online survey of 154 global executives in April 2012.

Similarly, TechAmerica Foundation defines big data as follows:

"Big data is a term that describes large volumes of high velocity, complex and variable data that require advanced techniques and technologies to enable the capture, storage, distribution, management and analysis of the information." (TechAmerica Foundation's Federal Big Data Commission, 2012)

We describe the Three V's below.

Volume refers to the magnitude of data. Big data sizes are reported in multiple terabytes and petabytes. A survey conducted by IBM in mid-2012 revealed that just over half of the 1144 respondents considered datasets over one terabyte to be big data (Schroeck, Shockley, Smart, Romero-Morales, &Tufano, 2012). One terabyte stores as much data as would fit on 1500 CDs or 220 DVDs, enough to store around 16 million Face book photographs. Beaver, Kumar, Li, Sobel, and Vajgel (2010) report that Face book processes up to one million photographs per second. One petabyte equals 1024 terabytes. Earlier estimates suggest that Face book stored 260 billion photos using storage space of over 20 petabytes.

Definitions of big data volumes are relative and vary by factors, such as time and the type of data. What may be deemed big data today may not meet the threshold in the future because storage capacities will increase, allowing even bigger data sets to be captured. In addition, the type of data, discussed under variety, defines what is meant by 'big'. Two datasets of the same size may require different data management technologies based on their type, e.g., tabular versus video data. Thus, definitions of big data also depend upon the industry. These considerations therefore make it impractical to define a specific threshold for big data volumes.

Variety refers to the structural heterogeneity in a dataset. Technological advances allow firms to use various types of structured, semi-structured, and unstructured data. Structured data, which constitutes only 5% of all existing data (Cukier, 2010), refers to the tabular data found in spreadsheets or relational databases. Text, images, audio, and video are examples of unstructured data, which sometimes lack the structural organization required by machines for analysis. Spanning a continuum between fully structured and unstructured data, the format of semi-structured data does not conform to strict standards. Extensible Markup Language (XML), a textual language for exchanging data on the Web, is a typical example of semi-structured data. XML documents contain user-defined data tags which make them machine-readable.

A high level of variety, a defining characteristic of big data, is not necessarily new. Organizations have been hoarding unstructured data from internal sources (e.g., sensor data) and external sources (e.g., social media). However, the emergence of new data management technologies and analytics, which enable organizations to leverage data in their business processes, is the innovative aspect. For instance, facial recognition technologies empower the brick-and-mortar retailers to acquire intelligence about store traffic, the age or gender composition of their customers, and their in-store movement patterns. This invaluable information is leveraged in decisions related to product promotions, placement, and staffing. Click stream data provides a wealth of information about customer behavior and browsing patterns to online retailers. Click stream advises on the timing and sequence of pages viewed by a customer. Using big data analytics, even small and medium-sized enterprises (SMEs) can mine massive volumes of semi-structured data to improve website designs and implement effective cross-selling and personalized product recommendation systems.

Velocity refers to the rate at which data are generated and the speed at which it should be analyzed and acted upon. The proliferation of digital devices such as smart phones and sensors has led to an unprecedented rate of data creation and is driving a growing need for real-time analytics and evidence-based planning. Even conventional retailers are generating high-frequency data. Wal-Mart, for instance, processes more than one million transactions per hour (Cukier, 2010). The data emanating from mobile devices and flowing through mobile apps produces torrents of information that can be used to generate real-time, personalized offers for everyday customers. This data provides sound information about customers, such as geospatial location, demographics, and past buying patterns, which can be analyzed in real time to create real customer value.

Given the soaring popularity of smart phones, retailers will soon have to deal with hundreds of thousands of streaming data sources that demand real-time analytics. Traditional data management systems are not capable of handling huge data feeds instantaneously. This is where big data technologies come into play. They enable firms to create real-time intelligence from high volumes of 'perishable' data.

In addition to the three V's, other dimensions of big data have also been mentioned. These include:

Veracity: IBM coined *Veracity* as the fourth V, which represents the unreliability inherent in some sources of data. For example, customer sentiments in social media are uncertain in nature, since they entail human judgment. Yet they contain valuable information. Thus, the need to deal with imprecise and uncertain data is another facet of big data, which is addressed using tools and analytics developed for management and mining of uncertain data.

Variability (and complexity): SAS introduced *Variability* and *Complexity* as two additional dimensions of big data. Variability refers to the variation in the data flow rates. Often, big data velocity is not consistent and has periodic peaks and troughs. Complexity refers to the fact that big data are generated through a myriad of sources. This imposes a critical challenge: the need to connect, match, cleanse and transform data received from different sources.

Value: Oracle introduced *Value* as a defining attribute of big data. Based on Oracle's definition, big data are often characterized by relatively "low value density". That is, the data received in the original form usually has a low value relative to its volume. However, a high value can be obtained by analyzing large volumes of such data.

The relativity of big data volumes discussed earlier applies to all dimensions. Thus, universal benchmarks do not exist for volume, variety, and velocity that define big data. The defining limits depend upon the size, sector, and location of the firm and these limits evolve over time. Also important is the fact that these dimensions are not independent of each other. As one-dimension changes, the likelihood increases that another dimension will also change as a result. However, a 'three-V tipping point' exists for every firm beyond which traditional data management and analysis technologies become inadequate for deriving timely intelligence. The Three-V tipping point is the threshold beyond which firms start dealing with big data. The firms should then trade-off the future value expected from big data technologies against their implementation costs.

3. Big data analytics

Big data are worthless in a vacuum. Its potential value is unlocked only when leveraged to drive decision making. To enable such evidence-based decision making, organizations need efficient processes to turn high volumes of fast-moving and diverse data into meaningful insights. The overall process of extracting insights from big data can be broken down into five stages (Labrinidis & Jagadish, 2012), shown in Figure 3. These five stages form the two main sub-processes: data management and analytics. Data management involves processes and supporting technologies to acquire and store data and to prepare and retrieve it for analysis. Analytics, on the other hand, refers to techniques used to analyze and acquire intelligence from big data. Thus, big data analytics can be viewed as a sub-process in the overall process of 'insight extraction' from big data.

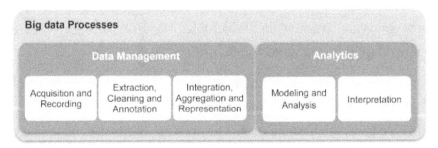

Figure 3: Processes for extracting insights from big data.

In the following sections, we briefly review big data analytical techniques for structured and unstructured data. Given the breadth of the techniques, an exhaustive list of techniques is beyond the scope of a single paper. Thus, the following techniques represent a relevant subset of the tools available for big data analytics.

3.1. Text analytics

Text analytics (text mining) refers to techniques that extract information from textual data. Social network feeds, emails, blogs, online forums, survey responses, corporate documents, news, and call center logs are examples of textual data held by organizations. Text analytics involve statistical analysis, computational linguistics, and machine learning. Text analytics enable businesses to convert large volumes of human generated text into meaningful summaries, which support evidence-based decision-making. For instance, text analytics can be used to predict stock market based on information extracted from financial news (Chung, 2014). We present a brief review of text analytics methods below.

Information extraction (*IE*) techniques extract structured data from unstructured text. For example, IE algorithms can extract structured information such as drug name, dosage, and frequency from medical prescriptions. Two sub-tasks in IE are Entity Recognition (ER) and Relation Extraction (RE) (Jiang, 2012). ER finds names in text and classifies them into predefined categories such as person, date, location, and organization. RE finds and extracts semantic relationships between entities (e.g., persons, organizations, drugs, genes, etc.) in the text. For example, given the sentence "Steve Jobs co-founded Apple Inc. in 1976", an RE system can extract relations such as Founder of [Steve Jobs, Apple Inc.] or Founded in [Apple Inc., 1976].

Text summarization techniques automatically produce a succinct summary of a single or multiple documents. The resulting summary conveys the key information in the original text(s). Applications include scientific and news articles, advertisements, emails, and blogs. Broadly speaking, summarization follows two approaches: the extractive approach and the abstractive approach. In extractive summarization, a summary is created from the original text units (usually sentences). The resulting summary is a subset of the original document. Based on the extractive approach, formulating a summary involves determining the salient units of a text and stringing them together. The importance of the text units is evaluated by analyzing their location and frequency in the text. Extractive summarization techniques do not require an 'understanding' of the text. In contrast, abstractive summarization techniques involve extracting semantic information from the text. The summaries contain text units that are not necessarily present in the original text. In order to parse the original text and generate the summary, abstractive summarization incorporates advanced Natural Language Processing (NLP) techniques. As a result, abstractive systems tend to generate more coherent summaries than the extractive systems do (Hahn & Mani, 2000). However, extractive systems are easier to adopt, especially for big data.

   Question answering (QA) techniques provide answers to questions posed in natural language. Apple's Siri and IBM's Watson are examples of commercial QA systems. These systems have been implemented in healthcare, finance, marketing, and education. Like abstractive summarization, QA systems rely on complex NLP techniques. QA techniques are further classified into three categories: the information retrieval (IR)-based approach, the knowledge-based approach, and the hybrid approach. IR-based QA systems often have three sub-components. First is the *question processing*, used to determine details, such as the question type, question focus, and the answer type, which are used to create a query. Second is *document processing* which is used to retrieve relevant pre-written passages from a set of existing documents using the query formulated in question processing. Third is *answer processing*, used to extract candidate answers from the output of the previous component, rank them, and return the highest-ranked candidate as the output of the QA system. Knowledge-based QA systems generate a semantic description of the question, which is then used to query structured resources. The Knowledge-based QA systems are particularly useful for restricted domains, such as tourism, medicine, and transportation, where large volumes of pre-written documents do not exist. Such domains lack data redundancy, which is required for IR-based QA systems. Apple's Siri is an example of a QA system that exploits the knowledge-based approach. In hybrid QA systems, like IBM's Watson, while the question is semantically analyzed, candidate answers are generated using the IR methods.

Sentiment analysis (opinion mining) techniques analyze opinionated text, which contains people's opinions toward entities such as products, organizations, individuals, and events. Businesses are increasingly capturing more data about their customers' sentiments that has led to the proliferation of sentiment analysis (Liu, 2012). Marketing, finance, and the political and social sciences are the major application areas of sentiment analysis. Sentiment analysis techniques are further divided into three sub-groups, namely document-level, sentence-level, and aspect-based. Document-level techniques determine whether the whole document expresses a negative or a positive sentiment. The assumption is that the document contains sentiments about a single entity. While certain techniques categorize a document into two classes, negative and positive, others incorporate more sentiment classes (like the Amazon's five-star system) (Feldman, 2013). Sentence-level techniques attempt to determine the polarity of a single sentiment about a known entity expressed in a single sentence. Sentence-level techniques must first distinguish subjective sentences from objective ones. Hence, sentence-level techniques tend to be more complex compared to document-level techniques. Aspect-based techniques recognize all sentiments within a document and identify the aspects of the entity to which each sentiment refers. For instance, customer product reviews usually contain opinions about different aspects (or features) of a product. Using aspect-based techniques, the vendor can obtain valuable information about different features of the product that would be missed if the sentiment is only classified in terms of polarity.

3.2. Audio analytics

Audio analytics analyze and extract information from unstructured audio data. When applied to human spoken language, audio analytics is also referred to as *speech analytics*. Since these techniques have mostly been applied to spoken audio, the terms audio analytics and speech analytics are often used interchangeably. Currently, customer call centers and healthcare are the primary application areas of audio analytics.

Call centers use audio analytics for efficient analysis of thousands or even millions of hours of recorded calls. These techniques help improve customer experience, evaluate agent performance, enhance sales turnover rates, monitor compliance with different policies (e.g., privacy and security policies), gain insight into customer behavior, and identify product or service issues, among many other tasks. Audio analytics systems can be designed to analyze a live call, formulate cross/up-selling recommendations based on the customer's past and present interactions, and provide feedback to agents in real time. In addition, automated call centers use the Interactive Voice Response (IVR) platforms to identify and handle frustrated callers.

In healthcare, audio analytics support diagnosis and treatment of certain medical conditions that affect the patient's communication patterns (e.g., depression, schizophrenia, and cancer) (Hirschberg, Hjalmarsson, &Elhadad, 2010). Also, audio analytics can help analyze an infant's cries, which contain information about the infant's health and emotional status (Patil, 2010). The vast amount of data recorded through speech-driven clinical documentation systems is another driver for the adoption of audio analytics in healthcare.

Speech analytics follows two common technological approaches: the transcript-based approach (widely known as large-vocabulary continuous speech recognition, LVCSR) and the phonetic-based approach. These are explained below.

LVCSR systems follow a two-phase process: indexing and searching. In the first phase, they attempt to transcribe the speech content of the audio. This is performed using automatic speech recognition (ASR) algorithms that match sounds to words. The words are identified based on a predefined dictionary. If the system fails to find the exact word in the dictionary, it returns the most similar one. The output of the system is a searchable index file that contains information about the sequence of the words spoken in the speech. In the second phase, standard text-based methods are used to find the search term in the index file.

Phonetic-based systems work with sounds or *phonemes*. Phonemes are the perceptually distinct units of sound in a specified language that distinguishes one word from another (e.g., the phonemes/k/and/b/differentiate the meanings of "cat" and "bat"). Phonetic-based systems also consist of two phases: phonetic indexing and searching. In the first phase, the system translates the input speech into a sequence of phonemes. This contrasts with LVCSR systems where the speech is converted into a sequence of words. In the second phase, the system searches the output of the first phase for the phonetic representation of the search terms.

3.3. Video analytics

Video analytics, also known as video content analysis (VCA), involves a variety of techniques to monitor, analyze, and extract meaningful information from video streams. Although video analytics is still in its infancy compared to other types of data mining (Panigrahi, Abraham, & Das, 2010), various techniques have already been developed for processing real-time as well as pre-recorded videos. The increasing prevalence of closed-circuit television (CCTV) cameras and the booming popularity of video-sharing websites are the two leading contributors to the growth of computerized video analysis. A key challenge, however, is the sheer size of video data. To put this into perspective, one second of a high-definition video, in terms of size, is equivalent to over 2000 pages of text (Manyika et al., 2011). Now consider that 100 hours of video are uploaded to YouTube every minute (YouTube Statistics, n.d.).

Big data technologies turn this challenge into opportunity. Obviating the need for cost-intensive and risk-prone manual processing, big data technologies can be leveraged to automatically sift through and draw intelligence from thousands of hours of video. As a result, the big data technology is the third factor that has contributed to the development of video analytics.

The primary application of video analytics in recent years has been in automated security and surveillance systems. In addition to their high cost, labor-based surveillance systems tend to be less effective than automatic systems (e.g., Hakeem et al., 2012 report that security personnel cannot remain focused on surveillance tasks for more than 20 minutes). Video analytics can efficiently and effectively perform surveillance functions such as detecting breaches of restricted zones, identifying objects removed or left unattended, detecting loitering in a specific area, recognizing suspicious activities, and detecting camera tampering, to name a few. Upon detection of a threat, the surveillance system may notify security personnel in real time or trigger an automatic action (e.g., sound alarm, lock doors, or turn on lights).

The data generated by CCTV cameras in retail outlets can be extracted for business intelligence. Marketing and operations management are the primary application areas. For instance, smart algorithms can collect demographic information about customers, such as age, gender, and ethnicity. Similarly, retailers can count the number of customers, measure the time they stay in the store, detect their movement patterns, measure their dwell time in different areas, and monitor queues in real time. Valuable insights can be obtained by correlating this information with customer demographics to drive decisions for product placement, price, assortment optimization, promotion design, cross-selling, layout optimization, and staffing.

Another potential application of video analytics in retail lies in the study of buying behavior of groups. Among family members who shop together, only one interacts with the store at the cash register, causing the traditional systems to miss data on buying patterns of other members. Video analytics can help retailers address this missed opportunity by providing information about the size of the group, the group's demographics, and the individual members' buying behavior.

Automatic video indexing and retrieval constitutes another domain of video analytics applications. The widespread emergence of online and offline videos has highlighted the need to index multimedia content for easy search and retrieval. The indexing of a video can be performed based on different levels of information available in a video including the metadata, the soundtrack, the transcripts, and the visual content of the video. In the metadata-based approach, relational database management systems (RDBMS) are used for video search and retrieval. Audio analytics and text analytics techniques can be applied to index a video based on the associated soundtracks and transcripts, respectively. A comprehensive review of approaches and techniques for video indexing is presented in Hu, Xie, Li, Zeng, and Maybank (2011).

In terms of the system architecture, there exist two approaches to video analytics, namely server-based and edge-based:

Server-based architecture: In this configuration, the video captured through each camera is routed back to a centralized and dedicated server that performs the video analytics. Due to bandwidth limits, the video generated by the source is usually compressed by reducing the frame rates and/or the image resolution. The resulting loss of information can affect the accuracy of the analysis. However, the server-based approach provides economies of scale and facilitates easier maintenance.

Edge-based architecture: In this approach, analytics are applied at the 'edge' of the system. That is, the video analytics is performed locally and on the raw data captured by the camera. As a result, the entire content of the video stream is available for the analysis, enabling a more effective content analysis. Edge-based systems, however, are costlier to maintain and have a lower processing power compared to the server-based systems.

3.4. Social media analytics

Social media analytics refer to the analysis of structured and unstructured data from social media channels. Social media is a broad term encompassing a variety of online platforms that allow users to create and exchange content. Social media can be categorized into the following types: Social networks (e.g., Face book and LinkedIn), blogs (e.g., Blogger and Word Press), microblogs (e.g., Twitter and Tumblr), social news (e.g., Digg and Reddit), social bookmarking (e.g., Delicious and Stumble Upon), media sharing (e.g., Instagram and YouTube), wikis (e.g., Wikipedia and Wiki how), question-and-answer sites (e.g., Yahoo! Answers and Ask.com) and review sites (e.g., Yelp, TripAdvisor) (Barbier& Liu, 2011; Gundecha& Liu, 2012). Also, many mobile apps, such as Find My Friend, provide a platform for social interactions and, hence, serve as social media channels.

Although the research on social networks dates to early 1920s, nevertheless, social media analytics is a nascent field that has emerged after the advent of Web 2.0 in the early 2000s. The key characteristic of the modern social media analytics is its data-centric nature. The research on social media analytics spans across several disciplines, including psychology, sociology, anthropology, computer science, mathematics, physics, and economics. Marketing has been the primary application of social media analytics in recent years. This can be attributed to the widespread and growing adoption of social media by consumers worldwide (He, Zha, & Li, 2013), to the extent that Forrester Research, Inc., projects social media to be the second-fastest growing marketing channel in the US between 2011 and 2016 (VanBoskirk, Overby &Takvorian, 2011).

User-generated content (e.g., sentiments, images, videos, and bookmarks) and the relationships and interactions between the network entities (e.g., people, organizations, and products) are the two sources of information in social media. Based on this categorization, the social media analytics can be classified into two groups:

Content-based analytics: Content-based analytics focuses on the data posted by users on social media platforms, such as customer feedback, product reviews, images, and videos. Such content on social media is often voluminous, unstructured, noisy, and dynamic. Text, audio, and video analytics, as discussed earlier, can be applied to derive insight from such data. Also, big data technologies can be adopted to address the data processing challenges.

Structure-based analytics: Also referred to as *social network analytics*, this type of analytics is concerned with synthesizing the structural attributes of a social network and extracting intelligence from the relationships among the participating entities. The structure of a social network is modeled through a set of nodes and edges, representing participants and relationships, respectively. The model can be visualized as a graph composed of the nodes and the edges. We review two types of network graphs, namely *social graphs* and *activity graphs* (Heidemann, Klier, & Probst, 2012). In social graphs, an edge between a pair of nodes only signifies the existence of a link (e.g., friendship) between the corresponding entities. Such graphs can be mined to identify communities or determine hubs (i.e., the users with a relatively large number of direct and indirect social links). In activity networks, however, the edges represent actual interactions between any pair of nodes. The interactions involve exchanges of information (e.g., likes and comments). Activity graphs are preferable to social graphs, because an active relationship is more relevant to analysis than a mere connection.

Various techniques have recently emerged to extract information from the structure of social networks. We briefly discuss these below.

Community detection, also referred to as community discovery, extracts implicit communities within a network. For online social networks, a community refers to a sub-network of users who interact more extensively with each other than with the rest of the network. Often containing millions of nodes and edges, online social networks tend to be colossal in size. Community detection helps to summarize huge networks, which then facilitates uncovering existing behavioral patterns and predicting emergent properties of the network. In this regard, community detection is similar to clustering (Aggarwal, 2011), a data mining technique used to partition a data set into disjoint subsets based on the similarity of data points. Community detection has found several application areas, including marketing and the World Wide Web (Parthasarathy, Ruan, &Satuluri, 2011). For example, community detection enables firms to develop more effective product recommendation systems.

Social influence analysis refers to techniques that are concerned with modeling and evaluating the influence of actors and connections in a social network. Naturally, the behavior of an actor in a social network is affected by others. Thus, it is desirable to evaluate the participants' influence, quantify the strength of connections, and uncover the patterns of influence diffusion in a network. Social influence analysis techniques can be leveraged in viral marketing to efficiently enhance brand awareness and adoption.

A salient aspect of social influence analysis is to quantify the importance of the network nodes. Various measures have been developed for this purpose, including degree centrality, between's centrality, closeness centrality, and eigenvector centrality (for more details refer to Tang & Liu, 2010). Other measures evaluate the strength of connections represented by edges or model the spread of influence in social networks. The Linear Threshold Model (LTM) and Independent Cascade Model (ICM) are two well-known examples of such frameworks (Sun & Tang, 2011).

Link prediction specifically addresses the problem of predicting future linkages between the existing nodes in the underlying network. Typically, the structure of social networks is not static and continuously grows through the creation of new nodes and edges. Therefore, a natural goal is to understand and predict the dynamics of the network. Link prediction techniques predict the occurrence of interaction, collaboration, or influence among entities of a network in a specific time interval. Link prediction techniques outperform pure chance by factors of 40–50, suggesting that the current structure of the network surely contains latent information about future links (Liben-Nowell & Kleinberg, 2003).

In biology, link prediction techniques are used to discover links or associations in biological networks (e.g., protein–protein interaction networks), eliminating the need for expensive experiments (Hasan &Zaki, 2011). In security, link prediction helps to uncover potential collaborations in terrorist or criminal networks. In the context of online social media, the primary application of link prediction is in the development of recommendation systems, such as Face book's "People You May Know",

YouTube's "Recommended for You", and Netflix's and Amazon's recommender engines.

3.5. Predictive analytics

Predictive analytics comprise a variety of techniques that predict future outcomes based on historical and current data. In practice, predictive analytics can be applied to almost all disciplines – from predicting the failure of jet engines based on the stream of data from several thousand sensors, to predicting customers' next moves based on what they buy, when they buy, and even what they say on social media.

At its core, predictive analytics seek to uncover patterns and capture relationships in data. Predictive analytics techniques are subdivided into two groups. Some techniques, such as moving averages, attempt to discover the historical patterns in the outcome variable(s) and extrapolate them to the future. Others, such as linear regression, aim to capture the interdependencies between outcome variable(s) and explanatory variables, and exploit them to make predictions. Based on the underlying methodology, techniques can also be categorized into two groups: regression techniques (e.g., multinomial legit models) and machine learning techniques (e.g., neural networks). Another classification is based on the type of outcome variables: techniques such as linear regression addresses continuous outcome variables (e.g., sale price of houses), while others such as Random Forests are applied to discrete outcome variables (e.g., credit status).

Predictive analytics techniques are primarily based on statistical methods. Several factors call for developing new statistical methods for big data. First, conventional statistical methods are rooted in statistical significance: a small sample is obtained from the population and the result is compared with chance to examine the significance of a relationship. The conclusion is then generalized to the entire population. In contrast, big data samples are massive and represent the majority of, if not the entire, population. As a result, the notion of statistical significance is not that relevant to big data. Secondly, in terms of computational efficiency, many conventional methods for small samples do not scale up to big data. The third factor corresponds to the distinctive features inherent in big data: heterogeneity, noise accumulation, spurious correlations, and incidental endogeneity (Fan, Han, & Liu, 2014). We describe these below.

Heterogeneity: Big data are often obtained from different sources and represent information from different sub-populations. As a result, big data are highly heterogeneous. The sub-population data in small samples are deemed outliers because of their insufficient frequency. However, the sheer size of big data sets creates the unique opportunity to model the heterogeneity arising from sub-population data, which would require sophisticated statistical techniques.

Noise accumulation: Estimating predictive models for big data often involves the simultaneous estimation of several parameters. The accumulated estimation error (or noise) for different parameters could dominate the magnitudes of variables that have true effects within the model. In other words, some variables with significant explanatory power might be overlooked because of noise accumulation.

Spurious correlation: For big data, spurious correlation refers to uncorrelated variables being falsely found to be correlated due to the massive size of the dataset. Fan and Lv (2008) show this phenomenon through a simulation example, where the correlation coefficient between independent random variables is shown to increase with the size of the dataset. As a result, some variables that are scientifically unrelated (due to their independence) are erroneously proven to be correlated as a result of high dimensionality.

Incidental endogeneity: A common assumption in regression analysis is the exogeneity assumption: the explanatory variables, or predictors, are independent of the residual term. The validity of most statistical methods used in regression analysis depends on this assumption. In other words, the existence of incidental endogeneity (i.e., the dependence of the residual term on some of the predictors) undermines the validity of the statistical methods used for regression analysis. Although the exogeneity assumption is usually met in small samples, incidental endogeneity is commonly present in big data. It is worthwhile to mention that, in contrast to spurious correlation, incidental endogeneity refers to a genuine relationship between variables and the error term.

The irrelevance of statistical significance, the challenges of computational efficiency, and the unique characteristics of big data discussed above highlight the need to develop new statistical techniques to gain insights from predictive models.

4. Concluding remarks

The objective of this paper is to describe, review, and reflect on big data. The paper first defined what is meant by big data to consolidate the divergent discourse on big data. We presented various definitions of big data, highlighting the fact that size is only one dimension of big data. Other dimensions, such as velocity and variety are equally important. The paper's primary focus has been on analytics to gain valid and valuable insights from big data. We highlight the point that predictive analytics, which deals mostly with structured data, overshadows other forms of analytics applied to unstructured data, which constitutes 95% of big data. We reviewed analytics techniques for text, audio, video, and social media data, as well as predictive analytics. The paper makes the case for new statistical techniques for big data to address the peculiarities that differentiate big data from smaller data sets. Most statistical methods in practice have been devised for smaller data sets comprising samples.

Technological advances in storage and computations have enabled cost-effective capture of the informational value of big data in a *timely* manner. Consequently, one observes a proliferation in real-world adoption of analytics that were not economically feasible for large-scale applications prior to the big data era. For example, sentiment analysis (opinion mining) has been known since the early 2000s (Pang & Lee, 2008). However, big data technologies enabled businesses to adopt sentiment analysis to glean useful insights from millions of opinions shared on social media. The processing of unstructured text fueled by the massive influx of social media data is generating business value by adopting conventional (pre-big data) sentiment analysis techniques, which may not be ideally suited to leverage big data.

Although major innovations in analytical techniques for big data have not yet taken place, one anticipates the emergence of such novel analytics in the near future. For instance, real-time analytics will likely become a prolific field of research because of the growth in location-aware social media and mobile apps. Since big data are noisy, highly interrelated, and unreliable, it will likely lead to the development of statistical techniques more readily apt for mining big data while remaining sensitive to the unique characteristics. Going beyond samples, additional valuable insights could be obtained from the massive volumes of less 'trustworthy' data.

Acknowledgment

The authors would like to acknowledge research and editing support provided by Ms. Ioana Moca.

References

Aggarwal, 2011

C.C. Aggarwal. **An introduction to social network data analytics** C.C. Aggarwal (Ed.), Social network data analytics, Springer, U.S. (2011), pp. 1-15

Barbier and Liu, 2011

G. Barbier, H. Liu **Data mining in social media** C.C. Aggarwal (Ed.), Social network data analytics, Springer, United States (2011), pp. 327-352

Beaver et al., 2010

D. Beaver, S. Kumar, H.C. Li, J. Sobel, P. Vajgel **Finding a needle in haystack: Face book's photo storage** Proceedings of the ninth USENIX conference on operating systems design and implementation, USENIX Association, Berkeley, CA, USA (2010), pp. 1-8

Chen et al., 2012

H. Chen, R.H.L. Chiang, V.C. Storey **Business intelligence and analytics: From big data to big impact** MIS Quarterly, 36 (4), pp. 1165-1188

Chung, 2014

W. Chung **Biz Pro: Extracting and categorizing business intelligence factors from textual news articles** International Journal of Information Management, 34 (2) (2014), pp. 272-284

ArticlePDF (1MB)

Cukier, 2010

Cukier K., The Economist, Data, data everywhere: A special report on managing information, 2010, February 25, Retrieved from http://www.economist.com/node/15557443.

Diebold, 2012

F.X. Diebold **A personal perspective on the origin(s) and development of "big data": The phenomenon, the term, and the discipline (Scholarly Paper No. ID 2202843)** Social Science Research Network (2012) Retrieved from http://papers.ssrn.com/sol3/papers.cfm?abstract_id=2202843

Fan et al., 2014

J. Fan, F. Han, H. Liu **Challenges of big data analysis** National Science Review, 1 (2) (2014), pp. 293-314

Fan and Lv., 2008

J. Fan, J. Lv., **Sure independence screening for ultrahigh dimensional feature space** Journal of the Royal Statistical Society: Series B (Statistical Methodology), 70 (5) (2008), pp. 849-911

Feldman, 2013

R. Feldman **Techniques and applications for sentiment analysis** Communications of the ACM, 56 (4) (2013), pp. 82-89

Gartner IT Glossary, n.d.

Gartner IT Glossary (n.d.) Retrieved from http://www.gartner.com/it-glossary/big-data/.

Gundecha and Liu, 2012

P. Gundecha, H. Liu **Mining social media: A brief introduction** Tutorials in Operations Research, 1 (4) (2012)

Hahn and Mani, 2000

U. Hahn, I. Mani. **The challenges of automatic summarization** Computer, 33 (11) (2000), pp. 29-36

Hakeem et al., 2012

A. Hakeem, H. Gupta, A. Kanaujia, T.E. Choe, K. Gunda, A. Scanlon, *et al.* **Video analytics for business intelligence** C. Shan, F. Porikli, T. Xiang, S. Gong (Eds.), Video analytics for business intelligence, Springer, Berlin, Heidelberg (2012), pp. 309-354

Hasan and Zaki, 2011

M.A. Hasan, M.J. Zaki **A survey of link prediction in social networks** C.C. Aggarwal (Ed.), Social network data analytics, Springer, United States (2011), pp. 243-275

Heidemann et al., 2012

J. Heidemann, M. Klier, F. Probst **Online social networks: A survey of a global phenomenon** Computer Networks, 56 (18) (2012), pp. 3866-3878

Article PDF (437KB)

He et al., 2013

W. He, S. Zha, L. Li **Social media competitive analysis and text mining: A case study in the pizza industry** International Journal of Information Management, 33 (3) (2013), pp. 464-472

Article PDF (736KB)

Hirschberg et al., 2010

J. Hirschberg, A. Hjalmarsson, N. Elhadad **"You're as sick as you sound": Using computational approaches for modeling speaker state to gauge illness and recovery** A. Neustein (Ed.), Advances in speech recognition, Springer, United States (2010), pp. 305-322

Hu et al., 2011

W. Hu, N. Xie, L. Li, X. Zeng, S. Maybank **A survey on visual content-based video indexing and retrieval** IEEE Transactions on Systems, Man, and Cybernetics, Part C: Applications and Reviews, 41 (6) (2011), pp. 797-819

Jiang, 2012

J. Jiang **Information extraction from text** C.C. Aggarwal, C. Zhai (Eds.), Mining text data, Springer, United States (2012), pp. 11-41

Kwon et al., 2014

O. Kwon, N. Lee, B. Shin **Data quality management, data usage experience and acquisition intention of big data analytics** International Journal of Information Management, 34 (3) (2014), pp. 387-394
Article PDF (561KB)
Labrinidis and Jagadish, 2012
A. Labrinidis, H.V. Jagadish **Challenges and opportunities with big data** Proceedings of the VLDB Endowment, 5 (12) (2012), pp. 2032-2033
Laney, 2001
D. Laney **3-D data management: Controlling data volume, velocity and variety** Application Delivery Strategies by META Group Inc. (2001, February 6), p. 949 Retrieved from http://blogs.gartner.com/doug-laney/files/2012/01/ad949-3D-Data-Management-Controlling-Data-Volume-Velocity-and-Variety.pdf
Liben-Nowell and Kleinberg, 2003
D. Liben-Nowell, J. Kleinberg. **The link prediction problem for social networks** Proceedings of the twelfth international conference on information and knowledge management, ACM, New York, NY, USA (2003), pp. 556-559
Liu, 2012
B. Liu **Sentiment analysis and opinion mining** Synthesis Lectures on Human Language Technologies, 5 (1) (2012), pp. 1-167
Manyika et al., 2011
J. Manyika, M. Chui, B. Brown, J. Bughin, R. Dobbs, C. Roxburgh, *et al.* **Big data: The next frontier for innovation, competition, and productivity** McKinsey Global Institute (2011) Retrieved from http://www.citeulike.org/group/18242/article/9341321
Pang and Lee, 2008
B. Pang, L. Lee **Opinion mining and sentiment analysis** Foundations and Trends in Information Retrieval, 2 (1–2) (2008), pp. 1-135
Panigrahi et al., 2010
B.K. Panigrahi, A. Abraham, S. Das **Computational intelligence in power engineering** Springer (2010)
Parthasarathy et al., 2011
S. Parthasarathy, Y. Ruan, V. Satuluri **Community discovery in social networks: Applications, methods and emerging trends** C.C. Aggarwal (Ed.), Social network data analytics, Springer, United States (2011), pp. 79-113
Patil, 2010

H.A. Patil **"Cry baby": Using spectrographic analysis to assess neonatal health status from an infant's cry** A. Neustein (Ed.), Advances in speech recognition, Springer, United States (2010), pp. 323-348

Schroeck et al., 2012

M. Schroeck, R. Shockley, J. Smart, D. Romero-Morales, P. Tufano **Analytics: The real-world use of big data. How innovative enterprises extract value from uncertain data** IBM Institute for Business Value (2012) Retrieved from http://www-03.ibm.com/systems/hu/resources/the_real_word_use_of_big_data.pdf

SMC, 2012

Small and midsize companies look to make big gains with "big data," according to recent poll conducted on behalf of SAP (2012, June 26) Retrieved from http://global.sap.com/corporate-en/news.epx?PressID= 19188

Sun and Tang, 2011

J. Sun, J. Tang **A survey of models and algorithms for social influence analysis** C.C. Aggarwal (Ed.), Social network data analytics, Springer, United States (2011), pp. 177-214

Tang and Liu, 2010

L. Tang, H. Liu **Community detection and mining in social media** Synthesis Lectures on Data Mining and Knowledge Discovery, 2 (1), pp. 1-137

TechAmerica Foundation's Federal Big Data Commission, 2012

TechAmerica Foundation's Federal Big Data Commission **Demystifying big data: A practical guide to transforming the business of Government** (2012) Retrieved from http://www.techamerica.org/Docs/fileManager.cfm?f= techamerica-bigdatareport-final.pdf

VanBoskirk et al., 2011

S. VanBoskirk, C.S. Overby, S. Takvorian **US interactive marketing forecast 2011 to 2016** Forrester Research, Inc. (2011) Retrieved from https://www.forrester.com/US+Interactive+Marketing+Forecast+2011+To+2016/ fulltext/-/E-RES59379

YouTube Statistics, n.d.

YouTube Statistics (n.d.) Retrieved from http://www.youtube.com/ yt/press/statistics.html.

Vitae

Amir Gandomi is an assistant professor at the Ted Rogers School of Information Technology Management, Ryerson University. His research lies at the intersection of marketing, operations research and IT. He is specifically focused on big data analytics as it relates to marketing. His research has appeared in journals such as OMEGA - The International Journal of Management Science, The International Journal of Information Management, and Computers & Industrial Engineering.

Murtaza Haider is an associate professor at the Ted Rogers School of Management, Ryerson University, in Toronto. Murtaza is also the Director of a consulting firm Regionomics Inc. He specializes in applying statistical methods to forecast demand and/or sales. His research interests include human development in Canada and South Asia, forecasting housing market dynamics, transport and infrastructure planning and development. Murtaza Haider is working on a book, ***Getting Started with Data Science: Making Sense of Data with Analytics*** (ISBN 9780133991024), which will be published by Pearson/IBM Press in spring 2015. He is an avid blogger and blogs weekly about socio-economics in South Asia for the Dawn newspaper and for the Huffington Post.

1.21 Seven Unusual Uses of Big Data

Within the last decade, we've seen companies in every industry leverage big data to become more efficient, save money, and connect with customers. However, the most common uses of big data aren't the only exciting developments in the field—the massive potential of big data lies in its diverse applications. There are so many opportunities for the technology to improve our lives in many ways—some of which may surprise you. Here are just 7 of the countless unusual ways big data can make a big impact.

1. Animal populations and migrations

As habitat destruction, climate change, and a growing human population (around 7.4 billion in 2016), more and more species all the time are becoming endangered or extinct altogether. By understanding more about current populations and how they move in their natural habitats, conservationists can help protect them. But how can researchers accurately study animals in harsh environments that are often difficult to navigate? Big data, of course. Using cameras to capture animal migration paths and other behavior, big data tools can be used to sift through all the information these cameras provide, giving researchers insights about animals in their natural habitats.

2. Billboards

Long gone are the days when companies would simply rent space on a billboard and just hope potential customers driving by would take notice. Instead of simply estimating how many people had seen the ad to set prices, new analytical tools can provide engagement statistics. Using eye-tracking devices and GPS, modern billboard owners can track how many people looked at and engaged with the ad, assess traffic patterns, and dynamically price the billboard space based on these statistics. It's much easier for advertisers to know the kind of impact a billboard is having, and it's easier for billboard owners to price appropriately.

3. Reducing emergency room visits

Many people head to the emergency room simply because they don't know of other options or don't have them. Often, they wind up in the emergency room far too often, sometimes in multiple hospitals on an almost daily basis. Because healthcare organizations don't usually share information, a repeat visitor might go unnoticed for months at a time. Big data is playing a role in changing that. Some hospitals are stepping up early interventional medicine to provide better care for chronic emergency users and to cut down on costs. Companies are using this tactic too—Caesar's Entertainment Corp. estimates it saved about $4.5 million by reducing emergency room visits through education for its employees.

4. Pro sports ticket pricing

Airlines aren't the only companies using predictive analytics to dynamically price tickets. Sports officials have one goal: to sell as many tickets as possible, at the highest possible price. Because of this, they leverage big data to figure out when to rise or lower prices for the highest profit margin overall. While these tactics might make sports fans grumble, it's a way for teams to bring in the most revenue—something that is every business's goal.

5. Ski safety and patrolling

Skiing is a dangerous sport, and it's crucial that resort operators to whatever they can to reduce injury and fraud. Many resorts now provide visitors with RFID chip-enabled lift tickets. These tickets allow the resort to analyze lift usage based on time of day and day of the week. In addition, the smart tickets cut down on fraud and can help locate lost or injured skiers who might need assistance. Some resorts even provide visitors with statistics for their day of skiing, a fun extra that wouldn't be possible without big data.

6. Optimizing Energy Usage

In order to reduce our global carbon footprint and ensure that everyone has access to the resources they need, optimizing and cutting down on energy use is crucial. Smart grids are a good step in the right direction toward smart cities—these devices analyze energy usage based on time of day, and distribute resources where they're needed. Other devices, like smart water meters, are helping in areas of drought to cut down on illegal watering. In Long Beach, CA, some homeowners have cut down their water usage by as much as 80% thanks to big data.

7. Urban Foraging

The middle of the city probably isn't your first thought when you think of the word "foraging". However, thanks to big data, the website Falling Fruit is helping urban residents see the bounty available in their neighborhood. An interactive map shows users where fruit and other edibles are likely to be growing in their area. It's just one of the many ways big data is making our world a better place!

Consultant – Speaker – Writer - Andrew Deen is always happy to share his knowledge about developing news stories in big data, IoT and business. He has been a consultant in almost every industry from retail to medical devices and everything in between. He implements lean methodology and currently writing a book about scaling up businesses.

https://datafloq.com/read/7-unusual-uses-of-big-data/3381?utm_source=
Datafloq%20newsletter&utm_campaign=368972258b-EMAIL_CAMPAIGN_
2017_07_24&utm_medium=email&utm_term=0_655692fdfd-368972258b-
93913053

1.22 Ten reasons why Data Scientist is the sexiest job of the 21st century (or not)

Isabel Caballero **Data Scientist, Travel Intelligence, Amadeus IT Group**

I joined Amadeus's team of data scientists coming from an Astrophysics background. Although I enjoyed my work, at some point I became interested in ways I could apply the skills I acquired working in Astrophysics to areas outside of academic research. I wanted to directly apply what I had always done (which included a lot of analysis of large amounts of data, programming, modeling, interpretation of results etc.). It was at that time I became interested in Big Data and data science, which is meant to be a very sexy job. Here's why (or why not!):

Photo: NASA

1. It is very rewarding to see how **the output of my work directly addresses customers' needs.** Having actual feedback from them (as opposed to stars or galaxies) adds motivation to keep working.

2. One of the reasons working as a Data Scientist is very exciting is the possibility **to tell a story from data**. This is something that I also enjoyed while I was working in Astrophysics. From the simple light collected by a telescope, one can extrapolate the whole story of an emitting star or galaxy. When I joined the Amadeus Travel Intelligence team, I exchanged photons for passengers, but this aspect of my daily work has otherwise remained unchanged.

3. Big Data is a rather new field and it is constantly evolving, making it a very exciting time to work in it. It's very challenging to keep learning and **to stay up to date**, plus it's necessary to remain flexible and to be able to adapt to new tools and technologies when needed.

4. Data Science **can be applied to very diverse fields** including the travel industry, of course, but it can also help people make better (and better-informed) decisions in other areas such as healthcare, manufacturing, retail, education, public administrations, and economic development.

5. I cannot forget perhaps the most obvious reason; There is **an increasing demand** for Data Scientists (the McKinsey Global Institute estimates that the "United States alone faces a shortage of 140,000 to 190,000 people [by 2018] with deep analytical skills"). This makes it very exciting, as there are many diverse opportunities and fields where it is possible to work as a Data Scientist.

6. Data Science is **accessible to everyone.** Today it is very easy to have access to computing resources and large amounts of public data. Almost anyone can do interesting and different things with data.

7. There are **many opportunities** for people with research and academic backgrounds to contribute to Big Data projects. Many programs have been set up to help with the transition from academia to data science, for instance the *Insight Data Science Fellows Program* in the US and *Science to Data Science* in Europe. Data Science is also increasingly present in university programs.

8. There are other aspects of working as a Data Scientist which are **less sexy**, but still important. A very harsh part of the work, which is both fundamental and time-consuming, is the process of **cleaning the data, dealing with inconsistencies, and assessing the data quality.** It is not a very visible part of the work, and not one that is a lot of fun, but it is necessary in order to obtain reliable results.

9. *Fortune* magazine called Data Scientist *"the nerdy-cool job that companies are scrambling to fill"*. **It can be challenging to integrate academic research aspects into a corporate culture.** Often, we don´t have the option or the space to explain the details of the methods that

were used to achieve a result. Therefore, the ability to communicate with different teams is a fundamental part of a Data Scientist's work.

10. The term **'Data Scientist' has several meanings and interpretations.** When I decided to look for a job in data science, I had many interviews for positions with Data Scientist in the title. But every job offer was completely different, ranging from data base administrator to business analyst. Tom Davenport, who described the role and called it the sexiest job of the 21st century, has more recently written that *It's already time to kill the Data Scientist title*. It is therefore important to know what you want to do when you search for a position in Data Science, as Data Scientist is a very broad and ambiguous term!

Editor's note: It's been labeled the sexiest profession of the 21st Century, one where demand has raced ahead of supply, a hybrid of data hacker, analyst, communicator, and trusted advisor. Data Scientists are people with the skill set (and the mind-set) to tame Big Data technologies and put them to good use. But what kind of person does this? Who has that powerful –and rare- combination of skills? In this series, Amadeus' team of Data Scientists seeks to unlock the answers to those questions and their impact on travel.

http://www.amadeus.com/blog/18/06/10-reasons-why-data-scientist-is-the-sexiest-job-or-not/

1.23 What is Data Science? 24 Fundamental Articles Answering This Question

Posted by Vincent Granville on October 18, 2016

Many people new to data science might believe that this field is just about R, Python, Hadoop, SQL, and traditional machine learning techniques or statistical modeling. Below you will find fundamental articles that show how modern, broad and deep the field is. Some data scientists are doing none of the above. In my case, I don't even code, but instead, I make various applications talk to each other, in a machine-to-machine communication framework. It is true though that most data scientists use R, Python and Hadoop-related systems.

The article on deep data science (see below) shows that data science is also about automating the tasks that many people (calling themselves data scientists) do routinely. And it can be done using very little mathematical / traditional statistical science. I like to put it this way: data science is about automating data science, and much of what I do consists of designing systems that automate what I do.

Many of these articles below are a few years old, but their content is even more relevant today than ever before. These articles should help the beginner have a better idea about what data science is. Some are technical, but most can be understood by the layman.

24 Articles about Core Data Science

(i)   Data Science Compared to 16 Analytic Disciplines
(ii)   10 types of data scientists
(iii)   40 Techniques Used by Data Scientists
(iv)   50 Questions to Test True Data Science Knowledge -- also read this article
(v)   24 Uses of Statistical Modeling
(vi)   21 data science systems used by Amazon to operate its business
(vii)   10 Modern Statistical Concepts Discovered by Data Scientists
(viii)   8 Deep Data Science Articles
(ix)   22 tips for better data science
(x)   How to detect spurious correlations, and how to find the real ones

Two New Articles Posted This Week

- Building an Algorithm to Break Strong Encryption
- More on 3rd Generation Spiking Neural Nets

Announcement

- The 5 Key Challenges to Building a Successful Data Lab - Whitepaper

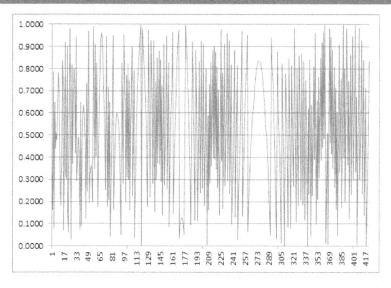

Source for picture: see next article below

Top DSC Resources

- **Article:** What is Data Science? 24 Fundamental Articles Answering This Question
- **Article:** Hitchhiker's Guide to Data Science, Machine Learning, R, Python
- **Tutorial:** Data Science Cheat Sheet
- **Tutorial:** How to Become a Data Scientist - On Your Own
- **Categories:** Data Science - Machine Learning - AI - IoT - Deep Learning
- **Tools:** Hadoop - DataViZ - Python - R - SQL - Excel
- **Techniques:** Clustering - Regression - SVM - Neural Nets - Ensembles - Decision Trees
- **Links:** Cheat Sheets - Books - Events - Webinars - Tutorials - Training - News - Jobs
- **Links:** Announcements - Salary Surveys - Data Sets - Certification - RSS Feeds - About Us

- Newsletter: Sign-up - Past Editions - Members-Only Section - Content Search - For Bloggers
- DSC on: Ning - Twitter - LinkedIn – Face book – Google Plus

http://www.datasciencecentral.com/profiles/blogs/20-articles-about-core-data-science

1.24 Analytics and Data Science India Jobs Study 2017- by Edvancer & AIM

With its increasing relevance across various sectors, the global demand for big data, analytics and data science professionals are on a rise. Piling data along with a surge in fields such as AI, machine learning and data science, has made analytics the most sought-after professions in India as well. There is an increase in demand for highly skilled professionals and companies are on a constant lookout for professionals who can fill the gap.

This brings us to our yearly study around the scenario of analytics jobs in the country. Titled: "Analytics and Data Science India Jobs Study 2017", it taps into this very aspect and evaluates the scenario of analytics and data science hiring across various industries such as retail, telecom, e-commerce etc, across cities, requirements in terms of experience & education, hiring trends and much more.

This year's study brought to you in association with **Edvancer**, a leading institute offering a wide range of online big data analytics training courses for all levels, brings a complete picture of the analytics and data science job scenario in India, in the form of eye-opening statistics and visuals.

Top Trends in Analytics jobs-

- The number of analytics jobs almost doubled from April 2016 to April 2017.

- This is in sharp contrast to the percentage increase in analytics job inventory a year back. The number of analytics jobs increased by **52%** from April 2015 to April 2016, and by **40%** from April 2014 to April 2015.

- While, it is difficult to ascertain the exact number of analytics jobs openings; by our estimates, close to **50,000** positions related to analytics are currently available to be filled in India.

- Compared to worldwide estimates, India contributes just **12%** of open jobs opening currently. The no. of jobs in India are likely to increase much faster vs. the rest of the world as more analytics projects get outsourced to India due to lack of skills across the world.

- 10 leading organizations with the most number of analytics opening this year are – Amazon, Citi, HCL, Goldman Sachs, IBM, JPMorgan Chase, Accenture, KPMG, E&Y & Capgemini.

Analytics jobs by cities-

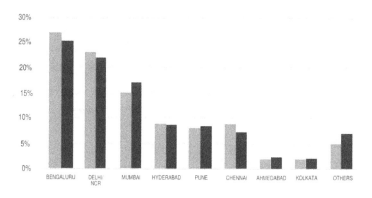

Percentage of Analytics Jobs by Cities

2016   2017

- In terms of cities, Bengaluru accounts for around **25%** of analytics jobs in India. This is down from **27%** a year earlier.1

- Delhi/ NCR comes second contributing **22%** analytics jobs in India, down slightly from **23%** a year ago.

- Approximately **17%** of analytics jobs are from Mumbai. This is up from **15%** from last year.

- The contribution of tier-B cities in analytics jobs have increased this year, from 5% in 2016 to **7%** this year due to the increased number of start-ups operating in tier 2 cities.

Analytics jobs by industry-

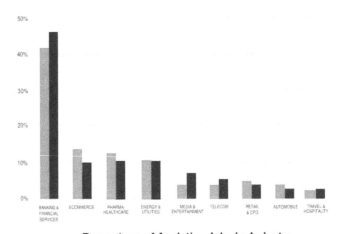

Percentage of Analytics Jobs by Industry

- Banking & Financial sector continues to be the biggest influence in Analytics job market. **46%** of all jobs posted on analytics were from the banking sector. This is an increase from **42%** a year ago.

- E-commerce has dipped in terms of analytics jobs this year. Just **10%** of analytics jobs were in ecommerce sector as opposed to **14%** a year ago.

- Media / entertainment sector seems to have an uptick in analytics jobs this year, contributing to **7%** of all analytics jobs as opposed to **4%** a year ago. The sector has been traditionally a late adopter of analytics.

Education requirement by analytics jobs-

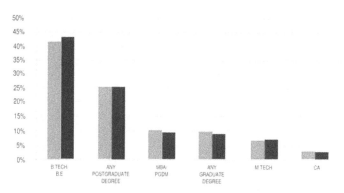

Percentage of hiring based on Educational Qualification

Education requirements for analytics recruiters have remai1ned the same since last year. Almost **42%** of analytics job openings are looking for a B.E. / B. tech. degree in the incumbent.

- **26%** analytics job openings are looking for a postgraduate degree and **10%**are looking for an MBA or PGDM.

- So, overall, **80%** of all employers are looking to hire analytics professionals with either an engineering degree or a postgraduate degree.

- **9%** analytics jobs are fine with any graduate degree.

- Job openings looking for a CA account for merely **3%**.

Experience requirement by analytics jobs-

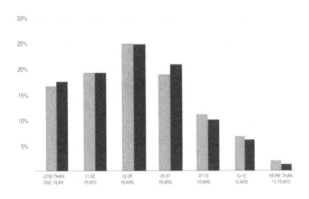

Percentage of hiring by Experiecnce

Around **61%** of analytics requirements are looking for candidates with less than 5 years' experience.

- **17%** analytics jobs are for freshers.

- **39%** analytics job openings are for professionals with more than 5 years job experience.

- There has been a significant increase in the requirement for senior analytics professionals last year. Job requirements for professionals more than 7 years' experience increased from **17%** of all analytics jobs in 2016 to **20%**this year.

Analytics jobs in cities by experience level-

- 2-5 years of experience continues to be the most demanded experience level across all cities, averaging at **24%** of job openings.

- This is followed by 5-7 years of experience level for most cities, except Chennai where analytics recruiter is looking for mostly 1-2 years' experience after 2-5 years.

- In terms of change from last year, Delhi/ NCR saw the most change from 2016. There has been a significant increase in the demand for 2-7 years of experience level in Delhi/ NCR whereas the demand for less than two years' experience shrank.

- Pune also saw a dip in demand for 0-2 years analytics professionals – from **42%** of analytics openings in 2016 to **33%** this year.

Analytics jobs across tools & skills-

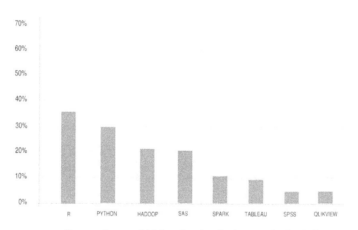

Percentage of hiring by Analytics tools & skills

- The demand for R professionals is the highest among all analytics recruiters. Almost **36%** of all advertised analytics jobs in India demand for R as a core skill.

- Python skills come second at **30%** of all analytics jobs looking for Python professionals. Among statistical tools, open source programming tools have picked up the most in recent years.

- Among visualization tools, Tableau skills are most in demand with **9%** of analytics jobs looking for Tableau professionals.

Analytics jobs by salaries-

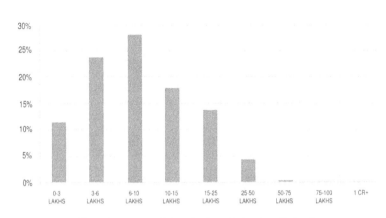

Percentage of Analytics Jobs by Salaries

- The median salaries being offered by advertised analytics jobs in India is INR **10.5 Lakh/ annum**.

- Advertised salaries tend to be lower than actual salaries. We have earlier reported the median salaries of analytics professionals in India to be **11.7 Lakh**.

- **28%** of all analytics jobs offer a salary range of 6 to 10 Lakh, followed by **24%** for 3-6 Lakh.

- Almost **40%** of all advertised analytics jobs in India are offering a salary of more than 10 Lakh

Analytics jobs across company type-

- Captive centers/ GIC's/ Back office has seen the highest growth in terms of analytics in last few years. Almost **56%** of all analytics demand is with Captive centers in India. These are organizations that mostly utilize analytics for internal consumption (for primarily their global businesses).

• MNC IT & KPO service providers follow next with **18%** of all analytics jobs advertised this year. Domestic IT & KPO service providers and consulting firms follow at **15%** & **11%** respectively.

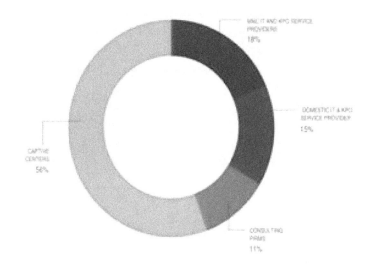

Percentage of hiring by Company type

Conclusion-

The fact that the number of analytics jobs has almost doubled from April 2016 to April 2017, is indicative of a positive trend that India is witnessing in terms of analytics and data science hiring. The study also throws an interesting perspective on the analytics hiring scenario as there are close to 50,000 positions in this field that are waiting for skilled analytics professionals. This brings good news for newcomers as out of the total number of openings, 17% of companies are looking for fresher, whereas 39% of analytics and data science job openings are for professionals with around 5 years job experience.

Overall, it brings a constructive picture of analytics and data science jobs in India this year, especially for freshers or for professionals who are looking to make a shift into analytics industry.

http://analyticsindiamag.com/analytics-and-data-science-india-jobs-study-2017-by-edvancer-aim/

Chapter-2: Machine Learning

Enterprises Must Possess the Power to Predict in the Age of the Customer

Machine learning is often used to build predictive models by extracting patterns from large datasets. These models are used in predictive data analytics applications including price prediction, risk assessment, predicting customer behavior, and document classification. Four approaches to machine learning: information-based learning, similarity-based learning, probability-based learning, and error-based learning. Predictive analytics applications use machine learning to build predictive models for applications including price prediction, risk assessment, and predicting customer behavior. Machine learning is often used to build predictive models by extracting patterns from large datasets. These models are used in predictive data analytics applications including price prediction, risk assessment, predicting customer behavior, and document classification.

2.1 Explaining Basics of Machine Learning, Algorithms and Applications

Posted on June 21, 2017 by Techno Jeder

"Data is abundant and cheap but knowledge is scarce and expensive."

In last few years, the sources of data capturing have evolved overwhelmingly. No longer have companies limited themselves to surveys, questionnaire and other traditional forms of data collection.

Smartphone, online browsing activity, drones, cameras are the modern form of data collection devices. And, believe me, that data is enormous.

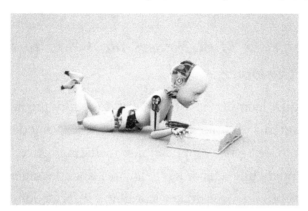

There is no way a human can look at such huge amounts of data and make sense out of it. Even if it is possible, it would be prone to irresistible errors. Is there a way out? Yes, Machine Learning has enabled humans to make intelligent real-life decision by making relatively less errors.

Have a look at the exciting ~ 4mins video below. It gives an idea of how machine learning is making computers, and many of the things like maps, search, recommending videos, translations, etc. better.

At the end of this article, you will be familiar with the basic concepts of machine learning, types of machine learning, its applications, and a lot more. Let us begin by addressing the elephant in the room.

What is Machine Learning (ML)?

The search engines (Google, Bing, Duckduckgo) have become the new knowledge discovery platforms. They have answers (probably accurate) to almost every silly question you can think of? But, how did it become so intelligent? Think about it!

In the meanwhile, let us first look at a few definitions of machine learning.

The term "machine learning" was coined by Arthur Samuel in 1959. According to him,

"Machine learning is the subfield of computer science that gives computers the ability to learn without being explicitly programmed."

Tom M. Mitchell provided a more formal definition, which says,

"A computer program is said to learn from experience *E* with respect to some class of tasks *T* and performance measure *P* if its performance at tasks in *T*, as measured by *P*, improves with experience *E*."

In simple words, machine learning is a set of techniques used to program computers and make decisions automatically. How does it make decisions? It makes decisions by detecting (or learning) pattern in the past data and generalizing it on the future data. There can be different forms of decisions such as predictions of the house prices or the weather or customer behavior, or classifications, like whether a spoken word in a recording is "world" or whether a photograph contains a face.

An ideal example for practical use of machine learning is email spam filters. Services like Google, yahoo, Hotmail etc. uses machine learning to detect if an email is spam or not. Furthermore, there are numerous other applications that as well which we'll look at later in this article.

"True loneliness is when you don't even receive spam emails."

What are the different types of ML algorithms?

There are several types of ML algorithms and techniques that you can easily get lost. Therefore, for better understanding, they have been divided into 3 major categories. Following is a list of different categories and types of machine learning algorithms:

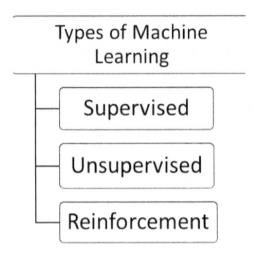

1. Supervised Learning

It is one of the most commonly used types of machine learning algorithms. In these types of ML algorithms, we have input and output variables and the algorithm generate a function that predicts the output based on given input variables. It is called 'supervised' because the algorithm learns in a supervised (given target variable) fashion. This learning process iterates over the training data until the model achieves an acceptable level. Supervised learning problems can be further divided into two parts:

- **Regression:** A supervised problem is said to be regression problem when the output variable is a continuous value such as "weight", "height" or "dollars."

- **Classification:** It is said to be a classification problem when the output variable is a discrete (or category) such as "male" and "female" or "disease" and "no disease."

A real-life application of supervised machine learning is the recommendation system used by Amazon, Google, Face book, Netflix, YouTube, etc. Another example of supervised machine learning is fraud detection. Let's say, a sample of the records is collected, and it is manually classified as "fraudulent or non-fraudulent". These manually classified records are then used to train a supervised machine learning algorithm, and it can be further used to predict frauds in the future. Some examples for supervised algorithms include Linear Regression, Decision Trees, Random Forest, k nearest neighbours, SVM, Gradient Boosting Machines (GBM), Neural Network etc.

2. Unsupervised Learning

In unsupervised machine learning algorithms, we only have input data and there is no corresponding output variable. The aim of these type of algorithms is to model the underlying structure or distribution in the dataset so that we can learn more about the data. It is called so because unlike supervised learning, there is no teacher and there are no correct answers. Algorithms are left to their own devices to discover and present the structure in the data. Similar to supervised learning problems, unsupervised learning problems can also be divided into two groups, namely Cluster analysis and Association.

- **Cluster analysis:** A cluster analysis problem is where we want to discover the built-in groupings in the data.

- **Association:** An association rule learning problem is where we want to discover the existence of interesting relationships between variables in the dataset.

In marketing, unsupervised machine learning algorithms can be used to segment customers according to their similarities which in return are helpful in doing targeted marketing. Some examples for unsupervised learning algorithms would be k-means clustering, hierarchical clustering, PCA, Apriori algorithm, etc.

3. Reinforcement Learning

In reinforcement learning algorithm, the machine is trained to act given an observation or make specific decisions. It is learning by interacting with an environment. The machine learns from the repercussions of its actions rather than from being explicitly taught. It is essentially trial-and-error learning where the machine selects its actions on the basis of its past experiences and new choices. In this, machine learns from these actions and tries to capture the best possible knowledge to make accurate decisions. An example of reinforcement learning algorithm is Markov Decision Process.

In a nutshell, there are three different ways in which a machine can learn. Imagine yourself to be a machine. Suppose, in an exam you are provided with an answer sheet where the answers are given. After your calculations, if the answer is found correct you will do the same calculations for that particular type of question. This is when it is said that you have learned through **supervised learning**.

Imagine the situation where you are not provided with the answer sheet and you have to learn on your own whether the answer is correct or not. You may end up giving wrong answers to most questions in the beginning but, eventually, you will learn how to answer correctly. This will be called **unsupervised learning.**

Consider the third case where a teacher is standing next to you in the exam hall and looking at your answers as you write. Whenever you write a correct answer, she says "good" and whenever you write a wrong answer, she says "very bad," and based on the remarks she gives, you try to improve (i.e., score the maximum possible in the exam). This is called **reinforcement learning**.

Where are some real-life applications of machine learning?

There are numerous applications of machine learning. Here is a list of a few of them:

1. **Weather forecast**: ML is applied to software that forecasts weather so that the quality can be improved.

2. **Malware stop/Anti-virus:** With an increasing number of malicious files every day, it is getting impossible for humans and many security solutions to keep up, and hence, machine learning and deep learning are important. ML helps in training anti-virus software so that they can predict better.

3. **Anti-spam:** We have already discussed this use case of ML. ML algorithms help spam filtration algorithms to better differentiate spam emails from anti-spam mails.

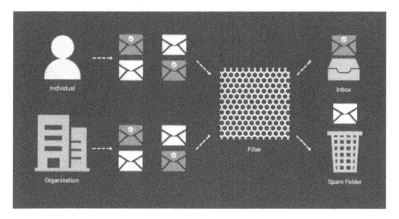

4. **Google Search:** Google search resulting in amazing results is another application of ML which we have already talked about.

5. **Game playing:** There can be two ways in which ML can be implemented in games, i.e., during the design phase and during runtime.

   • Designing phase: In this phase, the learning is applied before the game is rolled out. One example could be Live Move / Live AI products from Ai Live, which are the ML tools that recognize motion or controller inputs and convert them to game play actions.

   • Runtime: In this phase, learning is applied during runtime and fitted to a particular player or game session. Forza

Motorsports is one such example where an artificial driver can be trained on the basis of one's own style.

6. **Face detection/Face recognition:** ML can be used in mobile cameras, laptops, etc. for face detection and recognition. For instance, cameras snap a photo automatically whenever someone smiles much more accurately now because of advancements in machine learning algorithms.

7. **Speech recognition:** Speech recognition systems have improved significantly because of machine learning. For example, look at Google now.

8. **Genetics:** Clustering algorithms in machine learning can be used to find genes that are associated with a particular disease. For instance, me decision, a health management company, used a machine learning platform to gain a better understanding of diabetic patients who are at risk.

There are numerous other applications such as image classification, smart cars, increase cyber security and many more.

There are numerous other applications such as image classification, smart cars, increase cyber security and many more.

https://technojeder.wordpress.com/2017/06/21/explaining-the-basics-of-machine-learning-algorithms-and-applications/

2.2 Machine Learning Education: 3 Paths to Get Started

Alex Woodie

Machine learning is the predictive heart of big data analytics, and one of the key skills that separates data scientists from mere analysts. But getting started with machine learning can be a challenge. Here are a few ways beginners can get off the ground with their machine learning adventure.

Machine learning is a vast field with many different specialties, so it's quite easy for a beginner to get overwhelmed. For instance, one specialty called deep learning powers many of today's artificial intelligence breakthroughs. But without a background in basic machine learning approaches, a prospective data scientist would have zero chance of mastering this powerful but complex technology.

Here are three general paths that neophytes can get started with machine learning:

Take a Course Online

Udemy offers a beginner's course in machine learning called "Machine Learning A-Z: Hands-On Python and R in Data Science." The course costs $49 and is open to people who have a grasp on high school-level math.

Udacity has a course titled "Intro to Machine Learning" that covers the basics, such as extracting data, model selection, and performance evaluation. The self-paced course is free of charge and takes about 10 weeks.

While it may not be suitable for beginners, Coursera's machine learning class taught by renowned data scientists Andrew Ng is regarded as one of the top machine learning classes around. The course takes about

11 weeks and goes into considerable depth into machine learning topics. Students can access course material for free, but will need to pay to get a certificate upon completion.

(SFIO CRACHO / Shutter stock)

If you know R and statistics, but are completely new to machine learning, you might want to consider Data Camp's "Introduction to Machine Learning." Students can start the course — which covers basic ML algorithms like classification, regression, and clustering – for free, but getting a certificate will require payment.

Read a Book

If you want an in-depth descriptions into applies statistics, you could read "An Introduction to Statistical Learning with Applications in R," which is available as a free PDF download. The 440-page book from Springer is suitable for those with mathematical backgrounds as well as beginners from social sciences, although it assumes you have taken a class in basic statistics.

No treatment on this topic would be complete without a book from the "Dummies" series, and we don't disappoint. "Machine Learning for Dummies," which is available at Amazon for about $18, tackles the topic from both R and Python points of view, although readers don't have to have any computer science background to get something out of it.

The bestseller in this category may be "Machine Learning for Absolute Beginners: A Plain Introduction to Supervised and Unsupervised Learning Algorithms" ($10 at Amazon). Author Oliver Theobald covers the basic algorithms at play in this short, 132-page book, as well as some related facts, such as salaries that data scientists can expect.

Christopher Bishop's 2006 "Pattern Recognition and Machine Learning," also from Springer, is a highly regarded tome on the topic. Bishop's 758-page book goes in-depth into the theory behind the technology, including Bayesian probabilities and Gaussian distributions. He also covers some graphical models. It's not necessarily for the beginners though, as he assumes the reader has a firm grasp of calculus, linear algebra, and probability theory.

Watch a Video

You can access the video portions of Udacity's free online "Introduction to Machine Learning" course (mentioned above) via YouTube, which they are the top-viewed machine learning videos. Your host in the videos is Sebastian Thrun, who's the founder of Udacity and also a Google Fellow and Stanford professor.

Another source of machine learning videos is Kevin Markham, the founder of Data School and a former data science instructor at General Assembly and Coursera. Markham's Data School videos focus on learning to use the scikit-learn library for Python. No data science or statistical experience is expected.

Josh Gordon's "Machine Learning Recipes" video series offers a good introduction to machine learning. The Google Developer videos focus on using scikit-learn and Google's own Tensor Flow libraries to build basic machine learning models.

Andrew Ng's Stanford lectures on machine learning remain some of the most-viewed YouTube videos on the topic of machine learning; his first CS-229 lecture from way back in 2008 has more than 1.5 million views. You can watch it below:

https://www.datanami.com/2017/07/10/machine-learning-education-3-paths-get-started/

2.3   Machine Learning Best Practices: The Basics

By Wayne Thompson on Subconscious Musings JULY 12, 2017 Advanced Analytics

I started my training in machine learning at the University of Tennessee in the late 1980s. Of course, we didn't call it machine learning then, and we didn't call ourselves data scientists yet either. We used terms like statistics, analytics, data mining and data modeling.

Regardless of what you call it, I've spent more than 30 years building models that help global companies solve some of their most pressing problems. I've also had the good fortune to learn from some of the best data scientists on the planet, including Will Potts, Chief Data Scientist at Capital One, Dr. Warren Sarle, a distinguished researcher here at SAS, and Dr. William Sanders while I was at the University of Tennessee.

Through hundreds of projects and dozens of mentors over the years, I've caught on to some of the best practices for machine learning. I've narrowed those lessons down to my top ten tips. These are tips and tricks that I've relied on again and again over the years to develop the best models and solve difficult problems.

I'll be sharing my tips in a series of posts over the next few weeks, starting with the first three tips here. The next tips will be longer, but these first three are short and sweet, so I've included them in one post:

1. Look at your data

You spend 80 percent or more of your times preparing a training data set, so prior to building a model, please look at your data at the observational level. I always use PROC PRINT with OBS=20 in Base SAS®, the FETCH action in SAS® VIYA, and the HEAD or TAIL functions in Python to see and almost touch the observations. You can quickly discern if you have the right data in the correct form just by looking at it. It's not uncommon to make initial mistakes when building out your training data, so this tip can save you a lot of time. Naturally, you then want to generate measures of central tendency and dispersion. To isolate key trends and anomalies, compute summary statistics for your features with your label. If the label is categorical, compute summary measures using the label as a group by variable. If the label is interval, compute correlations. If you have categorical features, use those as your by group.

2. Slice and dice your data

Usually, there's some underlying substructure in your data. So I often slice my data up like a pizza – although the slices are not all the same size – and build separate models for each slice. I may use a group by variable like REGION or VEHICLE_TYPE that already provides built in stratification for my training data. When I have a target, I also build a shallow decision tree and then build separate models for each segment. I rarely use clustering algorithms to build segments if I have a target. I just don't like ignoring my target.

3. Remember Occam's Razor

The object of Occam learning is to output a succinct representation of the training data. The rational is, you want as simple a model as possible to make informed decisions. Many data scientists no longer believe in Occam's razor, since building more complex models to extract as much as you can from your data is an important technique. However, I also like to build simple, white-box models using regression and decision trees. Or I'll use a gradient boosting model as a quick check for how well my simple models are performing. I might add first order interactions or other basic transformations to improve the performance of my regression model. I commonly use L1 to shrink down the number of model effects in my model (watch for more about this in an upcoming post). Simpler models are also easier to deploy which makes the IT and systems operation teams happy. Finally, using the simplest model possible also makes it easier to explain results to business users, who will want to understand how you've arrived at a conclusion before making decisions with the results.

http://blogs.sas.com/content/subconsciousmusings/2017/07/12/machine-learning-best-practices-basics/

2.4   Machine Learning Best Practices: Combining Lots of Models

By Wayne Thompson on Subconscious Musings   JULY 25, 2017 Advanced Analytics

This is the third post in my series of machine learning techniques and best practices. If you missed the earlier posts, read the first one now, or review the whole machine learning best practices series.

Data scientists commonly use machine learning algorithms, such as gradient boosting and decision forests that automatically build lots of models for you. The individual models are then combined to form a potentially stronger solution. One of the most accurate machine learning classifiers is gradient boosting trees. In my own supervised learning efforts, I almost always try each of these models as challengers.

When using random forest, be careful not to set the tree depth too shallow. The goal of decision forests is to grow at random many large, deep trees (think forests, not bushes). Deep trees certainly tend to over fit the data and not generalize well, but a combination of these will capture the nuances of the space in a generalized fashion.

Some algorithms fit better than others within specific regions or boundaries of the data. A best practice is to combine different model in algorithms. You may also want to place more emphasis or weight on the modeling method that has the overall best classification or fit on the validation data. Sometimes two weak classifiers can do a better job than one strong classifier in specific spaces of your training data.

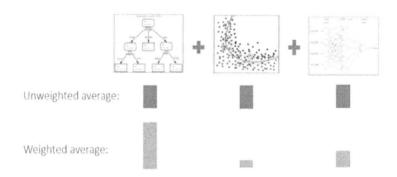

An ensemble model that combines a decision tree, support vector machine and neural network, either weighted or un-weighted.

As you become experienced with machine learning and master more techniques, you'll find yourself continuing to address rare event modeling problems by combining techniques.

Recently, one of my colleagues developed a model to identify <u>unlicensed money service businesses</u>. The event level was about 0.09%. To solve the problem, he used multiple techniques:

- First, he developed k-fold samples by randomly selecting a subsample of nonevents in each of his 200 folds, while making sure he kept all the events in each fold.

- He then built a random forest model in each fold.

- Lastly, his ensemble the 200-random forest, which ended up being the best classifier among all the models he developed.

This is a pretty big computational problem so it's important to be able to build the models in parallel across several data nodes so that the models train quickly. If there are other tips you want me to cover, or if you have tips of your own to share, leave a comment on this post.

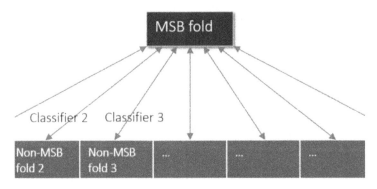

Build multiple base classifiers using subsamples for a rare events problem. Combine the base classifiers later.

My next post will be about model deployment, and you can click the image below to read all 10-machine learning best practices.

Wayne Thompson, Manager Data Science Technologies

Wayne Thompson, Chief Data Scientist at SAS, is a globally renowned presenter, teacher, practitioner and innovator in the fields of data mining and machine learning. He has worked alongside the world's biggest and most challenging organizations to help them harness analytics to build high performing organizations. Over the course of his 24 year tenure at SAS, Wayne has been credited with bringing to market landmark SAS analytics technologies, including SAS Text Miner, SAS Credit Scoring for Enterprise Miner, SAS Model Manager, SAS Rapid Predictive Modeler, SAS Visual Statistics and more. His current focus initiatives include easy to use self-service data mining tools along with deep learning and cognitive computing tool kits.

https://blogs.sas.com/content/subconsciousmusings/2017/07/25/machine-learning-best-practices-combining-lots-models/

2.5 Forrester's 2017 take on Tools for Data Science
Posted on March 16, 2017 by Bob Muenchen

In my ongoing quest to track The Popularity of Data Science Software, I've updated the discussion of the annual report from Forrester, which I repeat here to save you from having to read through the entire document. If your organization is looking for training in the R language, you might consider my books, R for SAS and SPSS Users or R for Stats Users, or my on-site workshops.

Forrester Research, Inc. is a company that provides reports which analyze the competitive position of tools for data science. The conclusions from their 2017 report, *Forrester Wave: Predictive* Analytics and Machine Learning Solutions are summarized in Figure 3b. On the x-axis they list the strength of each company's strategy, while the y-axis measures the strength of their current offering. The size and shading of the circles around each data point indicate the strength of each vendor in the marketplace (70% vendor size, 30% ISV and service partners).

As with Gartner 2017 report discussed above, IBM, SAS, KNIME, and Rapid Miner are considered leaders. However, Forrester sees several more companies in this category: Angoss, FICO, and SAP. This is quite different from the Gartner analysis, which places Angoss and SAP in the middle of the pack, while FICO is considered a niche player.

Forrester Wave plot of predictive analytics and machine learning software

In their Strong Performers category, they have H2O.ai, Microsoft, Statistic, Alpine Data, Dataiku, and, just barely, Domino Data Labs. Gartner rates Dataiku quite a bit higher, but they generally agree on the others. The exception is that Gartner dropped coverage of Alpine Data in 2017. Finally, Salford Systems is in the Contenders section. Salford was recently purchased by Minitab, a company that has never been rated by either Gartner or Forrester before as they focused on being a statistics package rather than expanding into machine learning or artificial intelligence tools as most other statistics packages have (another notable exception: Stats). It will be interesting to see how they're covered in future reports.

Compared to last year's Forrester report, KNIME shot up from barely being a Strong Performer into the Leader's segment. Rapid Miner and FICO moved from the middle of the Strong Performers segment to join the Leaders. The only other major move was a lateral one for Statistica, whose score on Strategy went down while its score on Current Offering went up (last year Statistica belonged to Dell, this year it's part of Quest Software.)

The size of the "market presence" circle for Rapid Miner indicates that Forrester views its position in the marketplace to be as strong as that of IBM and SAS. I find that perspective quite a stretch indeed!

Alteryx, Oracle, and Predixion were all dropped from this year's Forrester report. They mention Alteryx and Oracle as having "capabilities embedded in other tools" implying that that is not the focus of this report. No mention was made of why Predixion was dropped, but considering that Gartner also dropped coverage of then in 2017, it doesn't bode well for the company.

For a much more detailed analysis, see Thomas Dinsmore's blog.

http://r4stats.com/2017/03/16/forrester/

2.6 How Machine Learning Plus Predictive Analysis Boosts Business Performance

June 14, 2017 by Jennifer Hermes

David Vuong PM Analytics, Medgate

Machine learning can be used to reduce risks related to environmental, health, employee safety, and quality (EHSQ) issues; in general, though, it must be used in conjunction with predictive analysis if it is to be most effective. How can organizations start thinking about the best ways to harness machine learning as the technology advances? Begin by looking at the business issues that are most critical and the challenges that most affect an organization, and plan for technology that will address those issues first, suggests David Vuong, product manager of analytics at Medgate, an EHSQ software solutions company.

Machine learning is using artificial intelligence to allow machines to "learn" without being explicitly programmed. Examples of this in everyday life include Netflix (when suggested movies that you might like pop up based on your viewing history) and Google (when you begin typing a search term and it finishes your sentence for you). But machine learning is quantitative and isnot necessarily predictive analysis in its fullest form, says Vuong.

A predictive analytics program that harnesses machine learning capabilities, Vuong says, can use anonymous industry data and discover where risks related to EHSQ exist. EHSQ executives can then make decisions on how to reduce those risks, based on the available data. Within five years, companies that have systems connected via IoT will be able to benchmark themselves against others in their peer group, see correlations in their data that they may have not been aware of, and receive predictive and prescriptive insights that will help them improve their EHSQ programs, he says.

But in order to fully reap the rewards of machine learning and analytics in EHSQ, companies need to consider the best way to reach those goals early on. Companies should look at considerations such as security issues, the company's most pressing business problems, and, of course, the budget, said Stuart Payne of Gibson Energy during the recent Big Data, IoT and Machine Learning in Oil & Gas Conference.

But perhaps the biggest considerations when looking at the future of machine learning and analytics, in terms of how a company will be able to leverage those abilities in coming years, is to look at the organization's existing technologies and how they will interact with a new analytics program. Many companies are currently using a siloed approach to IoT, with various management systems working independently and not tied into each other. This could cause problems in the long run because it is difficult to pull data from the various systems together in order to analyze and use the data for EHSQ improvements. Carefully consider all new technology to ensure it can talk to other systems, thereby making it "future-proof" as well as scalable, Vuong suggests.

As machine-augmented decision making evolves and as organizations begin to take advantage of the technology, an EHSQ supervisor will be able to "see" and "hear" much more than before, leading to a more effective EHSQ team that can do more and miss less. "It will be a game changer," Vuong says.

David Vuong is the Product Manager of Analytics at Medgate, where he oversees the product development roadmap for Medgate's Analytics solution. He joined the Product Management team as the Product Manager of Business Intelligence in March 2015, where he developed a long-term plan to elevate Medgate's Business Intelligence suite to world-class levels. Prior to Medgate, David was in the Business Intelligence industry for over five years where he led new and established best practices in data visualization and design. He has worked with clients in industries such as mining, telecommunications, and logistics.

2.7 Machine Learning and Analytics: What's Your First Step?

Machine learning is a growing field, used in everything from the basics of anti-spam functions to the complexities of self-driving cars. As this is a constantly adapting technology, companies seeking to take advantage of the system for functions like analytics may have trouble finding the best place to begin.

So what is the first step for a tech department that wants to start using machine learning to improve its data analytics? Forbes Technology Council members have this to say:

1. Learn The Science

Even if you rely on outside expertise, it is important to understand what machine learning can and can't do with data. Stanford, Caltech and others offer online classes on Coursera that are very good. Even a little knowledge will go a long way towards helping you identify consultants and opportunities for analysis. - Manuel Vellon, Level 11

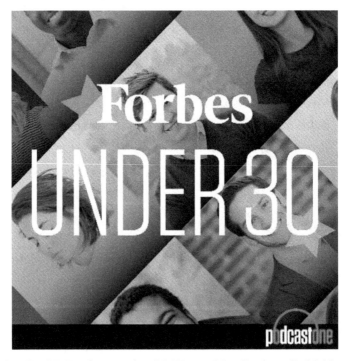

PODCAST *Forbes under 30* **Hosted by Steven Gold bloom**
Latest Episode **'The Minimalists' Approach to Everything**

2. Start With Basic Connectivity And Data Collection

The road to advanced analytics and machine learning starts with basic connectivity and data collection. This journey includes pinpointing the questions that need to be answered with data analysis, identifying the data needed to answer those questions, and putting processes in place to gather the correct type and amount of that data to properly support machine learning. - Mark Benson, Exosite, LLC

Have a Clear Goal

Ensure that you have a goal for the analytics. You need to train the machine. Ensure that you have the data and understanding of what the machine should learn, or it will be difficult to be successful. However, that doesn't mean you have to have a fully detailed plan either. The best project outcome may be that there's a positive surprise in the analytics. - George McKevitt, Compliance Science

Shutter stock

Start with an Internal Project

Find an interesting problem that the team wants to crack, and let them develop their skills in machine learning while they work on a problem they are passionate about. - Kurt Dykema, Twisthink

Hire an Expert

Get an expert data scientist to work with the tech department and business sponsor. Identify a small, "low-hanging fruit" first project that can show true business value. Choose a project where there is a sufficient amount of data and a well-defined outcome that can be demonstrated. (The data scientist can then validate the data's applicability.) - Leon Hounshell, Greenwave Systems

Learn to Crawl and Walk before You Sprint

"Big data" doesn't always mean zettabytes, but that more data always beats more complex algorithms. To improve analytics with machine learning, try to crawl before you sprint. To crawl: Collect all data in batch for a total historical analysis. To walk: Advance into real-time collection and descriptive analysis. To sprint: Use the same real-time collection framework for both prescriptive and predictive analytics - Don Brown, Rocana

Test Tools For Free

The best way is to get your hands on some actual products or technologies to test. Through both AWS and Azure, one can get free time to explore machine learning tools for data analytics by visiting sites such as this. By looking at the technologies that are out there, you can learn more and see the potential for your own organization. - George Teixeira, DataCore Software

Forbes Technology Council is an invitation-only community for world-class CIOs, CTOs and technology executives. ***Do I qualify?***

https://www.forbes.com/sites/forbestechcouncil/2017/02/02/machine-learning-and-analytics-whats-your-first-step/#246022125899

2.8   How Businesses are Using Machine Learning and AI in 2017

Published January 12th, 2017 by Cathy Reisenwitz in IT Management

In 2013 director Spike Jonze made his solo screenwriting debut with *her*, a movie about an artificial-intelligence-powered bot.

Then, in April 2016, Face book launched a service that allowed brands to build AI-powered bots for Messenger. CIO Journal reported that Messenger powers at least 33,000 chatbots, including Kai from MasterCard. The future is now.

"The AI market has the potential for a steep growth trajectory," John Curran, Managing Director of Communications, Media, and Technology for Accenture wrote for RCR Wireless. Curran cites the Accenture Artificial Intelligence Report, which predicts that by 2035 AI could cause annual economic growth rates to double and boost productivity by nearly 40%. By the year 2020, BofA Merrill Lynch Global sees the market for AI reaching $70 billion.

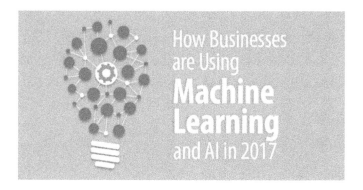

Today, CIOs are using artificial intelligence to automating existing work and to do new work, which cheaper and more powerful AI makes possible. And according to the Wall Street Journal, CIOs are saying the day is fast approaching when machine learning begins to impact core business functions.

Who can use machine learning?

Not every SaaS can make use of machine learning right now. Mikhail Naumov, Co-founder & CSO of venture-backed, AI Company Digital Genius, succinctly explained in Forbes what a business needs to start using machine learning today. First, you need large volumes of historical data. You can train a puppy with a bag of treats. To train a machine learning algorithm, you need reams and reams of human-corrected data.

The other thing you need is a business case for machine learning. Building an algorithm and training it isn't cheap. So you need a plan for making it pay for itself before you start. Will your machine learning algorithm find you ways to cut costs or ways to provide more value? For example, can your bot reduce your customer service department's average time to resolution? Or could it replace human insurance assessments?

On the "create more value" side, could AI help up sell your customers? Or could it make your marketing more effective at generating leads?

If so, you may be a match for machine learning. Even if you're not there, it's good to know what's on the horizon. So here are some ways businesses are utilizing machine learning in 2017.

Personalize

Curran: "Leveraging AI techniques, companies can move customer relationships beyond superficial to deeper, more meaningful interactions and experiences that engage customers at unprecedented and hyper-personalized levels such as proactively delivering an ad to a consumer on a Smartphone that is of high interest to them."

A great example of AI-powered personalization is Amazon's "Just Ask" feature on Echo. The Echo is the device powered by Amazon's bot,

Alexa. Because Alexa knows your buying history, delivery address, and shipping and payment preferences she can offer you daily promotions and special deals based on your needs. Customer Service Speaker and Author Richard Shapiro calls the "Just Ask" feature, "a game changer."

At CES this year, voice-controlled AI assistants were "everywhere," according to Jamie Condliffe, Associate Editor of news and commentary for MIT Technology Review. Consumers love devices with built-in speech-powered bots, and Condliffe writes that companies in 2017 are trying to put conversational interfaces "into as many pieces of hardware as possible."

Salesforce Einstein takes all your CRM data to make predictions about what's likely to happen and recommendations on what you should do next. Naumov offers the example of Einstein using email, calendar, and social data to send your email during the 20-minute time slot when your prospect is statistically most likely to open an email from you and respond positively.

Automate

Japanese company Fanuc sells robots to factories that can learn new skills on their own. In eight hours a Fanuc robot can learn how to complete a new task with 90 percent accuracy. Fanuc is the world's largest industrial robot producer, according to MIT Technology Review. And by partnering with a Japanese machine-learning company, it's been able to produce robots that come with artificial intelligence powered by machine learning algorithms. And you can even download apps into its robots.

But robots aren't content to just take factory jobs. Data science is in AI's crosshairs too. A Los Angeles-based startup called Bottlenose is aiming at automating data science, as investor Nova Spivack explained to the *Wall Street Journal*, this company is Meta as heck; because if you can use AI to automate data science suddenly, AI becomes much cheaper.

Predict

The *Wall Street Journal* reported that AIG invested hard in AI in 2016. AIG CEO Peter Hancock has put 125 people to work creating artificial intelligence models he hopes will make the company better at anticipating insurance claims and predicting outcomes.

"Rather than doing things on the back of an envelope, we've become more analytical and have started looking at statistics and performance to predict issues going forward," Senior Vice President and Deputy General Counsel Nicholas Kourides told Vanguard Law.

"We pay over $100 million a day in claims," Kourides said. "If we can get just a little better at that, we have the potential to save a huge amount of money."

Right now, AIG has five machine learning algorithms at work fixing tech glitches. Each so-called "co-bot" has a human handler who trains it to solve problems. The example the *Journal* uses is a network device outage. These once required 3.5 hours for an engineer to fix, but a co-bot needs just ten minutes to get devices up and running again. The machines solve most of the issues on their own, but the human is there to train it on anything it can't yet handle. More than 145,000 incidents have been solved this way, giving 23,000 hours of productivity back to AIG's humans.

Improve

Every year, vehicle crashes kill almost 1.3 million people, an average of 3,287 preventable deaths per day. Young adults between the ages of 15 and 44 make up more than half of these deaths. Vehicle crashes injure an additional 20-50 million.

The Toyota Research Institute is using artificial intelligence to make automobiles "safer, more affordable, and more accessible to everyone, regardless of age or ability." But machine learning and deep neural networks can do more than create self-driving vehicles. TRI is also working on robot assistants to help the elderly and differently able stay healthy, and at home, longer and is working to develop stronger, thinner, lighter, more flexible materials.

Conclusion

So, these are some of the ways businesses are utilizing machine learning in 2017.

Spoilers

In *Her*, our protagonist falls in love with his artificial- intelligence-powered bot. Companies are currently testing out AI, seeing how they feel about it. It's too soon to know which industries will fall in lasting love with AI, and which industries will see their love fizzle, like in *her*.

End spoilers

Either way, "AI is more than just a fad," wrote Ray Wang, Principal Analyst, Founder, and Chairman of Silicon Valley-based Constellation Research. "With a market size of \$100B by 2025, Constellation sees the AI subsets of machine learning, deep learning, natural language processing, and cognitive computing taking the market by storm."

"I think we are broadly entering the age in which technology will change fundamental aspects of society rather than improving prior functions and seeing changes around the edges," TawehBeysolow told me. Beysolow is currently writing a book about deep neural networks.

Gartner sees nearly a third of market-leading companies seeing artificial intelligence platform services cannibalizing revenues by 2019.

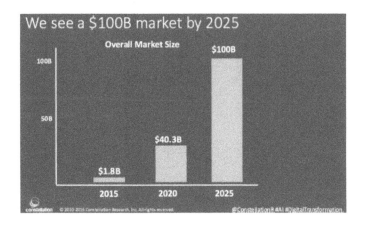

Again, not every SaaS business can try machine learning right now, and even fewer can use it profitably. But if you have large volumes of historical data (and humans to correct it) and a business case for machine learning, there are tons of possibilities out there.

To learn more about machine learning, deep neural networks, and AI,subscribe to the Capterra IT blog. Looking for IT Management software? Check out Capterra's list of the best IT Management software solutions. Share this article. Tags: How Businesses are Using Machine Learning

About the Author: Cathy Reisenwitz

Cathy Reisenwitz helps B2B software companies with their sales and marketing at Capterra. Her writing has appeared in The Week, Forbes, the Chicago Tribune, The Daily Beast, VICE Motherboard, Reason magazine, Talking Points Memo and other publications. She has been quoted by the New York Times Magazine and has been a columnist at Bitcoin Magazine. Her media appearances include Fox News and Al Jazeera America. If you're a B2B software company looking for more exposure, email Cathy at cathy@capterra.com. To read more of her thoughts, follow her on Twitter.

Join our software expert blogging community, learn more about our editorial guidelines, and propose a topic you'd like to write about.

http://blog.capterra.com/how-businesses-are-using-machine-learning-and-ai-in-2017/

2.9   7 Machine Learning Tools for IIoT

By Zayan Guedim; May 19, 2017

Machine learning is a branch of AI that enables AI to retain the memory of past computations and utilize those outcomes to inform current solutions to complex problems.

Companies at the forefront of the machine learning field offer open source libraries of solutions for companies and the average person.

IIOT refers to the Industrial Internet of Things.

Below is a list of seven open-source platforms that help businesses integrate machine learning into their production process. With these toolkits, businesses, regardless of their size, can get access to the same ML resources developed and used by prestigious companies.

The 7 Machine Learning Tools for IIoT:

1.   Amazon Machine Learning:

In 2015, Amazon's subsidiary **AWS** (Amazon Web Services) launched **Amazon Machine Learning** as part of its Cloud-based solutions. AML is a deliberately simplified platform intended for developers of any skill level to walk them through the creation of machine learning predictive models.

2.   Google's Tensor Flow:

Google uses Tensor Flow toolkit for its own products and services. Since 2015, Tensor Flow is an open source software library for deep learning. The updated version, Tensor Flow 1.0 is now available, with much faster calculations, more flexibility and features, and support for new languages.

Aleutie; Shutterstock.com

3. Microsoft's Azure:

The **Azure Machine Learning Studio** is Microsoft's Cloud-based platform that allows businesses and organizations to benefit from machine learning solutions that are easy to implement. With AMLS's collaborative, drag-and-drop machine learning tools, businesses can easily create, test, deploy and share predictive models.

4. H20:

Used by over 80,000 data scientists and 9,000 organizations around the world, H20.ai is the biggest open source AI platform that enables enterprises to get a "digital brain." An H20 product, such as Deep Water, makes the training and deployment of models easy with automatic tuning and a fast GPU-based system.

5. Caffe:

Built by **Berkeley Artificial Intelligence Research** (BAIR), **Caffe** is an open source **deep learning** framework already used for academic research projects, startup prototypes, and large-scale industrial applications.

The Caffe framework offers easy configuration, the ability to switch between GPU and CPU to train models before deployment. It is also one of the fastest systems.

6. M. L. lib.:

Apache Spark is a general-purpose cluster computing framework that, other than high-level APIs and tools, has an open-source machine learning library called **M. L. lib**. When you download Spark, M. L. lib. is included as a module, compatible with all APIs.

7. Torch:

Torch, an open-source ML platform, simplifies and speeds up the process of building algorithms.

Based on GPU/CPU and a simple scripting language, it is flexible and fast. Torch is already in use by major companies such as Google, Facebook, Twitter, Purdue, Yandex, NVIDIA, and others.

https://edgylabs.com/7-machine-learning-tools-iiot/

2.10 Six in Ten Manufacturers Will Have Fully Connected Factories by 2022

Zebra Technologies Corporation published the results of the Zebra's 2017 Manufacturing Vision Study, a body of research analyzing the emerging trends shaping the future of connected factories. The global study revealed manufacturers are adopting the IIoT to enhance visibility and improve quality.

Driven by globalization, intensifying competition and rising customer demand for more options and higher quality products, a connected plant floor has become a necessity. Zebra's survey shows the number of organizations achieving a fully connected factory is expected to rise dramatically over the next five years.

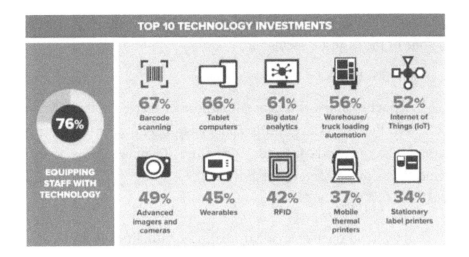

KEY SURVEY FINDINGS

• **Manufacturers will continue to adopt Industry 4.0 and the smart factory.** Workers will use a combination of radio frequency identification (RFID), wearable, automated systems and other emerging technologies to monitor the physical processes of the plant and enable companies to make decentralized decisions. By 2022, 64 percent of manufacturers expect to be fully connected compared to 43 percent today.

• **One-half of manufacturers plan to adopt wearable technologies by 2022.** And 55 percent of current wearable users expect to expand their level of usage in the next five years.

• **Manual processes are expected to dramatically decline.** Today, 62 percent use pen and paper to track vital manufacturing steps; this is expected to drop to one in five by 2022. The use of pen and paper to track work in progress (WIP) is highly inefficient and susceptible to error.

• **Executives across all regions cited achieving quality assurance as their top priority over the next five years.** Forward-looking manufacturers are embracing a quality-minded philosophy to drive growth, throughput and profitability. By 2022, only 34 percent expect to rate this as a top concern – signaling that improvements made by both suppliers and manufacturers will ultimately improve the quality of finished goods.

- **Manufacturers stated investments in visibility will support growth across their operation.**63% cited tracking as a core focus with a blend of technology (i.e. barcode scanning, RFID and real-time location systems [RTLS]) expected to be deployed to achieve the desired visibility.

- **51% of companies are planning to expand the use of voice technology in the next five years.** The most dramatic growth for voice technology will be in the largest companies (>$1 Billion) with a reported use growing to 55 percent by 2022.

REGIONAL FINDINGS

- On-demand, cloud, and Software as a Service (SaaS) solutions for Manufacturing Execution Systems (MES) are expected to grow rapidly with 58% of North American respondents expecting to use these services in 2022.

- By 2022, 54% of surveyed European manufacturers plan to use RTLS to collect critical data about assets including location, stage and condition.

- More than one-half (51 percent) of surveyed Latin American manufacturers and 48% of Asia-Pacific manufacturers plan to use RFID to optimize production WIP by 2022.

- Almost six-in-ten (58%) Latin American manufacturing executives cite improving quality assurance as their top priority over the next five years.

- Companies are focusing less on keeping materials on-hand and depending more on suppliers to provide goods on-demand. In five years, Just in Time (JIT) shipments will have the highest use in Latin America (42%) and Asia Pacific (40%).

SURVEY BACKGROUND AND METHODOLOGY

- 1 100 North American, Latin American, European and Asia Pacific decision makers who authorize or influence the purchase of relevant manufacturing technologies were interviewed by Peerless Insights.

- The online survey was fielded in the first quarter of 2017 across a wide range of segments, including automotive, high tech, food and beverage, tobacco and pharmaceuticals.

http://iiot-world.com/connected-industry/six-in-ten-manufacturers-will-have-fully-connected-factories-by-2022/

2.11 Three ways to visualize prediction regions for classification problems

By Rick Wicklin on The DO Loop JULY 17, 2017Advanced Analytics | Data Visualization

An important problem in machine learning is the "classification problem." In this supervised learning problem, you build a statistical model that predicts a set of categorical outcomes (responses) based on a set of input features (explanatory variables). You do this by training the model on data for which the outcomes are known. For example, researchers might want to predict the outcomes "Lived" or "Died" for patients with a certain disease. They can use data from a clinical trial to build a statistical model that uses demographic and medical measurements to predict the probability of each outcome.

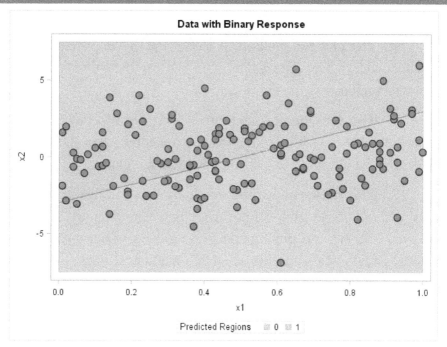

SAS software provides several procedures for building parametric classification models, including the LOGISTIC and DISCRIM procedures. SAS also provides various nonparametric models, such as spleen effects, additive models, and neural networks.

For each input, the statistical model predicts an outcome. Thus the model divides the input space into disjoint regions for which the first outcome is the most probable, for which the second outcomes is the most probable, and so forth. In many textbooks and papers, the classification problem is illustrated by using a two-dimensional graph that shows the prediction regions overlaid with the training data, as shown in the adjacent image which visualizes a binary outcome and a linear boundary between regions. (Click to enlarge.)

This article shows three ways to visualize prediction regions in SAS:

1. The polygon method: A parametric model provides a formula for the boundary between regions. You can use the formula to construct polygonal regions.

2. The contour plot method: If there are two outcomes and the model provides probabilities for the first outcome, then the 0.5 contour divides the feature space into disjoint prediction regions.

3. The background grid method: You can evaluate the model on a grid of points and color each point according to the predicted outcome. You can use small markers to produce a faint indication of the prediction regions, or you can use large markers if you want to tile the graph with color.

This article uses logistic regression to discriminate between two outcomes, but the principles apply to other methods as well. The SAS documentation for the DISCRIM procedure contains some macros that visualize the prediction regions for the output from PROC DISCRIM. I am grateful to my colleague Chris B. for discussions relevant to this topic.

A logistic model to discriminate two outcomes

To illustrate the classification problem, consider some simulated data in which the Y variable is a binary outcome and the X1 and X2 variable are continuous explanatory variables. The following call to PROC LOGISTIC fits a logistic model and displays the parameter estimates. The STORE statement creates an item store that enables you to evaluate (score) the model on future observations. The DATA step creates a grid of evenly spaced points in the (x1, x2) coordinates, and the call to PROC PLM scores the model at those locations. In the PRED data set, GX and GY are the coordinates on the regular grid and PREDICTED is the probability that Y=1.

```
proc logistic data=Logistic Data;
   model y(Event='1') = x1 x2;
```

```
    store work. Logi Model;
/* save model to item store */
run;


data Grid;  /* create grid in (x1,x2) co ords */
do x1 = 0 to 1by0.02;
do x2 = -7.5 to 7.5by0.3;
output;
end;
end;
run;


proc plm restore=work. Logi Model;
/* use PROC PLM to score model on a grid */
    score data=Grid out=Pred(rename=(x1=gx x2=gy)) / ilink;  /*
evaluate the model on new data */
    run;
```

The polygon method

This method is only useful for simple parametric models. Recall that the logistic function is 0.5 when its argument is zero, so the level set for 0 of the linear predictor divides the input space into prediction regions. For the parameter estimates shown to the right, the level set $\{(x1,x2) \mid 2.3565 -4.7618*x1 + 0.7959*x2 = 0\}$ is the boundary between the two prediction regions. This level set is the graph of the linear function $x2 = (-2.3565 + 4.7618*x1)/0.7959$. You can compute two polygons that represent the regions: let x1 vary between [0,1] (the horizontal range of the data) and use the formula to evaluate x2, or assign x2 to be the minimum or maximum vertical value of the data.

Analysis of Maximum Likelihood Estimates					
Parameter	DF	Estimate	Standard Error	Wald Chi-Square	Pr > ChiSq
Intercept	1	2.3565	0.5203	20.5157	<.0001
x1	1	-4.7618	0.9467	25.3005	<.0001
x2	1	0.7959	0.1445	30.3320	<.0001

After you have computed polygonal regions, you can use thePOLYGON statement in PROC SGPLOT to visualize the regions. The graph is shown at the top of this article. The drawbacks of this method are that it requires a parametric model for which one variable is an explicit function of the other. However, it creates a beautiful image!

The contour plot method

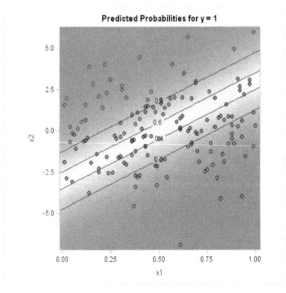

Given an input value, many statistical models produce probabilities for each outcome. If there are only two outcomes, you can plot a contour plot of the probability of the first outcome. The 0.5 contour divides the feature space into disjoint regions.

There are two ways to create such a contour plot. The easiest way is to use the EFFECTPLOT statement, which is supported in many SAS/STAT regression procedures. The following statements show how to use the EFFECTPLOT statement in PROC LOGISTIC to create a contour plot, as shown to the right:

```
proc logistic data=Logistic Data;
   model y(Event='1') = x1 x2;
   effect plot contour(x=x1 y=x2);
   /* 2. contour plot with scatter plot overlay */
run;
```

Unfortunately, not every SAS procedure supports the EFFECTPLOT statement. An alternative is to score the model on a regular grid of points and use the Graph Template Language (GTL) to create a contour plot of the probability surface. You can read my previous article about how to use the GTL to create a contour plot.

The drawback of this method is that it only applies to binary outcomes. The advantage is that it is easy to implement, especially if the modeling procedure supports the EFFECTPLOT statement.

The background grid method

In this method, you score the model on a grid of points to obtain the predicted outcome at each grid point. You then create a scatter plot of the grid, where the markers are colored by the outcome, as shown in the graph to the right.

When you create this graph, you get to choose how large to make the dots in the background. The image to the right uses small markers, which is the technique, used by Hastie, Tibshirani, and Friedman in their book *The Elements of Statistical Learning*. If you use square markers and increase the size of the markers, eventually the markers tile the entire background, which makes it look like the polygon plot at the beginning of this article. You might need to adjust the vertical and horizontal pixels of the graph to get the background markers to tile without overlapping each other.

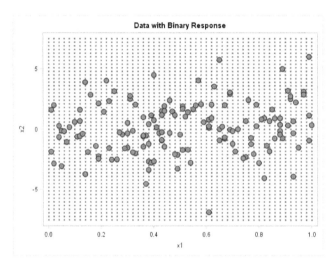

This method has several advantages. It is the most general method and can be used for any procedure and for any number of outcome categories. It is easy to implement because it merely uses the model to predict the outcomes on a grid of points. The disadvantage is that choosing the size of the background markers is a matter of trial and error; you might need several attempts before you create a graph that looks good.

Summary

This article has shown several techniques for visualizing the predicted outcomes for a model that has two independent variables. The first model is limited to simple parametric models, the second is restricted to binary outcomes, and the third is a general technique that requires scoring the model on a regular grid of inputs. Whichever method you choose, PROC SGPLOT and the Graph Template Language in SAS can help you to visualize different methods for the classification problem in machine learning.

You can download the SAS program that produces the graphs in this article. Which images do you like the best? Do you have a better visualization? Leave a comment?

http://blogs.sas.com/content/iml/2017/07/17/prediction-regions-classification.html

2.12 Big Data: The Golden Prospect of Machine Learning

The boom in the B2B big data market (from a sub-$100m industry in 2009 to $130bn today) mirrors an enterprise-led scramble to invest in data mining, reminiscent of the California gold rush, accompanied by a similar media buzz.

Although much is still written about the near-magical potential of data analytics for business, this fervor is now giving way to a more serious debate on where the real business value can actually be found. It's clear that data prospectors are diverging into two camps: the 'haves' and the 'have-not-yet'.

A recent KPMG survey showed only 40% of executives have a high level of trust in the consumer insights from their analytics, and most said their C-suite didn't fully support their current data analytics strategy. 58% of businesses told Teradata the impact of big data analytics on revenues was "3% or smaller". The real bonanza appears confined to banking, supply chains, and technical performance optimization – understandably some businesses feel left behind.

Guidance on using data analytics is aimed at companies with a massive pre-existing data hoard who wish to extract value from it – the equivalents of the gold rush's "49ers" that arrived in California early in

1849 to stake a claim on a good piece of prospecting land. Those struggling tend to be consumer-facing brands or marketers attempting to understand their customers' behaviour by panning vigorously in a shallow stream of aggregated sales data.

The first question these Argonauts need to ask themselves is whether there's really any difference between the 'data analytics' they are doing today and good old-fashioned business intelligence? The ubiquity of big data has led to a subtle shift in language use, whereby any information is now 'data' and analysis often simply means 'looking'.

Can human decision-makers find new actionable insights from just looking at data? Credible examples and detailed case studies are conspicuous by their absence, despite analytics vendors' repeated promises of golden nuggets of actionable insight at the end of the analytics journey (it should be noted that merchants made far more money in the gold rush than miners – its first millionaire, Samuel Bannon, sold prospecting tools and supplies, and was also the first to publicize the gold strike by running up and down the streets of San Francisco yelling: 'Gold! Gold in the American river!'

Attempting to squeeze insights out of small data has proven hazardous; to the extent it can lead one astray. Insight is defined as 'the understanding of a specific cause and effect in a specific context.'

Data cannot generate insight – insight is the conclusion people draw from evidence. Humans draw these conclusions, but in a deeply flawed way, simply because we've evolved to detect patterns everywhere.

We see faces in house fronts, mythical beasts in constellations and apparitions on toast. We inevitably draw statistical inferences that are invalid and cannot pick-out the 'random' scatter plot from an identity parade of graphs by sight alone. People know that statistical correlation doesn't imply causation, but they constantly behave as if it does. All these traits work against us when viewing data.

What about machine learning, then? Can dumb machines, invulnerable to the cognitive biases that afflict humans, uncover causal relationships from data which our puny minds are too feeble to compute? Typically, as an industry, we've found the answer is yes, but while predictive models can reliably forecast and simulate events, their complexity prevents easy interpretation.

For most business uses of prediction, this doesn't matter. Typically, it's been found that the forecast-and-simulate approach, particularly for marketing purposes, left unmet the fundamental need brands have to understand their customer and how to connect with them. In fact, there are platforms available in the market that apply machine learning to a particularly large pile of 'pay dirt' that any brand can access, but until recently had been considered impossible to mine.

These platforms make use of the natural-language text churned out by millions of people across social media, blogs, and discussion forums and turn it into 'data points' which can be clustered, filtered, and modeled, just like quantitative data.

This is a great leap forward in the big data era – the use of deep learning techniques such as neural nets to success transform 'unstructured' data (natural language, images, sound and video) into usable form. It's now possible to harvest online conversations and model them using standard data science techniques, telling marketers exactly what position a brand occupies in consumers' minds, what type of occasion and feelings they associate with a product, and giving a true understanding of how a target audience sees the brand.

You can identify the distinct communities discussing a subject on social media, the drivers of their collective attention, and who influences the influencers. Finally, once the conversational data has been processed in this way, algorithms can be used to identify the online trends and triggers which track real-world events.

These models are now used by marketers to uncover emerging consumer trends years before they show up in market research, test new product concepts, and determine the best copy for marketing materials.

Most importantly, mining web data this way gives consumer brands the chance to reap the same rewards from advances in big data analytics as the banks and web companies, without sacrificing understanding on the altar of automation. For the data-starved marketer, it's the mother lode.

https://econsultancy.com/blog/68995-big-data-the-golden-prospect-of-machine-learning-on-business-analytics/

Chapter-3: Artificial Intelligence

3.1 Defining AI, Machine Learning, and Deep Learning

February 15, 2017 by <u>Rich Brueckner</u>

The *inside BIGDATA Guide to Deep Learning & Artificial Intelligence* is a useful new resource directed toward enterprise thought leaders who wish to gain strategic insights into this exciting area of technology. In this guide, we take a high-level view of AI and deep learning in terms of how it's being used and what technological advances have made it possible. We also explain the difference between AI, machine learning and deep learning, and examine the intersection of AI and HPC. We also present the results of a recent *inside BIGDATA* survey to see how well these new technologies are being received. Finally, we take a look at a number of high-profile use case examples showing the effective use of AI in a variety of problem domains.

The Difference between AI, Machine Learning and Deep Learning

With all the quickly evolving nomenclature in the industry today, it's important to be able to differentiate between AI, machine learning and deep learning. The simplest way to think of their relationship is to visualize them as a concentric model as depicted in the figure below. Here, AI— the idea that came first—has the largest area, followed by machine learning—which blossomed later and is shown as a subset of AI. Finally deep learning—which is driving today's AI explosion— fits inside both.

AI has been part of our thoughts and slowly evolving in academic research labs since a group of computer scientists first defined the term at the Dartmouth Conferences in 1956 and provided the genesis of the field of AI. In the long decades since, AI has alternately been heralded as an all-encompassing holy grail, and thrown on technology's bit bucket as a mad conception of overactive academic imaginations. Candidly, until around 2012, it was a bit of both.

Over the past few years, especially since 2015, AI has exploded on the scene. Much of that enthusiasm has to do with the wide availability of GPUs that make parallel processing ever faster, cheaper, and more powerful. It also has to do with the simultaneous one-two punch of practically infinite storage and a flood of data of every stripe including images, video, text, transactions, geospatial data, etc.

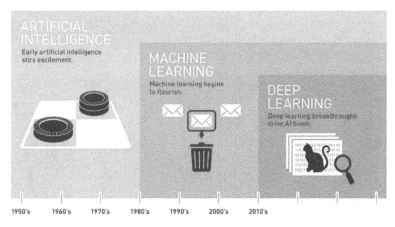

ARTIFICIAL
INTELLIGENCE
Early artificial intelligence
stirs excitement.

MACHINE
LEARNING
Machine learning begins
to flourish.

DEEP
LEARNING
Deep learning breakthroughs
drive AI boom.

1950's   1960's   1970's   1980's   1990's   2000's   2010's

Since an early flush of optimism in the 1950s, smaller subsets of artificial intelligence – first machine learning, then deep learning, a subset of machine learning – have created ever larger disruptions.

On the same trajectory, deep learning has enabled many practical applications of machine learning and by extension the overall field of AI. Deep learning breaks down tasks in ways that make all kinds of machine assists seem possible, even likely. Driverless cars, better preventive healthcare, even better movie recommendations, are all here today or on the horizon. AI is the foundation for the present and the future.

Download the *inside BIGDATA Guide to Deep Learning & Artificial Intelligence*, courtesy of NVIDIA.

3.2 AI and Automation Will Make Many IT Jobs in India Obsolete in 5 Years
By Kirti Sharma - Aug 1, 2017

Humans adopted the route of digitization and automation so as to make it easier for businesses to interact with their customers and make their internal processes smoother and more organized. While the whole transformation did help humans in achieving what they set out to achieve, somewhere on the way, they ended up impacting the role they themselves were playing in the whole process.

If you or anyone related to you is working in IT space in India, you must be aware of the sudden pink slips and job cuts being handed over to people on a daily basis from last few year. No matter which firm you're part of or which position you hold, your job is one day away from being canned.

So, if you're in IT or considering making IT as your career choices, then a recent survey from simply learn on how the future of IT jobs is changing in India can help you decide your course. Titled **How Automation is Changing Work Choices: The Future of IT Jobs in India**, the survey reveals that the future of IT lies in Cyber Security, Big Data and Data Science, Big Data Architect, Big Data Engineer, Artificial Intelligence and IoT (Internet of Things) Architect, and Cloud Architect as these job profiles will be high in demand in the near future.

According to the survey report, the jobs that are in the jeopardy of getting extinct are the ones that have become repetitive and are most likely to be taken over by Artificial Intelligence (AI) in next five years or so. These include job profiles such as BPO, manual testing, system maintenance and infrastructure management etc.

The Simply learn survey report comes just a few months after an international survey found out that there is a 50% chance that Artificial Intelligence (AI) will surpass human intelligence in all areas within a period of about 45 years. The study was conducted by researcher Katja Grace at the University of Oxford's Future of Humanity Institute and it involved surveying a total of 1,634 artificial intelligence researchers from all around the world.

Commenting on the report, Kashyap Dalal, Chief Business Officer said that while the situation does look a little glum at the moment, core development jobs will not feel the impact of job loss. He added, "The IT industry is seeing the impact of two major trends – one, that of AI and machine learning. And second, that of legacy skill-sets going out of date. While there is risk to jobs due to these trends, the good news is that a huge number of new jobs are getting created as well in areas like Cyber Security, Cloud, Dev Ops, Big Data, Machine Learning and AI. It is clearly a time of career pivot for IT professionals, to make sure they are where the growth is."

Simply learn's report also highlighted the preferred technology skills based on a survey it conducted of 7,000 IT professionals from key metros. The survey found out that over 50 per cent of IT professionals in India with work experience in the bracket of 4–10 years have invested in courses and training programs that can help them better their knowledge and build new skills. Some of the top domains preferred by professionals for online training programs include Big Data & Analytics, Project Management, Cloud Computing, Cyber Security, Agile & Scrum, and Digital Marketing.

https://www.indianweb2.com/2017/08/01/ai-automation-will-make-many-jobs-india-obsolete-5-years/?utm_source=pushengage&utm_medium=push_notification&utm_campaign=push_engage

3.3   Businesses Need Artificial "Specialist" Intelligence, Not the Other Kind

Here is the stark reality about businesses; we need specialists to do almost all our jobs. What this means in terms of the development of Artificial Intelligence (AI), or more precisely Artificial General Intelligence (AGI), is that the real world need of narrow intelligence out sizes the need for smarter self-aware intelligences. So, the fear about the emergence of a sentient intelligence is completely misplaced. What we should really fear is the exponential pace of developing artificial specialist intelligence.

That is, the kind of intelligence that can do a job so damn well that we never need to pay a human anymore to perform the job. In the old days, the term "computer" was used for humans who would meticulously perform hand calculations. You would have rows of people that would do this kind of work:

Source: http://www.computerhistory.org/revolution/calculators/1/65/272

In fact, you couldn't hire just anybody off the street. These people had to be above average in their mathematical skills. Richard Feynman himself was known to be a very gifted "computer." Here's a story of

Feynman <u>besting the abacus</u> where Feynman describes his approximation technique:

> *The number was 1729.03. I happened to know that a cubic foot contains 1728 cubic inches, so the answer is a tiny bit more than 12. The excess, 1.03 is only one part in nearly 2000, and I had learned in calculus that for small fractions, the cube root's excess is one-third of the number's excess. So all I had to do is find the fraction 1/1728, and multiply by 4 (divide by 3 and multiply by 12). So I was able to pull out a whole lot of digits that way.*

So, when Google has its self-driving cars drive two million miles, it has driven more miles than the average human. A human who drives on average 13,000 miles in a year will need to drive for 153 years to reach two million miles. After 1.7 miles, Google had reported that its cars had 11 minor accidents. I've driven my cars at one tenth the amount that Google has done and I'm certain to have at least 11 minor accidents (i.e. scraped hubcaps, fender benders etc.). The point though here is that automation can easily become the safest and most likely the best kind of driver we will ever have. There are 3.5 million truck drivers in the U.S., and pretty soon they will be 3.5 million truck drivers that drive less safely and less efficiently than specialized driving automation.

As far as the "street smarts" or "common sense" that we expect from humans to do their job correctly, we might as well throw that out the door also. Let's look at the <u>infamous case of United Airlines</u>. A paying passenger was battered and dragged off a plane simply because common sense did not prevail. Surely all the flight attendants, ground crew and law enforcement were not complete idiots. Yet, a simple solution to the problem could not be found (i.e. raise the re-accommodation payment until someone accepts).

The reason we insert humans in our businesses is so that common sense will prevail. Unfortunately, the way we've mechanized most of our corporations, we know that we've thrown out all common sense. The popularity of the Dilbert cartoon strip is a testament of loss of common sense in our corporations. So let's not pretend here, a majority of corporations run without much common-sense, furthermore they are run mostly by warm body humans. Clearly, the presence of a warm-body does not guarantee the existence of 'common-sense'.

Most businesses don't require their employees to have common-sense, what they want their employees to have is mechanized efficiency. It just turns out that this mechanized efficient kind of job that is the easiest replaced with today's technology (not some future AGI).

American workers are now forced into the "Gig Economy" whether they like it or not. Let me make it perfectly clear, the gig economy is a knee-jerk reaction to the destruction of jobs (or more precisely, that of careers). It is the survival mechanism for people to become more adaptable in what they can provide as services. What we are losing are single professions that are able to support ourselves with. It means that there are fewer and fewer jobs that we can support ourselves by being just specialists. So what happens is that people have to become specialists in many other kinds of jobs. That portfolio diversity allows us to survive as each job incrementally gets extinguished by automation.

So we are forced now to become generalists that become masters of many skills. How can we master many skills? It turns out that automation is what allows us to master skills with less experience. The table has been flipped in that folks with "common sense" and "street sense" become critical. Folks with advanced "business intuition" are the ones that will continue to thrive (before AGI). That's because automation has given them superpowers (ask Andrew Ng).

So as we make rapid progress, expect to see more capable narrow intelligence applications created. The world will become even more competitive over time and anyone who doesn't understand how to implement and deploy Artificial Intelligence is going to be at a complete disadvantage. Leaders of business who have an intuition of how their markets operate and have the savvy to build the automation that can exploit opportunities are going to take over the world.

The main point I want to make is that debates about the possibility of AGI (or AI if you still want to use that antiquated term) are pointless. The present reality (or is it clear and present danger?) is that artificial narrow intelligence is going to clean up big time. The main blind spot of many is that AI will only be useful if it has general intelligence. On the contrary, it is more useful if it has specialized intelligence. This is not a new observation; Marc Andreessen has said many times that "software is eating the world." If is not obvious to you, Artificial Intelligence is software.

Mark Cuban has an even more surprising quote:

Artificial Intelligence, deep learning, machine learning—whatever you're doing if you don't understand it—learn it. Otherwise you're going to be a dinosaur within 3 years; If you love brutal assessments.

https://medium.com/intuitionmachine/businesses-need-artificial-specialist-intelligence-not-the-other-kind-b0c285c1586e

3.4 Artificial Intelligence: Monster or Mentor?
Posted by <u>Roy Wilds, PhD, PHEMI Systems</u> on June 8, 2017

Artificial Intelligence (AI) is everywhere these days. It's simultaneously heralded as both the greatest thing since sliced bread — freeing us from driving cars, diagnosing diseases better, and so on — and the worst thing imaginable— displacing millions of jobs, and a step towards the inevitable AI domination of humans.

Lost in this hyperbole are the many simple, yet effective, enabling innovations that AI makes possible. Just like we rely on machines in the physical world to excavate holes for buildings or transport people or cargo long distances, we increasingly rely on machine algorithms such as machine learning (ML) models in the online, networked world. These innovations enable us to keep our email from overflowing with spam and to index and catalog enormous volumes of text for simple and fast retrieval, along with a wide range of other efficiencies. A recent article in Harvard Business Review [1] touched on this, highlighting the risks of large – yet ambiguous – AI projects compared to the measured possibilities businesses can undertake.

Artificial intelligence is a hot topic right now. Driven by a fear of losing out, companies in many industries have announced AI-focused initiatives. Unfortunately, most of these efforts will fail. They will fail not because AI is all hype, but because companies are approaching AI-driven innovation incorrectly. And this isn't the first time companies have made this kind of mistake.

In this blog series we're going to dive deeper into several exciting examples where AI enables human workers to function at a far greater level of productivity than they would otherwise. The productivity gain is realized through three main mechanisms, which often overlap:

- **Distillation — the ultimate summarizer.** Crawling and analyzing enormous volumes of text, numbers, and data to generate a human-consumable concise summary.
- **Categorization — the ultimate sorter and router**. Finding global patterns in enormous datasets to allow you to organize data at large scales.
- **Prediction — the ultimate assistant**. Learning from human behavior and feedback to replicate and automate common tasks.

These mechanisms are the core conceptual elements of many AI applications, and they aren't new. However, here we're going to emphasize the machine-human interaction they involve.

All too often, we data scientists and engineers get lost in the technical details of our algorithms and codes, forgetting about the human that is intended to benefit from the work we immerse ourselves in. And I'm not just talking about ignoring the end-user interface. When we scientists and engineers focus on how end-users can benefit from AI capabilities throughout the process — as viewed through the lens of to distilling, categorizing, and predicting — we can genuinely help make people more productive.

The three case studies we're going to focus on will touch on each of these mechanisms in turn.

In the next article, we'll take a look at the first mechanism, **distillation**. We'll take as our example the **customer journey** challenge. We'll explore how, through combinations of network analysis, temporal pattern mining, and interactive analysis we can build AI-assisted technologies that enable humans to answer these questions and identify service optimizations and cost reductions, and deliver a better customer experience.

Subsequent articles will touch on:

- Categorization – exploring how email triage can enable fixed resource teams to grow with volumes of email traffic

- Prediction – reviewing an example of how AI-assisted medical diagnosis can enhance medical care and accuracy

http://www.datasciencecentral.com/profiles/blogs/artificial-intelligence-monster-or-mentor

3.5   The Race for AI: Google, Twitter, Intel, Apple in a Rush to Grab Artificial Intelligence Startups

Deepashri Varadharajan; Published on April 5, 2017; Featured in: Entrepreneurship, Technology, VC& Private Equity

Around 46% of the AI companies acquired since 2012 have had VC backing.

Corporate giants like Google, IBM, Yahoo, Intel, Apple and Sales force are competing in the race to acquire private AI companies, with Ford, Samsung, GE, and Uber emerging as new entrants. Over 200 private companies using AI algorithms across different verticals have been acquired since 2012, with over 30 acquisitions taking place in Q1'17 alone (as of 3/24/17). This quarter also saw one of the largest M&A deals: Ford's acquisition of Argo AI for $1B.

(For a list of acquired companies by geography, read the blog post here. To sign up for the AI webinar, click here.)

ARTIFICIAL INTELLIGENCE M&A ACTIVITY
Q1'12-Q1'17 YTD (as of 3/23/17)

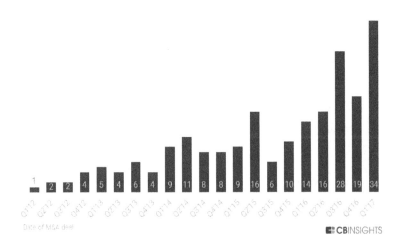

Date of M&A deal   **CB**INSIGHTS

In 2013, Google picked up deep learning and neural network startup DNN research from the computer science department at the University of Toronto. This acquisition reportedly helped Google make major upgrades to its image search feature. In 2014 Google acquired British company Deep Mind Technologies for some $600M (Google's Deep Mind program recently beat a human world champion in the board game "Go"). Last year, it acquired visual search startup Moodstock, and bot platform Api.ai. More recently, in Q1'17, Google acquired predictive analytics platform Kaggle.

Apple has been ramping up its M&A activity, and ranked second with a total of 7 acquisitions. It recently acquired Tel Aviv-based Real Face, valued at $2M.

Intel, Microsoft, and Face book are tied for third place. Intel acquired 3 startups in 2016 alone: Itseez, Nervana Systems, and Movidius, while Face book acquired Belarus-based Masquerade Technologies and Switzerland-based Zurich-Eye recently. Microsoft recently acquired Geneeand conversational AI startup Maluuba.

Twitter is the next most-active acquirer, with 4 major acquisitions, the most recent being image-processing startup Magic Pony.

Sales force, which joined the race in 2015 with the acquisition of Tempo AI, made two major acquisitions last year: Khosla Ventures-backed MetaMind and open-source machine-learning server PredictionIO. GE made 2 acquisitions in November 2016: AI-IoT startup Bit Stew Systems, and CRM-focused Wise.io.

The timeline below shows the M&A activity of corporations that have made 2 or more acquisitions since 2012. (Note: The exact dates for Apple's Novauris and Amazon's Orbeus acquisitions are not known. They are marked with a star to indicate approximate date of acquisition.)

https://www.linkedin.com/pulse/race-ai-google-twitter-intel-apple-rush-grab-startups-varadharajan

3.6   Artificial Intelligence (Chipsets) Market by Technology (Deep Learning, Robotics, Digital Personal Assistant, Querying Method, Natural Language Processing, Context Aware Processing), Offering, End-User Industry, and Geography - Global Forecast to 2022

By: marketsandmarkets.com; Publishing Date: November 2016; Report Code: SE 4053

The artificial intelligence (AI) market is expected to be worth USD 16.06 Billion by 2022, growing at a CAGR of 62.9% from 2016 to 2022. The base year used for this study is 2015 and the forecast period is from 2016 to 2022. This report provides a detailed analysis of the artificial intelligence market on the basis of technology, offering, end-user industry, and geography. Artificial intelligence is a consolidation of state-of-the-art technologies which are used to develop products which work similar to human intelligence.

Objectives of the Study

• To define, describe, and forecast the artificial intelligence (AI) market segmented on the basis of technology, offering, end-user industry, and geography.

• To forecast the market size, in terms of value, for various segments with regard to four main regions, namely, North America, Europe, Asia-Pacific (APAC), and Rest of the World (RoW)

• To provide detailed information regarding the major factors influencing the growth of the AI market (drivers, restraints, opportunities, and industry-specific challenges)

- To strategically analyze the micro markets with respect to the individual growth trends, future prospects, and contribution to the total market.

- To provide a detailed overview of the value chain of the AI market and analyze market trends through the Porter's five forces analysis.

- To strategically profile the key players and comprehensively analyze their market position in terms of ranking and core competencies, along with detailing the competitive landscape for the market leaders.

- To analyze competitive developments such as partnerships and joint ventures, mergers acquisitions, new product developments, expansions, and research and development in the AI market.

To estimate the size of the artificial intelligence market, top-down and bottom-up approaches have been followed in the study. This entire research methodology includes the study of annual and financial reports of top players, presentations, press releases; journals such as "The Zettabyte Era: Trends and Analytics" by Cisco Systems, Inc. (U.S.), Big Data (Artificial Intelligence) by EU Business Innovation Industry, The New Wave of Artificial Intelligence by Every A/S (Norway), AI Meets Big Data by Umbel (U.S.), and Deep Learning Methods and Applications by Li Deng and Dong Yu; paid databases such as Google Finance, Factiva (By Dow Jones & Company), Yahoo Finance; and interviews with industry experts. Also, the average revenue generated by the companies according to the region was used to arrive at the overall artificial intelligence market size. This overall market size was used in the top-down procedure to estimate the sizes of other individual markets via percentage splits from secondary and primary research.

To know about the assumptions considered for the study, **download the pdf brochure**.

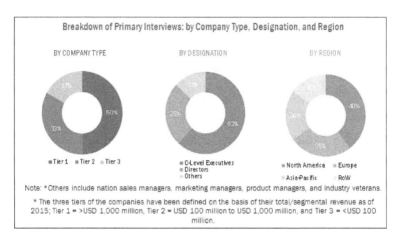

The artificial intelligence ecosystem comprises hardware and platforms/services/software solutions providers such as Google Inc. (U.S.), IBM Corp. (U.S.), Microsoft Corporation (U.S.), General Vision Inc. (U.S.), Intel Corporation (U.S.), Numenta, Inc. (U.S.), Baidu, Inc. (China), Inbenta Technologies, Inc. (U.S.), and NVIDIA Corporation (U.S.).

Target Audience:

- Artificial Intelligence module designers and manufacturers
- Research organizations and consulting companies
- Associations, forums, and alliances related to artificial intelligence
- Investors
- Startup companies
- Raw material suppliers
- Government and other regulatory bodies
- Market research and consulting firms

Artificial Intelligence Market Scope:

By Technology

- Deep Learning

- Robotics
- Digital Personal Assistant
- Querying Method
- Natural Language Processing
- Context-Aware Processing

By Offering

- Products

  o Hardware
  o Software

- Services

  o Installation
  o Training
  o Support and Maintenance

By End-User Industry

- Agriculture

  o Crop Monitoring
  o Automated Irrigation/Harvesting (GPS-Enabled) Systems
  o AI-Guided Drones

- BFSI

  o Wealth Management
  o Fraud Detection
  o Automated Virtual Assistants

- Manufacturing

  o Robot-Integrated CIM systems

- Healthcare

  o Health Assistance and Medical Management
  o Drug Development

- Oil and Gas

  - Exploration and Production (E&P) Life Cycle

- Media and Advertising

  - Facial Recognition Advertising
  - Customer Self-Service

- Transportation and Automotive

  - Autonomous Guided Vehicles
  - Infotainment Human-Machine Interface

- Retail

  - Product Recommendations
  - Autonomous In-Store Robots

- Others (Law, Education)

  - Legal Informatics
  - Virtual Mentor

By Geography

- North America

  - U.S.
  - Canada
  - Mexico

- Europe

  - U.K.
  - Germany
  - France
  - Rest of Europe

- APAC

- o China
- o Japan
- o South Korea
- o India
- o Rest of APAC

- Rest of the World

- o Middle East
- o Africa
- o Latin America

Available Customizations:

With the given market data, Markets and Markets offers customizations according to the clients' specific needs. The following customization options are available for the report:

http://www.marketsandmarkets.com/Market-Reports/artificial-intelligence-market-74851580.html

3.7 The Rise of AI Is Forcing Google and Microsoft to Become Chipmakers

By now our future is clear: We are to be cared for, entertained, and monetized by artificial intelligence. Existing industries like healthcare and manufacturing will become much more efficient; new ones like augmented reality goggles and robot taxis will become possible.

But as the tech industry busies itself with building out this brave new artificially intelligent, and profit boosting, world, it's hitting a speed bump: Computers aren't powerful and efficient enough at the specific kind of math needed. While most attention to the AI boom is understandably focused on the latest exploits of algorithms beating humans at poker or piloting juggernauts, there's a less obvious scramble going on to build a new breed of computer chip needed to power our AI future.

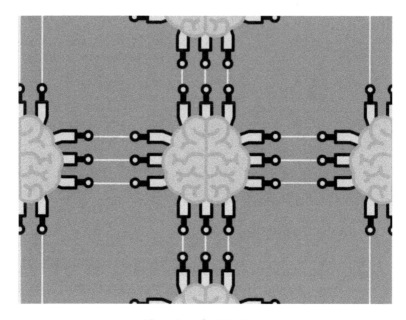

Hot Little Potato

One data point that shows how great that need is: software companies Google and Microsoft have become entangled in the messy task of creating their own chips. They're being raced by a new crop of startups peddling their own AI-centric silicon—and probably Apple, too. As well as transforming our lives with intelligent machines, the contest could shake up the established chip industry.

Microsoft revealed its AI chip-making project late on Sunday. At a computer vision conference in Hawaii, Harry Shum, who leads Microsoft's research efforts, showed off a new chip created for the HoloLens augmented reality googles. The chip, which Shum demonstrated tracking hand movements, includes a module custom-designed to efficiently run the deep learning software behind recent strides in speech and image recognition. Microsoft wants you to be able to smoothly reach out and interact with the virtual objects overlaid on your vision and says nothing on the market could run machine learning software efficiently enough for the battery-powered device that sits on your head.

Microsoft's project comes in the wake of Google's own deep learning chip, announced in 2016. The TPU, for tensor processing unit, was created to make deep learning more efficient inside the company's cloud. The company told WIRED earlier this year that it saved the company from building 15 new datacenters as demand for speech recognition soared. In May Google announced it had made a more powerful version of its TPU and that it would be renting out access to the chips to customers of its cloud computing business.

News that Microsoft has built a deep learning processor for Hololens suggests Redmond wouldn't need to start from scratch to prep its own server chip to compete with Google's TPUs. Microsoft has spent several years making its cloud more efficient at deep learning using so-called field-programmable gate arrays, a kind of chip that can be reconfigured after it's manufactured to make a particular piece of software or algorithm run faster. It plans to offer those to cloud customers next year. But when asked recently if Microsoft would make a custom server chip like Google's, Doug Burger, the technical mastermind behind Microsoft's roll out of FPGAs, said he wouldn't rule it out. Pieces of the design and supply chain process used for the HoloLens deep learning chip could be repurposed for a server chip.

Google and Microsoft's projects are the most visible part of a new AI-chip industry springing up to challenge established semiconductor giants such as Intel and Nvidia. Apple has for several years designed the processors for its mobile devices, and is widely believed to be working on creating a new chip to make future iphones better at artificial intelligence. Numerous startups are working on deep learning chips of their own, including Groq, founded by ex-Google engineers who worked on the TPU. "Companies like Intel and Nvidia have been trying to keep on selling what they were already selling," says Linley Gwennap, founder of semiconductor industry analysts the Linley Group. "We've seen these leading cloud companies and startups moving more quickly because they can see the need in their own data centers and the wider market."

Graphics chip maker Nvidia has seen sales and profits soar in recent years because its chips are better suited than conventional processors to training deep learning software. But the company has mostly chosen to modify and extend its existing chip designs rather than making something tightly specialized to deep learning from scratch, Gwennap says.

You can expect the established chip companies to fight back. Intel, the world's largest chipmaker, bought an AI chip startup called Nervana last summer and is working on a dedicated deep learning chip built on the company's technology. The company has the most sophisticated and expensive chip manufacturing operation on the planet. But representatives of the large and small upstarts taking on the chip industry say they have critical advantages. One is that they don't have to make something that fits within an existing ecosystem of chips and software originally developed for something else.

"We've got a simpler task because we're trying to do one thing and can build things from the ground up," says Nigel Toon, CEO and co-founder of Graph core, a UK startup working on a chip for artificial intelligence. Last week the company disclosed $30 million of new funding, including funds from Demis Hassabis, the CEO of Google's Deep Mind AI research division. Also in on the funding round: several leaders from Open AI, the research institute co-founded by Elon Musk.

At the other end of the scale, the big cloud companies can exploit their considerable experience in running and inventing machine learning services and techniques. "One of the things we really benefited from at

Google was we could work directly with the application developers in, say, speech recognition and Street View," says Norm Jouppi, the engineer who leads Google's TPU project. "When you're focused on a few customers and working hand in hand with them it really shortens the turnaround time to build something."

Google and Microsoft built themselves up by inventing software that did new things with chips designed and built by others. As more is staked on AI, the silicon substrate of the tech industry is changing—and so is where it comes from.

https://www.wired.com/story/the-rise-of-ai-is-forcing-google-and-microsoft-to-become-chipmakers/?mbid=nl_72517_p2&CNDID=50292723

3.8   Artificial Intelligence Is Stuck. Here's How to Move It Forward

Gray Matter by GARY MARCUS JULY 29, 2017

Artificial Intelligence is colossally hyped these days, but the dirty little secret is that it still has a long, long way to go. Sure, A.I. systems have mastered an array of games, from chess and Go to "Jeopardy" and poker, but the technology continues to struggle in the real world. Robots fall over while opening doors, prototype driverless cars frequently need human intervention, and nobody has yet designed a machine that can read reliably at the level of a sixth grader, let alone a college student. Computers that can educate themselves — a mark of true intelligence — remain a dream.

Even the trendy technique of "deep learning," which uses artificial neural networks to discern complex statistical correlations in huge amounts of data, often comes up short. Some of the best image-recognition systems, for example, can successfully distinguish dog breeds, yet remain capable of major blunders, like mistaking a simple pattern of yellow and black stripes for a school bus. Such systems can neither comprehend what is going on in complex visual scenes ("Who is chasing whom and why?") nor follow simple instructions ("Read this story and summarize what it means").

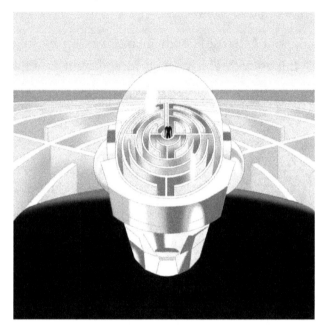

Credit: Jun Cen

Although the field of A.I. is exploding with micro discoveries, progress toward the robustness and flexibility of human cognition remains elusive. Not long ago, for example, while sitting with me in a cafe, my 3-year-old daughter spontaneously realized that she could climb out of her chair in a new way: backward, by sliding through the gap between the back and the seat of the chair. My daughter had never seen anyone else disembark in quite this way; she invented it on her own — and without the benefit of trial and error, or the need for terabytes of labeled data.

Presumably, my daughter relied on an implicit theory of how her body moves, along with an implicit theory of physics — how one complex object travels through the aperture of another. I challenge any robot to do the same. A.I. systems tend to be passive vessels, dredging through data in search of statistical correlations; humans are active engines for discovering how things work.

To get computers to think like humans, we need a new A.I. paradigm, one that places "top down" and "bottom up" knowledge on equal footing. Bottom-up knowledge is the kind of raw information we get directly from our senses, like patterns of light falling on our retina. Top-down knowledge comprises cognitive models of the world and how it works.

Deep learning is very good at bottom-up knowledge, like discerning which patterns of pixels correspond to golden retrievers as opposed to Labradors. But it is no use when it comes to top-down knowledge. If my daughter sees her reflection in a bowl of water, she knows the image is illusory; she knows she is not actually in the bowl. To a deep-learning system, though, there is no difference between the reflection and the real thing, because the system lacks a theory of the world and how it works. Integrating that sort of knowledge of the world may be the next great hurdle in A.I., a prerequisite to grander projects like using A.I. to advance medicine and scientific understanding.

I fear, however, that neither of our two current approaches to funding A.I. research — small research labs in the academy and significantly larger labs in private industry — is poised to succeed. I say this as someone who has experience with both models, having worked on A.I. both as an academic researcher and as the founder of a start-up company, Geometric Intelligence, which was recently acquired by Uber.

Academic labs are too small. Take the development of automated machine reading, which is a key to building any truly intelligent system. Too many separate components are needed for any one lab to tackle the problem. A full solution will incorporate advances in natural language processing (e.g., parsing sentences into words and phrases), knowledge representation (e.g., integrating the content of sentences with other sources of knowledge) and inference (reconstructing what is implied but not written). Each of those problems represents a lifetime of work for any single university lab.

Corporate labs like those of Google and Facebook have the resources to tackle big questions, but in a world of quarterly reports and bottom lines, they tend to concentrate on narrow problems like optimizing advertisement placement or automatically screening videos for offensive content. There is nothing wrong with such research, but it is unlikely to lead to major breakthroughs. Even Google Translate, which pulls off the neat trick of approximating translations by statistically associating sentences across languages, doesn't understand a word of what it is translating.

I look with envy at my peers in high-energy physics, and in particular at CERN, the European Organization for Nuclear Research, a huge, international collaboration, with thousands of scientists and billions of dollars of funding. They pursue ambitious, tightly defined projects (like using the Large Hadron Collider to discover the Higgs boson) and share their results with the world, rather than restricting them to a single country or corporation. Even the largest "open" efforts at A.I., like Open AI, which has about 50 staff members and is sponsored in part by Elon Musk, is tiny by comparison.

An international A.I. mission focused on teaching machines to read could genuinely change the world for the better — the more so if it made A.I. a public good, rather than the property of a privileged few.

Gary Marcus is a professor of psychology and neural science at New York University.

https://www.nytimes.com/2017/07/29/opinion/sunday/artificial-intelligence-is-stuck-heres-how-to-move-it-forward.html?_r=0

3.9   The Seven I's of Big Data Science Methodology

Industry press is enamored by the 4 V's of Big Data. These are Volume, Velocity, Variety and Veracity. Volume is referring to the size of the data. Velocity is referring to the speed of how data is collected and consumed. Variety is referring to the different kinds of data consumed, from structured data, unstructured data and sensor data. Veracity is referring to the trustworthiness of the data.

IBM (source) has a nice infographic that highlights the problem space of Big Data:

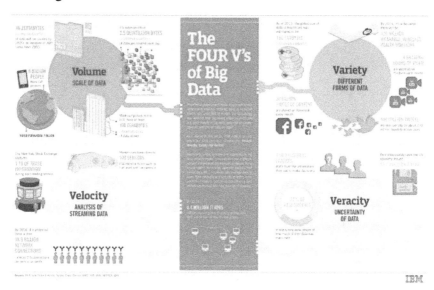

Readers however are left perplexed as how best to discover value given these tremendous data complexities. Alluviate is focused on formulating a Big Data Methodology (specifically we call it **The Data Lake Methodology**) for creating valuable and actionable insight. There certainly can be other Big Data methodologies, but we believe that the Data Lake approach leads to a more agile and lean process.

The current standard process for Data Mining is CRISP-DM. It involves 5 major phases:

The core value of Big Data is not just the ability to store lots of data in cheap commodity hardware. The real value, which many vendors seem to have missed the point entirely, is the ability to process that data to gain insight. This is Data Mining in the traditional sense and it is Machine Learning in the more advanced sense. Therefore, as a starting CRISP-DM is a good starting point for defining a new process. This new process however needs to get an upgrade. That is, we can't ignore advanced in technology since 1999 when CRISP-DM was originally defined.

A Data Lake approach to Big Data has the following features:

- The ingestion step requires zero ceremony. There is no need for upfront schema design or ETL development.

- Access to analytics is democratized by providing ease of use self-service tools.

- The process is entirely incremental and iterative, rather than a boil the ocean approach of previous data warehousing.

- The approach employs Big Data processing to creates data profile and provides recommendation to support the discovery of insight.

Given this context of a new kind of way of doing data integration, I propose the Seven I's of the Data Lake Methodology:

1. Ingest

Ingest the data sources that you require. Data that comes from multiple data silos are placed in a single name space to allow ease of exploration.

2. Integrate

Data that is ingested from multiple source can gain immense value through data linkage and fusion processes. This usually requires a combination of massive process and machine learning. Other aspects of integration may include the necessary data preparation required for downstream analytics processes like predictive analytics or OLAP cubes. Essentially, we are leveraging Big Data technologies to prepare data to make it easier for humans to explore and investigate Big Data.

3. Index

The Data ingested and integrated inside a Data Lake needs to be further processed into a structure that enables the user to explore the Data Lake in a responsive manner. Technologies like search engines (inverted indices) and OLAP databases provide the capability for users to slice and dice through the data. It is not enough to provide a SQL interface into the Hadoop file system.

4. Investigate

This is the process of exploring through data building an understanding and creating of models the data. This phase is enhanced by the previous Index phase by accelerating the number of iterations of investigations that can be performed.

5. Discover Insight

When valuable insight is uncovered; the process requires that this insight be validated. The thought here is that the process should lean towards rapidly discover the Minimum Valuable Insight. This is analogous to the idea of Minimum Viable Product.

6. Invest

Insights are a nice to have, but can't be made valuable unless an enterprise invests energy and resources to act on that insight. This requires that insights discovered are implemented and deployed into the organization.

7. Iterate

This is actually a "meta" phase for the entire process, but I prefer the number seven over the number six. It is of course important to emphasize the point that it is not enough to deploy your analytics solution just once. The world is a dynamic place and lots of things change. You world will operate in such a way that the original veracity of your source will change and new models will have to be built to compensate and adapt.

I hope that the Big Data industry will move beyond discussing the problem of the Four V's of Big Data. The Seven I's of Big Data Science instead focuses on the more valuable process of discovering actionable insight. This is a better place to revolve the discussion around.

https://medium.com/intuitionmachine/the-seven-is-of-big-data-science-methodology-711af03ef5b

3.10 Google's AI Processor's (TPU) Heart Throbbing Inspiration

Google has finally released the technical details of its Tensor Process Unit (TPU) ASIC. Surprisingly, at its core, you find something that sounds like it's inspired by the heart and not the brain. It's called a "Systolic Array" and this computational device contains 256 x 256 8bit multiply-add computational units. That's a grand total of 65,536 processors capable of cranking out 92 trillion operations per second! A systolic array is not a new thing; it was described way back in 1982 by Kung from CMU in "Why Systolic Architectures?" Just to get myself dated, I still recall a time when Systolic machines were all the rage.

Unlike other computational devices that treat scalar or vectors as primitives, Google's TPU treats matrices as primitives. The TPU is designed to perform matrix multiplication at a massive scale. If you look at the diagram above, you notice that that the device doesn't have high bandwidth to memory. It uses DDR3 with only 30GB/s to memory. Contrast that to the Nvidia Titan X with GDDR5X hitting transfer speeds of 480GB/s. The systolic array trades off speed for throughput. A Titan X has 3,583 CUDA cores. The CUDA cores are 32bit and are more general purpose than 8bit cores of the TPU. Apparently, Google knew likely way back in 2014 that 8bit was good enough (note: Google had deployed TPU as early as 2015).

Here's a diagram of Google's TPU:

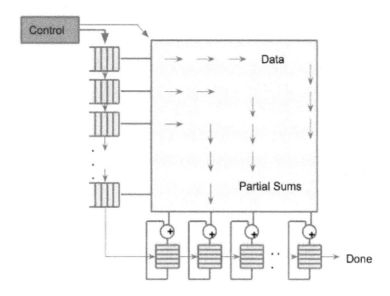

Google TPU with its 2D Systolic Array

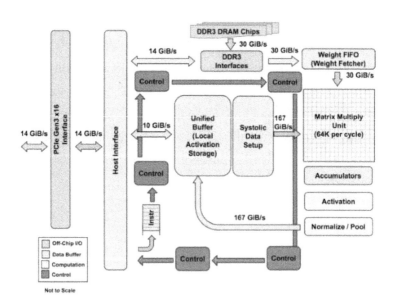

Source: https://drive.google.com/file/d/0Bx4hafXDDq2EMzRNcy1vSUx tcEk/view

Systolic arrays are heavily pipelined, given that it is 256 units wide, it takes 256 cycles from the time the first element gets into the array to the time it comes out. Twice that many cycles for everything that needs to get it, to all come out. However, at its peak, you'll get 65k processors all cranking together. Here's a slide that shows how a systolic array performs matrix multiplication:

Systolic Array Example:
3x3 Systolic Array Matrix Multiplication

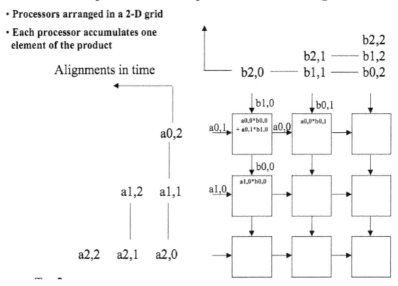

Source: http://web.cecs.pdx.edu/~mperkows/temp/May22/0020.Matrix-multiplication-systolic.pdf

Notice how the how the matrix elements have to be staggered as they work their way into the array. Another interesting thing about the TPU is that its DDR3 memory seems to be used exclusively for weights. Instructions and data come through the PCIe interface. It surely doesn't use all of its DDR3 memory for a single DL network. What it may appear to be doing is that it could be switching context between different DL networks. You can find some explanation of this design here: "Outrageously Large Neural Network".

Anyway, very interesting architecture, unfortunately it works well only for inference and not for training. However, you just never know if Google already has built something that can also work well for training.

Here's the floor plan for the device:

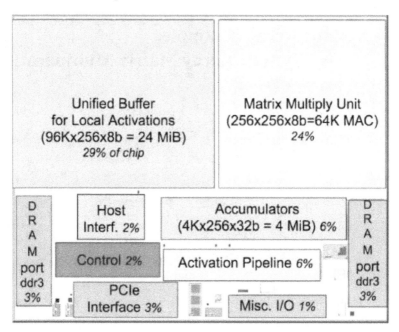

ASIC development is a high risk and expensive proposition. Google had no issue deciding on implementing this in 2014 because, not only did it have the money, but rather they had a captive user base that would have a use for this. However, this design can easily be copied by the many wannabe AI chip vendors.

We could see the same thing that happened in the world of Bitcoin. In that field, miners rapidly moved from CPU; to GPU; to FPGA and then ASICs. The big leaps in performance occurred in the transitions from CPU to GPU and from FPGA to ASICs. The FPGA route was interesting and served as a good test-phase for ASICs but the gains were negligible. So those betting on FPGAs to bring value to Deep Learning (i.e. Xilinx and

Intel), they should sell their longs and go short. It'll only be useful for niche and novel use-cases, in short, markets too small to care about.

The design is something that's going to be replicated because everyone will want a low powered DL component. It doesn't require high memory bandwidth. It's a CISC device so the instructions sets are quite compact requiring an average of 10–20 cycles per instruction, with only a dozen (12) instructions (hint: microcode folks, looks like there's future opportunity here!). 29% of the die is memory, 24% of it is all 8 bit MACs so the semiconductor design isn't rocket science.

In typical Google fashion, that is use simple hardware and crack the problem in software, the secret sauce here is in the software. To pull this off, you have to have an intimate understanding of Deep Learning workloads. How else do you figure out what CISC instructions are important? You also need a bit of compiler design, because apparently the host CPU seems to be doing a lot of prep works to align data and manage results.

ASIC systolic arrays are going to flood the market with likely Chinese government subsidized hardware manufacturers cranking this stuff out. It just takes someone to come up with an open source reference design. Just like what happened in the Bitcoin world. This stuff is ancient design stuff, and I'm sure someone has the old iWarp designs and compilers in their basement somewhere!

Well, before you go, make sure you "heart" this post!

Update 1: TPU developers raise $10m to start a TPU company.

Update 2: Interesting take https://www.linkedin.com/pulse/should-we-all-embrace-systolic-arrays-chien-ping-lu

Update 3: NVIDIA just unveiled their V100with 120 trillion operations per second for matrix-matrix multiplicationshttps://devblogs.nvidia.com/parallelforall/inside-volta/?ncid=so-lin-vt-13919 .

Update 4: Google just announced their 2nd generation TPU (https://cloud.google.com/tpu/) with 180 trillion ops per second and 64GB of ultra high bandwidth ram.

https://medium.com/intuitionmachine/googles-ai-processor-is-inspired-by-the-heart-d0f01b72defe

Chapter-4: Deep Learning

4.1   Deep Teaching: The Sexiest Job of the Future

Credit: https://unsplash.com/@stilclassics

Microsoft Research has a recent paper (Machine Teaching: A New Paradigm for Building Machine Learning Systems) that explores the eventual evolution of Machine Learning. The paper makes a clear distinction between Machine Learning and Machine Teaching. The authors explain that Machine Learning is what is practiced in research organizations and Machine Teaching is what will eventually practiced by engineering organizations. The teaching perspective is not only different from the learning perspective, but there are obvious advantages in that concept disentanglement is known a priori:

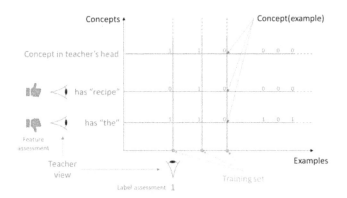

Source: Machine Teaching: A New Paradigm
for Building Machine Learning Systems

The paper concludes with three key developments that will be required by Machine Teaching to make progress:

To truly meet this demand, we need to advance the discipline of machine teaching. This shift is identical to the shift in the programming field in the 1980s and 1990s. This parallel yields a wealth of benefits. This paper takes inspiration from three lessons from the history of programming.

The first one is problem decomposition and modularity, which has allowed programming to scale with complexity.

The second lesson is the standardization of programming languages: write once, run everywhere.

The final lesson is the process discipline, which includes separation of concerns, and the building of standard tools and libraries.

If you have been actively following this blog, it should be apparent by now that it has a distinctly software engineering spin towards the application of Deep Learning technology. We are inundated on a daily basis with plenty of astonishing discoveries in Deep Learning. To avoid being overwhelmed, we are specifically seeking the kinds of discoveries that can lead to accelerated development of Deep Learning solutions. This accelerated development, as also alluded to the paper above, will likely mirror the history of Software Engineering.

In any new science or technology, as humans we attempt to frame new concepts into a framework that is more familiar. Deep Learning is one of those newer sciences that many experts are having trouble getting a good grasp of. This is due to our lack of understanding of not only how it works but also the limits of the technology. Our collective theoretical understanding of the field is at its infancy. Most progress has been spearheaded by experimentation and not theory.

Software Engineering (SE) practices have been developed over the past several decades with the primary objective to control complexity. SE is driven by the goal of 'keeping reasoning under control'. That is, the practice of SE focuses on information boundaries, separation of concerns, modularity and composition to build systems that we can evolve in the context of increasing complexity. Software engineering understands how different components of a system evolve over time at different rates. The principle of loose coupling is what enables this, which I have written about earlier in the context of Deep Learning.

Peter Norvig of Google has a short video on the difference between conventional software engineering and this new paradigm of Deep Learning development:

Artificial intelligence in the software engineering workflow

Monolithic Deep Learning networks that are trained end-to-end as we typically find today are intrinsically immensely complex such that we are incapable of interpret its inference or behavior. There are recent researches that have shown that an incremental training approach is viable. Networks have been demonstrated to work well by training with smaller units and then subsequently combining them to perform more complex behavior.   Google's <u>Deep   Mind</u> and   Microsoft's <u>Maluuba</u> have   made significant progress this year in the above research.

To enable Software Engineering practices in the realm of Deep Learning requires mechanism that supports <u>Modularity</u>. This is still a topic of research and there are many recent advances in this area. Research that focuses on Domain Adaptation, Transfer Learning, Meta-learning, Multi-objective systems and Curriculum learning are the key areas.

Francois Collet, developer of Keras, wrote a recent piece on the "<u>Future of Deep Learning</u>" where he makes some speculative predictions on the future. He writes:

At a high-level, the main directions in which I see promise are:

Models, closer to general-purpose computer programs, are built on top of far richer primitives than our current differentiable layers.

Models that require less involvement from human engineers—it shouldn't be your job to tune knobs endlessly.

Greater, systematic reuse of previously learned features and architectures; meta-learning systems based on reusable and modular program subroutines.

All of this reflects the current pain points of Deep Learning development being at an extremely experimental and the desire for higher abstractions that lead to increased productivity.

Although Collet starts his presentation from the perspective of a programmer, he concludes with the idea of 'growing' a system. Deep Learning systems will most likely not be programmed in the manner that we do today. Rather, it will be more like working with a biological system where we purposely condition the system to achieve our objectives.

The Japanese have an art form called Bonsai where miniature trees are grown. Bonsai doesn't use genetically dwarfed trees; rather it uses cultivation techniques like pruning and grafting to create trees the mimic adult trees in the small. Wired has an article "Soon We Won't Program Computers. We'll Train Them Like Dogs" that alludes to the change in paradigm from that of coding into that of teaching.

So rather than having a library of modular programs that we compose together, we rather have a library of teaching programs that we compose together to train a new system.

The second lesson from the history of programming that Microsoft Researchers allude to is the need for a universal machine that permits the easy porting of Deep Learning models to different servers or devices. I have written previously about the current developments in Deep Learning Virtual Machines. The most active projects in this space is Google's Tensorflow's XLA project and Intel Nervana's NNVM project. In the next few years, we will see the introduction of specialized Deep Learning hardware from many companies (see: Graph Core, Wave Computing, Groq, Fujistu DLU, and Microsoft HPU etc.). This new hardware can be exploited only if adequate high level frameworks are available. Many hardware vendors will likely be hit by the brutal reality that they need to spend a significant level of investment in porting existing Deep Learning frameworks to support their hardware. Targeting a universal virtual machine is the easiest route to this; unfortunately the present reality is that this approach is very far from being ready.

The final lesson from the Microsoft Research paper is the need for process methodology. Most of what has been explored to this date focuses on training of Deep Learning systems (see: "Best Practices for Training Deep Learning Networks"). There is very little on the process method of 'Teaching'. This is of course understandable because our "teaching methods" are still being discovered in Deep Learning laboratories and I predict that it will require at least a year for these tools to achieve a level of maturity required by engineering teams.

Back in 2012, Data Science was labeled as the sexiest job of the 21st century. That prediction was of course before the emergence of Deep Learning into the scene. The sexiest job of the 21st century is likely to be teaching, however not teaching humans, but teaching automation to perform jobs that need to be done. With this, permit me the luxury to coin a new term "Deep Teaching."

https://medium.com/intuitionmachine/why-teaching-will-be-the-sexiest-job-of-the-future-a-i-economy-b8e1c2ee413e

4.2   The Emerging Information Geometric Approach to Deep Learning

Classical Statistics addresses systems involving large numbers, however Statistics breaks down in a domain of high dimensional inputs and models with a high number of parameters. In this domain, new theories and methods are being developed using new insights discovered though the use of massive computational systems. The field of Deep Learning is spearheading these discoveries; however there is a pressing need to have an overarching framework. Such a framework is at the core of our development efforts at Alluviate.

The study of Deep Learning at its foundations is based on Probability Theory and Information Theory. For a probabilistic treatment, the book "The Elements of Statistical Learning" is suggested. From a Information Theoretic viewpoint, David MacKay's book and his video lectures are a great place to start (see: Information Theory, Inference, and Learning Algorithms). Joshua Bengio's upcoming book on Deep Learning also has a dedicated a chapter to cover two fields.

The Count Bayesie blog has a very intuitive tutorial that is worth a quick read. It introduces probability theory and provides a generalization of the equation for expectation :

$$E[X] = \int_{\Omega} X(\omega)P(d\omega) $$

Where the author employs the Lebesque Integral that defines probability in a space and that could otherwise be non-Euclidean. This is a hint to the realization that probability may not need to define a non-Euclidean space. If Non-Euclidean then perhaps there may be other Non-Euclidean metrics that could be employed in the study of Deep Learning?

The dynamics of a Neural Network is usually framed in the context of optimizing a convex or non-convex non linear problem. This involves the minimization/maximization of an objective function. The formulation of the objective function is a bit arbitrary but it is typically the squared error between the actual and estimated values:

$$ \sum_x [\hat{q}(x) — q(x)]^2 $$

The solution to the optimization problem is typically a simple gradient descent approach. What is surprising here is that Deep Learning systems are highly successful despite such a simple approach. One would have thought that gradient descent would be all too often stuck often many local minima one would expect in a non-convex space. However, the intuition of low dimensions does not convey to higher dimensions, where local minima are actually saddle points and a simple gradient descent can escape given enough patience!

However, without an overarching theory or framework, a lot of the techniques employed in Deep Learning (i.e. SGD, Dropout, Normalization, hyper-parameter search etc) all seem to be arbitrary techniques (see: http://arxiv.org/abs/1206.5533).

At Alluviate we build of Information Theoretic approach with the primary notion of employing metrics that distinguish between an estimated distribution and an actual distribution. We use this knowledge to drive more efficient training.

In Information Theory there is the Kullback-Leibler Divergence $D_{KL} (p\|q) = \sum^x p(x) \log \left(\frac{p(x)}{q(x)} \right)$ which is a measure of the difference between two probability distributions. (Note: Shannon's Entropy is a special case of the KL divergence where q is constant). If one takes a distribution and its infinitesimal difference, one arrives as the following equation:

$$ D_{KL}(p_{\theta}\|q_{\theta + \delta\theta}) = g_{ij}\Delta\theta^{i}\Delta\theta^{j} + O\delta\theta^3 $$

Where g_{ij} is the Fisher Information Matrix (FIM):

$$ g_{ij} = -\sum_x P_{\theta}(x) \frac{\partial}{\partial\theta i}\frac{\partial}{\partial\theta^j} \log P_{\theta}(x) $$

The Cramér–Rao lower bound is an estimate of the lower bound of the variance of an estimator. It is related to the FIM $I(\theta)$ in scalar form: $$ Var(\hat{\theta}) >= \frac {1}{I(\theta)} $$

So the above equation says that the FIM has an effect on minimizing the variance between estimated and actual values.

There exists a formulation by Sun-Ichi Amari in a field called Information Geometry that casts the FIM as a metric. Amari shows in his paper "Natural Gradient works Efficiently in Learning", and speculates that natural gradient may more effectively navigate out of plateaus than conventional stochastic gradient descent. The FIM Information Geometry shares some similarity with Einstein's General Theory of Relativity in that the dynamics of a system follows a non-Euclidean space. So rather than observing the curvature of light as a consequence of gravity, one would find a curvature of information in the presence of knowledge.

Although the Information Geometry theory is extremely elegant, the general difficulty with the FIM is that is is expensive to calculate. However recent developments (all in 2015) have shown various approaches to calculating an approximation that leads to very encouraging results.

Parallel training of DNNs with Natural Gradient and Parameter Averaging from the folks developing the Speech Recognizer Kaldi have developed a stochastic gradient technique that employs an approximation of the FIM. Their technique not only improves over standard SGD, but allows for parallelization.

Youshua Bengio and his team at the University of Montreal have a paper Topmoumoute online natural gradient algorithm TONGA have developed a low-rank approximation of FIM with an implementation that beats stochastic gradient in speed and generalization.

Finally Google's Deep Mind team have published a paper "Natural Neural Networks". In this paper they describe a technique that re-parameterizes the neural network layers so that the FIM is effectively the identity matrix. It is a novel technique that has similarities to the Batch Normalization that was previously proposed.

We still are in an early stage for a theory of Deep Learning using Information Geometry, however recent developments seem show the promise of employing a more abstract theoretical approach. Abstract mathematics like Information Geometry should not be dismissed as impractical to implement but rather used as a guide towards building better algorithms and analytic techniques. As in High Energy physics research, there is undeniable value in the interplay between the theoretical and the experimental physicists.

https://medium.com/intuitionmachine/the-emerging-information-geometric-approach-to-deep-learning-a39235716a95

4.3   The Deep Learning Roadmap

It just occurred to me, that after a couple of years tracking Deep Learning developments, that nobody has even bothered to create a map of what's going on! So, I quickly decided to come up with a Deep Learning roadmap. A word of warning, this is just a partial map and doesn't cover the latest developments. Many of the ideas I write on this blog isn't even covered by this map. Anyway, here's a start of this and hope people start coming out of their labs to further expand on it.

The "Unsupervised Learning" part is from a talk by Russ Salakhutdinov and the "Reinforcement Learning" part is from a talk by Pieter Abbeel.

There are a ton of other ideas that are coming out of the edges as well as the center of this diagram. Also, I did not show the connections between the 3 center concepts. For example, you can use CNNs for Value Iteration and GAN and VAEs use DL networks. It's a wild world in the Deep Learning space and you just never know how all of this gets re-arranged.

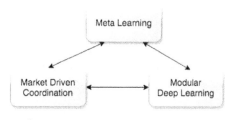

I've got a higher-level map that starts off with this:

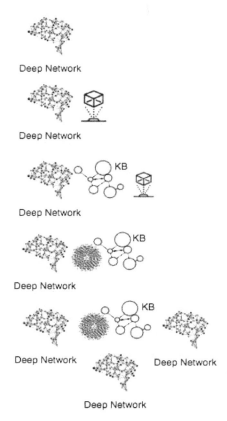

That possibly can stitch everything together in one "grand unified theory". This is how I think it will all play out:

Unsupervised learning is the 'dark matter' where we need a lot more clarity. It's my conjecture that meta-learning (with context) is the approach to this. There is some evidence that is developing, but I cannot know for sure. Modular Deep Learning is already in the cards. There is sufficient evidence that this works well. Market Driven Coordination is still early stages, but I believe that the only real way forward is to have diverse architectures working on the same problem and "markets" are a known decentralized way to coordinate actions.

There's still a lot to be done though and we just in the early stages of Deep Learning evolution:

See: https://medium.com/intuitionmachine/five-levels-of-capability-of-deep-learning-ai-4ac1d4a9f2be

One additional key issue outside of unsupervised learning is the need to bridge the semantic gap between connectionist and symbolic architectures. If you think there's a demand for more clarity in Deep Learning, then support this kind of effort by buying the "Deep Learning Playbook".

https://medium.com/intuitionmachine/the-deep-learning-roadmap-f0b4cac7009a

4.4   Next AI Milestone: Bridging the Semantic Gap

John Launchbury of DARPA has an excellent video that I recommend everyone watch (viewing just the slides will give one a wrong impression of the content). The video distills the current state of AI into 3 waves.

Handcrafted Knowledge—where programmers craft sets of rules to represent knowledge in well-defined domains

Statistical Learning—where programmers create statistical models for specific problem domains and train them on big data.

Contextual Adaptation—where systems construct contextual explanatory models for classes of real world phenomena.

It's a bit of a simplified presentation because it lumps all of machine learning, Bayesian methods and Deep Learning into a single category. There are many more approaches to AI that don't fit within DARPA's 3 waves.

Pedro Domingos author of the "The Master Algorithm". He talks about the 5 Tribes of AI: **Connectionists, Symbolists, Evolutionaries, Bayesians and Analogizers** (I discuss something like 17 tribes of AI).

But let's give DARPA the luxury of simplifying their presentation of the current state of the field.

They do cover some of the known problems of Deep Learning such as adversarial features. Unfortunately, from this point is where the press took off with their presentation and ran with it. Creating titles like "Understanding the Limits of Deep Learning" (Venture Beat).

The key slide though out of the presentation is this:

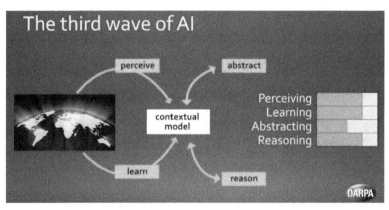

DARPA's third wave model takes a lot of inspiration from some of their previously announced research initiatives such as Explanatory interfaces and Meta-Learning. I write about these two in previous articles (see: "The Only Way to Make Deep Learning Interpretable is to have it Explain Itself" and "The Meta Model and Meta Meta Model of Deep Learning" DARPA's presentation nails it, by highlighting what's going on in current state-of-the-art research. If anyone is seeking out a short explanation of what's going on in the field, then this is the video to watch.

The main problem that we face today is bridging the semantic gap between what I would call Artificial Intuition and rational (symbolic) machines. Deep Learning systems have flaws analogous to our own intuitions having flaws. When you have cognitive processes that have limits on memory and time in the context information overload and lack of meaning, then you are bound to have flaws. These flaws are however caught by logical systems. That's why bridging the gap can have some profound effects.

One reason that the semantic gap wasn't address as vigorously before was that Connectionist systems (i.e. Artificial Neural Networks) did not historically work well. With the advent of Deep Learning, there's a new emphasis in finding a solution that melds Symbolic and Connectionist systems. That's where a lot of research is chipping away at the problem. The excitement here though is that it appears that the researchers are making outstanding progress!

Just to recap, here's the roadmap that I have (explained here):

1. **Classification Only (C)**
2. **Classification with Memory (CM)**
3. **Classification with Knowledge (CK) ←This is what DARPA is talking about.**
4. **Classification with Imperfect Knowledge (CIK)**
5. **Collaborative Classification with Imperfect Knowledge (CCIK)**

One disclaimer regarding this roadmap - It's a Deep Learning roadmap and does not cover developments in other AI fields. One point however that I want to make here is that, achieving the 3rd wave is likely to be an evolution of how we do Deep Learning.

I suspect the solution to this problem will have something to do with "Late Binding". It is very impressive that DARPA actually chose a very precise phrase to describe this (i.e. Contextual Adaptation). Which does imply adapting behavior depending on context?

A question that is very important to ask is "how far away are we from bridging the semantic gap?" Given the brisk pace of DL development; understand here for a moment that some of the techniques mentioned in the video (i.e. few-shot learning and generative models) are being refined in the last year or so. I would not be surprised that within 2–3 years that the gap will be bridged! That's just how crazy the developments in Deep Learning are.

https://medium.com/intuitionmachine/the-first-rule-of-agi-is-bc8725d21530

4.5 Biologically Inspired Software Architecture for Deep Learning

Credit: *https://unsplash.com/search/butterfly?photo=7q9L5nxbz78*

With the emergence of Deep Learning as the dominant paradigm for Artificial Intelligence based systems, one open question that seems to be neglected is "What guidelines do we have in architecting software that uses Deep Learning?" If all the innovative companies like Google are on a exponential adoption curve to incorporate Deep Learning in everything they do, then what perhaps is the software architecture that holds this all together?

The folks at Google wrote a paper (a long time ago, meaning 2014); "Machine Learning: The High-Interest Credit Card of Technical Debt" that enumerates many of the difficulties that we need to consider when building software that consists of machine learning or deep learning sub-components. Contrary to popular perception those Deep Learning systems can be "self-driving". There is a massive ongoing maintenance cost when machine learning is used. In the Google paper, the authors enumerate many risk factors, design patterns, and anti-patterns to needs to be taken into consideration in an architecture. These include design patterns such as : boundary erosion, entanglement, hidden feedback loops, undeclared consumers, data dependencies and changes in the external world.

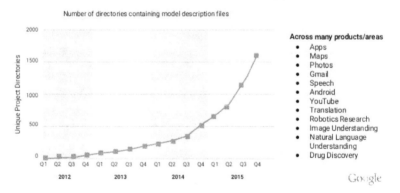

The Google "Technical Debt" article should be required reading for anyone involved in operationalizing Deep Learning systems. For easy reference and to aid in discussion, lets detail the important risk factors and design patterns in that paper.

Software architect involves patterns to ensure software code is modular and thus have minimal dependencies with each other. By contrast, Deep Learning systems (applies equally to machine learning), code is created from training data. This is the key difference between classical software and Deep Learning systems.

1. Complex Models Erode Boundaries

There are few mechanisms to separate data dependencies in data.

Entanglement—Deep learning models and the data used to train them is naturally entangled.

Hidden Feedback Loops—Systems that learn from the world are in a feedback loop with its actions and its observations.

Undeclared Consumers—Predictions made by a machine may be used by other systems.

2. Data Dependencies Dominate over Code Dependencies

Data dependencies have greater importance unfortunately it is far less common to find tools to discover data dependencies.

Unstable Data Dependencies—Data behavior inevitably changes over time. A mitigation strategy is to use versioned copies of data.

Underutilized Data Dependencies—Regularly evaluate the effect of removing features from a model whenever possible.

Static Analysis of Data Dependencies—Annotate data and features to allow automatic dependency checking.

Correction Cascades—Using models in a domain different from its original domain. Annotate the model to allow inspection of its original use.

3. System Level Spaghetti

Glue Code—Only 5% of the code is machine learning, 95% of code is glue code and thus should be treated with conventional software architecture approaches.

Pipeline Jungles—Invest engineering resources so that maintaining pipelines (code for data collection and feature extraction) can be made sustainable.

Dead Experimental Codepaths—A famous example of this was Knight Capital's system losing $465 million in 45 minutes dues to an obsolete experimental codepath.

Configuration Debt—Machine learning algorithms can be elegant, but a lot of real world messiness can be found in their configuration.

4. Changes in the External World

The world is rarely stable and therefore these system need to be adaptive.

Fixed Threshold in Dynamic Systems—This applies to classical machine prediction models where arbitrary thresholds are defined rather than learned from the data.

When Correlations no longer Correlate—Models that assume correlation may break when the correlations no longer hold.

Monitoring and Testing—Live monitoring of behavior is critical.

As you can see, the problems are vast and the solutions are quite limited. However, as we explore newer architectures (i.e. "Modular Deep Learning" and "Meta-Learning") we can begin to seek out newer solutions. A good inspiration that I stumbled upon can be found in this insightful blog (Scientific American) that describes "Building a Resilient Business Inspired by Biology". The author describes 6 features found in biology and applied it to business processes. I will take the same approach and see how it may apply to Deep Learning systems.

1. Redundancy. Duplication of components may be inefficient however it provides the mechanism to handle the unexpected. In addition, functional redundancy offers a way to repurpose components to reduce costs.

2. Heterogeneity. Different predictive machines make it possible to react to a more diverse range of change as well as avoid correlated behavior that can lead to total system failure. Diversity is required for evolutionary learning and adaptation.

3. Modularity. Decoupling of components act like firewalls between components and help mitigate against total collapse. Individual component damage can be tolerated while the integrity of other components is preserved. In general, a distributed loosely coupled system has higher survivability that a centralized tightly coupled system.

4. Adaptation. A systems needs to be sufficiently flexible and agile to adjust to changes in the environment. Adaptive approaches that involve simulation, selection, and amplification of successful strategies are important. Self-learning is requirement to achieve adaptability.

5. Prudence. The environment is unpredictable and thus the management of uncertainty should be built in. Thus continuous simulations that stress test the system as well as the development of alternative scenarios and contingent plans are necessary.

6. Embeddedness. Systems do not exist in isolation and are embedded in a much larger ecosystem. Therefore these systems require behavior that works in a way that is of mutual benefit to the ecosystem as a whole.

These 6 features are excellent guidelines on how to build not only adaptable systems, but one's that are ultimately sustainable. It is important to note the importance of "loose coupling" in biology.

A recent paper from the folks at Berkeley is exploring the requirements for building these new kinds of systems (see: "Real-Time Machine Learning: The Missing Pieces"). The project is Ray from Berkeley's RISELab, although they don't mention it in their paper. They make the argument that systems are increasingly deployed in environments of "tightly-integrated components of feedback loops involving dynamic, real-time decision making." and thus require "a new distributed execution framework". The difference between the classical machine learning system and their new framework is depicted by this graphic:

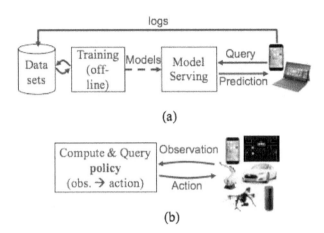

(a)

(b)

The authors spell out 7 requirements that this new kind of architecture needs to support:

1. Low Latency—millisecond ends to end latency.

2. High Throughput—millions of tasks per second.

3. Dynamic Task Creation—the number of tasks required needs to be dynamically allocated.

4. Heterogeneous Tasks—the resources and execution time required by tasks vary wildly.

5. Arbitrary Dataflow Dependencies

6. Transparent Fault Tolerance

7. Debug ability and Profiling

What was just described was the state-of-the-art thinking in design. Clearly, we have a very long way to go in terms of architectures that are adaptive to the environment; although the prescription does address other aspects such as heterogeneity, redundancy and modularity.

Present day software architectures are clearly not up to the task in accommodating systems that employ Deep Learning components. A new kind of architecture is clearly demanded. It is very early, but this is a very important area and it is essential that our Deep Learning systems have manageability built in. After all, every complex technology requires manageability to be economically sustainable.

Update:

It has come to my attention that DARPA has a new program "Toward Machines that Improve with Experience" that "seeks to develop the foundations for systems that might someday learn in much the way biological organisms do":

> *Concepts from nature could include but are not limited to:*
>
> *(1) Mechanisms for evolving networks;*
> *(2) Memory stability in adaptive networks;*
> *(3) Goal-driven behavior mechanisms;*
> *(4) Learning rules and plasticity mechanisms;*
> *(5) Modulation of local processing based on global context, neuro-modulators and hormones;*
> *(6) Minimizing resources use in processing and learning;*

https://medium.com/intuitionmachine/biologically-inspired-software-architecture-for-deep-learning-e64db295bb2f

4.6 One Deep Learning Virtual Machine to Rule Them All

The current state of Deep Learning frameworks is similar to the fragmented state like LLVM before the creation of common code generation backend. In the chaotic good old days, every programming language had to re-invent its way of generating machine code. With the development of LLVM, many languages now share the same backend code. Many programming languages use LLVM as their backend. Several well known examples of this are Ada, C#, Common Lisp, Delphi, Fortran, Haskell, Java bytecode, Julia, Lua, Objective-C, Python, R, Ruby, Rust, and Swift. The frontend code only needs to parse and translate source code to an intermediate representation (IR).

Credit: https://unsplash.com/search/machinery?photo=PmrwuizKUq0

Deep Learning frameworks will eventually need their own "IR". The IR for Deep Learning is of course the computational graph. Deep learning frameworks like Caffe and Tensorflow have their own internal computational graphs. These frameworks are all merely convenient fronts to the internal graph. These graphs specify the execution order of mathematical operations, analogous to what a dataflow graph does. The graph specifies the orchestration of collections of CPUs and GPUs. This execution is highly parallel. Parallelism is the one reason why GPUs are ideal for this kind of computation. There are however plenty of untapped opportunities to improve the orchestration between the CPU and GPU.

New research is exploring ways to optimize the computational graph in way that go beyond just single device optimization and towards more global multi-device optimization. An example of this is the research project XLA (Accelerated Linear Algebra) from Google. XLA supports both Just in Time (JIT) or Ahead of Time (AOT) compilation. It is a high level optimizer that performs its work in optimizing the interplay of GPUs and CPUs. The optimizations that are planned include the fusing of pipelined operations, aggressive constant propagation, reduction of storage buffers and fusing of low-level operators.

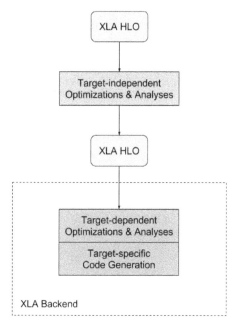

Google's XLA

Not to be outdone, two other open source projects that are also exploring computational graph optimization. NNVM from MXNet (Supported by Amazon) is another computation graph optimization framework that similar to XLA focuses on the need for an intermediate representation. The goal of the NNVM optimizer is to reduce memory and device allocation while preserving the original computational semantics.

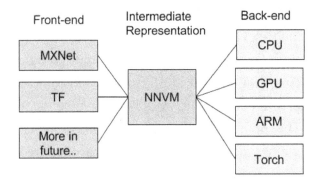

MxNet's   NNVM: http://tqchen.github.io/2016/10/01/build-your-own-tensorflow-with-nnvm-and-torch.html

NGraph from Intel is also exploring optimizations that include even more extensive optimizations: kernel fusion, buffer allocation, training optimizations, inference optimizations, data layout and distributed training. There are certainly plenty of ideas of how to improve the performance and the space is heating up with a lot of activity.

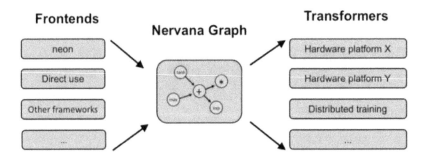

Intel's NGraph

In addition to these approaches that originate from the DL community, other approaches to optimizing machine learning algorithms have been developed by other companies. HP has developed the Cognitive Computing Toolkit (CCT) and IBM has developed System ML.

HP's CCT simplifies the development of HPC routines by compiling high-level abstractions down to optimized GPU kernels. Typically, the development of GPU kernels is a laborious process. However, if the algorithms can be expressed using combinations of high-level operators then it should be possible to generate the GPU kernel. This is what CCT is designed to do.

An offshoot of CCT is the <u>Operator Vectorization Library</u> (OVL). OVL is a python library that does the same a CCT but for TensorFlow framework. Custom TensorFlow operators are written in C++. OVL enables TensorFlow operators to be written in Python without sacrificing performance. This improves productivity and avoids the cumbersome process of implementing, building, and linking custom C++ and CUDA code.

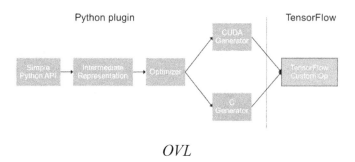

OVL

IBM' a System ML is a high-level declarative language with an R-like and Python-like syntax. Developers express machine learning algorithms using this declarative language. System ML takes care of generating the execution plan. The system supports optimizations on single nodes as well as distributed computations on platforms like Hadoop and Spark. Rule-based and cost-based optimization techniques are used to optimize the execution plan. System ML comes with an existing suite of algorithms that include Descriptive Statistics, Classification, Clustering, Regression, Matrix Factorization, and Survival Analysis.

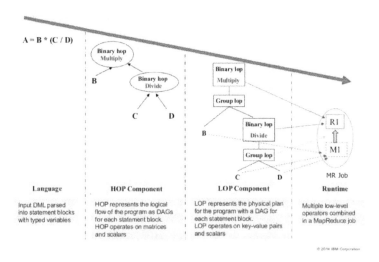

SystemML

Source: https://www.slideshare.net/YunyaoLi/20140829declarative-thinkingfinal

These five open source projects (XLA, NNVM, NGraph, CCT and System ML) all perform optimizations in a global manner across either the computational graph or an alternative declarative specification. The current DL frameworks however have code generation and execution all intertwined with their code base, making opportunities to develop optimization solutions less portable. Ideally, one would like to see a common standard, a DL virtual machine instruction set, where the community can collective contribute optimization routines. Right now however is a competitive race to become the ruling standard. That is, one computational graph to rule them all. A common standard deep learning virtual machine is a futuristic dream. One obvious idea is to leverage deep learning itself to optimize its own computations. That is, deep learning to "Learn to Optimize" itself. There have been current Meta-level research that are exploring this self-improvement approach, however, not at the level of fine-grained memory access and assembly level code.

https://medium.com/intuitionmachine/on-deep-learning-virtual-machines-153168fa144b

Info graphic: Best Practices for Training Deep Learning Networks

Background Information:

https://medium.com/intuitionmachine/10-lessons-learned-from-building-deep-learning-systems-d611ab16ef66#.gbhf6hlqd and

https://medium.com/intuitionmachine/infographic-best-practices-in-training-deep-learning-networks-b8a3df1db53

4.7 Deep Learning is Transformative, Data Science is Just Informative

Carlos E. Perez Follow - Deep Learning Patterns, Methodology and Strategy @ IntuitionMachine.com Jan 7

One of the biggest misconceptions in the market place is that a Data Science or Data Analytics practice is the same thing as a Deep Learning practice. Let me explain to you why it indeed is radically different.

The difference is most easily explained by the difference in business intelligence and business process reengineering. The latter analyzes business processes to pinpoint areas of restructuring and improvement. The former analyzes business data with the intent of informing stakeholders and executives. The former is informational and the latter is transformative.

Deep Learning as Mark Cuban has quipped is "Automating Automation"(See: Mark Cuban points to Deep Learning as the next 'grand slam' in technology start at 6:30 mark):

Credit: http://www.cnbc.com/2016/10/04/mark-cuban-points-to-machine-learning-as-the-next-grand-slam-in-technology.html

Mark Cuban points to deep learning as the next 'grand slam' in technology Pokémon Go may have sparked the world's craving for augmented reality, but billionaire Mark Cuban says the industry has a long way to go. He is banking on deep learning…www.cnbc.com

Think about for example previous technologies like the web and mobile. Now think of how many changes to our business processes were introduced by these two innovations. With the web, customer service became self-serviced. With mobile, customer service could become always a few swipes away. Deep Learning is disruptive technology at equal or even greater level. That's because it is not just a customer facing technology, but rather one that affects backend activities is so many ways.

The confusion that most organizations have is that data is critical in both practices and therefore make the incorrect conclusion that they are the same activity. This is a fatal mistake because it blinds decision makers from seeing the disruptive potential of Deep Learning. Deep Learning is about leveraging narrow intelligence to augment complex workflow tasks.

It is an ever present, ambient technology that exists to help run daily businesses activities. Data science and analytics are important, but aren't able to effectively deliver insight into beneficial action. The other disconnect is that the data logistics practice for Deep Learning differs from that of Data Science. We'll discuss this is a subsequent article.

Deep Learning is an entirely new field that has its genesis from Machine Learning. This is also the root of confusion since it is likely the only people exposed to machine learning in an organization are data scientists. This however should not imply that a group that saw it first is the same group that should be responsible for its deployment. The skill sets are entirely different. The skills required for business process re-engineering are entirely different from that of business intelligence. So why would one assume that data scientists would have the right skill set to work on a deep learning deployment?

The learning from data aspect also gets many confused. Deep Learning learns from data just as Machine Learning learns from data. How it learns of course is entirely different, but for argument's sake, let's not bothers with the subtle scientific differences. The key difference is Machine Learning only digests data, while Deep Learning can generate and enhance data. It is not only predictive but also generative. One example of this is the business context is that it is able to generate designs:

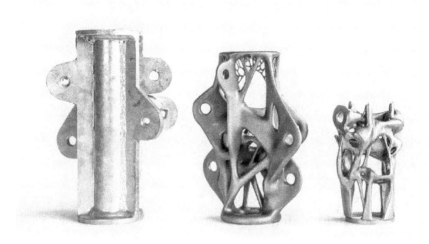

See: https://medium.com/intuitionmachine/the-alien-look-of-deep-learning-generative-design-5c5f871f7d10#.6fk9keqax for discussion.

Designs that a knowledge worker can leverage to iteratively explore and select are the best options. The same idea can be generalized to many other kinds of activities that a business is involved in. Think for example the notion of generating plans (i.e. sets of activities). A planner can ask a Deep Learning system to provide a recommendation of various plans. A planner can then take those recommendations and iteratively perform improvements. This kind of capability can be very valuable in fast moving reactive environments.

There certainly is a lot more to talk about Deep Learning, so I recommend that you continue the conversation by reaching out to us at Intuition Machine and let us know if you are interested in receiving the "Deep Learning Playbook for Enterprises"

https://medium.com/intuitionmachine/data-science-is-informative-but-deep-learning-is-transformative-316e61871dd8

4.8 The Five Capability Levels of Deep Learning Intelligence

Credit: https://unsplash.com/search/stairs?photo=YfCVCPMNd38

Arend-Hintze has a good short article on "Understanding the four types of AI, from reactive robots to self-aware beings" where he outlines the following types:

Reactive Machine—It's the most basic type that is unable to form memories and use past experiences to inform decisions. They can't function outside the specific tasks that they were designed for.

Limited Memory—Are able to look into the past to inform current decisions. The memory however is transient and isn't used for future experiences.

Theory of Mind—These systems are able to form representations of the world as well as other agents that it interacts with.

Self-Awareness- Mostly speculative description here.

I like his classification much better than the "Narrow AI" and "General AI" dichotomy. This classification makes an attempt to break down Narrow AI into 3 categories. This gives us more concepts to differentiate different AI implementations. My reservation though of the definition is that they appear to come from a GOFAI mindset. Furthermore, the leap from limited memory able to employ the past to theory of mind seems to be an extremely vast leap.

I however would like to take this opportunity to come up with my own classification, more targeted towards the field of Deep Learning. I hope my classification is a bit more concrete and helpful for practitioners. This classification gives us a sense of where we currently are and where we might be heading.

We are inundated with all the time with AI hype that we fail to good conceptual framework for making a precise assessment of the current situation. This may simply be due to the fact that many writers have trouble keeping up with the latest development in Deep Learning research. There's too much to read to keep up and the latest discoveries continue to change our current understanding. See "Rethinking Generalization" as one of those surprising discoveries.

Five Capability Levels of Deep Learning

1. Classification Only (C)

This level includes the fully connected neural network (FCN) and the convolution network (CNN) and various combinations of them. These systems take a high dimensional vector as input and arrive at a single result, typically a classification of the input vector. You can consider these systems as being stateless functions, meaning that their behavior is only a function of the current input. Generative models are one of those hotly researched areas and these also belong to this category. In short, these systems are quite capable by themselves.

2. Classification with Memory (CM)

This level includes memory elements incorporated with the C level networks. LSTMs are example of these with the memory units are embedded inside the LSTM node. Other variants of these are the Neural

Turing Machine (NMT) and the Differentiable Neural Computer (DNC) from Deep Mind. These systems maintain state as they compute their behavior.

3. Classification with Knowledge (CK)

This level is somewhat similar to the CM level, however rather than raw memory, the information that the C level network is able to access is a symbolic knowledge base. There are actually three kinds of symbolic integration that I have found, a transfer learning approach, a top-down approach, a bottom up approach. The first approach uses a symbolic system that acts as regularize. The second approach has the symbolic elements at the top of the hierarchy that are composed at the bottom by neural representations. The last approach has it reversed, where a C level network is actually attached to a symbolic knowledge base.

4. Classification with Imperfect Knowledge (CIK)

At this level, we have a system that is built on top of CK, however is able to reason with imperfect information. An example of this kind of system would be AlphaGo and Poker playing systems. AlphaGo however does not employ CK but rather CM level capability. Like AlphaGo, these kinds of systems can train it by running simulation of it against itself.

5. Collaborative Classification with Imperfect Knowledge (CCIK)

This level is very similar to the "theory of mind" where we actually have multiple agent neural networks combining to solve problems. These systems are designed to solve multiple objectives. We actually dose primitive versions of this in adversarial networks, that learn to perform generalization with competing discriminator and generative networks Expand that concept further into game-theoretic driven networks that are able to perform strategically and tactically solving multiple objectives and you have the making of these kind of extremely adaptive systems. We aren't at this level yet and there's still plenty of research to be done in the previous levels.

Different level brings about capabilities that don't exist in the previous level. C level systems for example are only capable of predicting anti-causal relationships. CM level systems are capable of very good translation. CIK level systems are capable of strategic game play.

We can see how this classification somewhat aligns with Hinzte classification, with the exception of course of self-awareness. That's a capability that I really have not explored and don't intend to until the pre-requisite capabilities have been addressed. I've also not addressed zero-shot or one-shot learning or unsupervised learning. This is still one of the fundamental problems, as Yann LeCun has said:

If intelligence was a cake, unsupervised learning would be the cake, supervised learning would be the icing on the cake, and reinforcement learning would be the cherry on the cake. We know how to make the icing and the cherry, but we don't know how to make the cake.

LeCun has also recently started using the phrase "predictive learning" in substitution of "unsupervised learning". This is an interesting change and indicates a subtle change in his perspective as to what he believes is required to implement the "cake". In LeCun's view, the foundation needs to be built before we can make substantial progress in AI. In other words, building off current supervised learning by adding more capabilities like memory, knowledge bases and cooperating agents will be a slog until we are all able to build that "predictive foundational layer". In the most recent NIPS 2016 conference he posted this slide:

One accelerator technology in all of this however is that when the capabilities are used in a feedback loop. We actually have seen instance of this kind of 'meta-learning' or 'learning to optimize' in current research. I cover these developments in another article "Deep Learning can Now Design Itself!" The key take away with meta-methods is that our own research methods become much more powerful when we can train machines to actually discover better solutions that we otherwise could find.

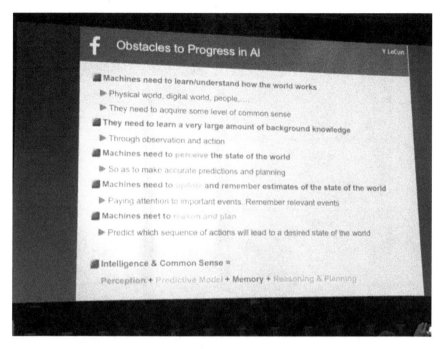

Credit: https://twitter.com/data_beth

This is why, despite formidable problems in Deep Learning research, we can't really be sure how rapid progress may proceed.

To understand better how Deep Learning capabilities fit with your enterprise, visit Intuition Machine or discuss on the FaceBook Group on Deep Learning.

http://csc.ucdavis.edu/~cmg/papers/et1.pdf Computational Mechanics of Input-Output Processes: Structured transformations and the e-transducer

https://medium.com/intuitionmachine/five-levels-of-capability-of-deep-learning-ai-4ac1d4a9f2be

4.9   Why Deep Learning is Radically Different from Machine Learning

There is a lot of confusion these days about Artificial Intelligence (AI), Machine Learning (ML) and Deep Learning (DL). There certainly is a massive uptick of articles about AI being a competitive game changer and that enterprises should begin to seriously explore the opportunities. The distinction between AI, ML and DL are very clear to practitioners in these fields. AI is the all-encompassing umbrella that covers everything from Good Old Fashion AI (GOFAI) all the way to connectionist architectures like Deep Learning. ML is a sub-field of AI that covers anything that has to do with the study of learning algorithms by training with data. There are whole swaths (not swatches) of techniques that have been developed over the years like Linear Regression, K-means, Decision Trees, Random Forest, PCA, SVM and finally Artificial Neural Networks (ANN). Artificial Neural Networks is where the field of Deep Learning had its genesis from.

Some ML practitioners who have had previous exposure to Neural Networks (ANN), after all it was invented in the early 60's, would have the first impression that Deep Learning is nothing more than ANN with multiple layers. Furthermore, the success of DL is more due to the availability of more data and the availability of more powerful computational engines like Graphic Processing Units (GPU). This of course is true; the emergence of DL is essentially due to these two advances; however, the conclusion that DL is just a better algorithm than SVM or Decision Trees is akin to focusing only on the trees and not seeing the forest.

To coin and reesen who said, "Software is eating the world", "Deep Learning is eating ML". Two publications by practitioners of different machine learning fields have summarized it best as to why DL is taking over the world. Chris Manning an expert in NLP writes about the "Deep Learning Tsunami:

Deep Learning waves have lapped at the shores of computational linguistics for several years now, but 2015 seems like the year when the full force of the tsunami hit the major Natural Language Processing (NLP) conferences. However, some pundits are predicting that the final damage will be even worse.

Nicholas Paragios writes about the "Computer Vision Research: the Deep Depression":

It might be simply because deep learning on highly complex, hugely determined in terms of degrees of freedom graphs once endowed with massive amount of annotated data and unthinkable—until very recently—computing power can solve all computer vision problems. If this is the case, well it is simply a matter of time that industry (which seems to be already the case) takes over, research in computer vision becomes a marginal academic objective and the field follows the path of computer graphics (in terms of activity and volume of academic research).

These two articles do highlight how the fields of Deep Learning are fundamentally disruptive to conventional ML practices. Certainly, it should be equally disruptive in the business world. I am however stunned and perplexed that even Gartner fails to recognize the difference between ML and DL. Here is Gartner's August 2016 Hype Cycle and Deep Learning isn't even mentioned on the slide:

Figure 1. Hype Cycle for Emerging Technologies, 2016

Source: Gartner (August 2016)

What a travesty! It's bordering on criminal that they their customers have a myopic notion of ML and are going to be blindsided by Deep Learning.

Anyway, despite being ignored, DL continues to by hyped. The current DL hype tends to be that we have this commoditized machinery that given enough data and enough training time, is able to learn on its own. This is of course either an exaggeration of what the state-of-the-art is capable of or an over simplification of the actual practice of DL. DL has over the past few years given rise to a massive collection of ideas and techniques that were previously either unknown or known to be untenable.

At first this collection of concepts, seems to be fragmented and disparate. However, over time patterns and methodologies begin to emerge and we are frantically attempting to cover this space in "Design Patterns of Deep Learning".

Periodic Table of Deep Learning Patterns

Deep Learning today goes beyond just multi-level perceptions but instead is a collection of techniques and methods that are used to building compos able differentiable architectures. These are extremely capable machine learning systems that we are only right now seeing just the tip of the iceberg. The key take away from this is that, Deep Learning may look like alchemy today, but we eventually will learn to practice it like chemistry. That is, we would have a more solid foundation so as to be able to build our learning machines with greater predictability of its capabilities.

BTW, if you are interested in finding out how Deep Learning can help you in your work, please feel to leave your email at: www.intuitionmachine.com or join the discussion in Face book: https://www.facebook.com/groups/deeplearningpatterns/ or for the more technically inclined join at LinkedIn: https://www.linkedin.com/groups/8584076.

https://medium.com/intuitionmachine/why-deep-learning-is-radically-different-from-machine-learning-945a4a65da4d

Deep Learning Exponential Growth Trends

Some people just don't grow it, no matter how hard you bang the table. But maybe some hockey stick graphs will help.

It all begins with this chart:

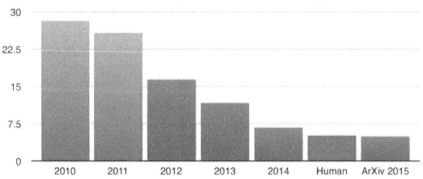

In 2010 image recognition would fail at least on fourth of the time, but by 2015, image recognition surpassed human recognition! What is driving this? Something definitely is brewing.

DEEP LEARNING FOR VISUAL PERCEPTION
Going from strength to strength

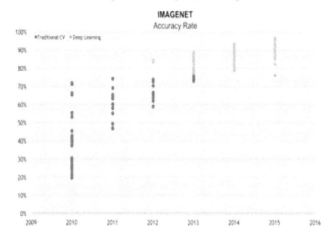

Something called "Deep Learning" began emerging in 2012. So let's check Google search trends that track interest:

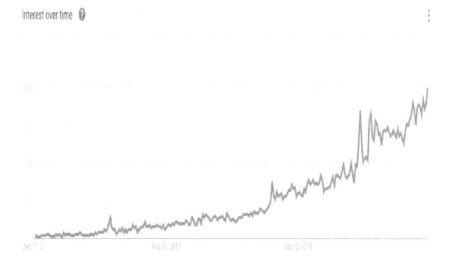

It turns out that the academic community has something really brewing.

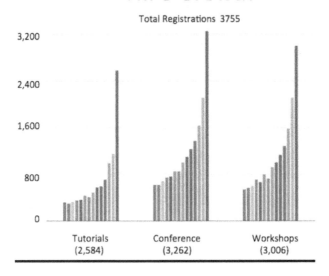

Here is another conference but with some commentary:

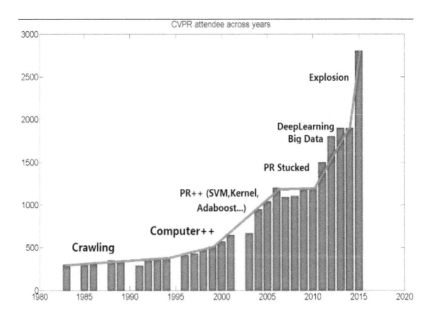

But is this all theory? Let's take a peek inside Google:

Growing Use of Deep Learning at Google

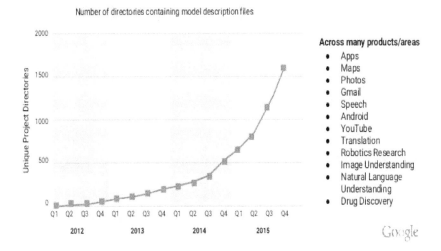

What's the demand for talent like?

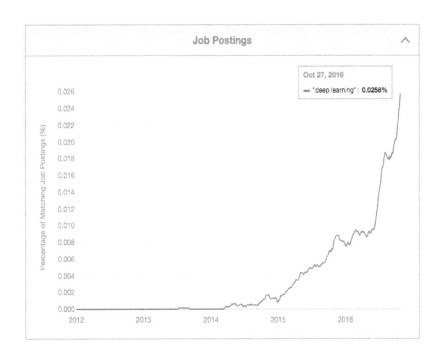

What about what the 1%ers are investing in?

Global Quarterly AI Funding
In millions (USD)

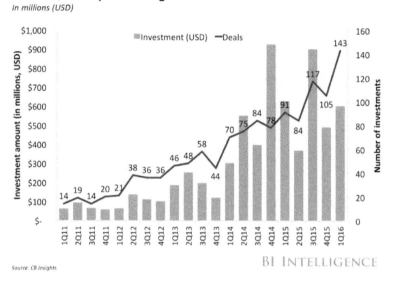

Source: CB Insights

BI INTELLIGENCE

Source: http://www.businessinsider.com/microsoft-bets-on-ai-2016-12

What are the companies acquiring?

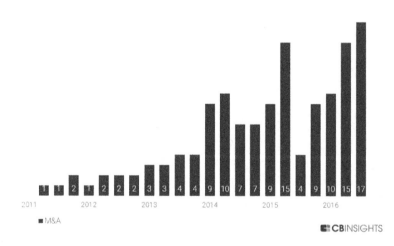

What are the masses investing in?

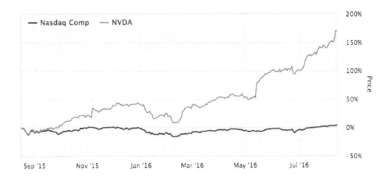

Is Deep Learning the main driver of Artificial Intelligence?

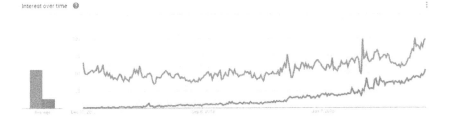

Blue is "Artificial Intelligence" and red is "Deep Learning"

Now for the most important trend:

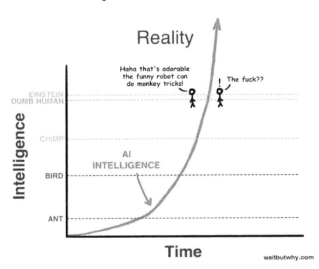

Now, the fact that you are reading this tells me that you've heard of "Deep Learning". It is likely 99.9% of the population have no clue as to what it is. This gives you a head start and I do recommend that you take action on this knowledge advantage.

https://medium.com/intuitionmachine/8-exponential-hockey-stick-charts-for-deep-learning-74bba7a0284c

4.10 10 Deep Learning Trends and Predictions for 2017

Credit: https://unsplash.com/search/road?photo=c0I4ahyGIkA

I used to write predictions for the upcoming year in my previous blog. The last one I recall writing was "Software Development Trends and Predictions for 2011". That's quite a long time ago. Just to recap, out of 10 predictions, I gather that I got 6 accurately (i.e. JavaScript VM, NoSQL, Big Data Analytics, Private Clouds, Inversion of Desktop Services, Scala), however the remaining 4 have not gained enough traction (i.e. Enterprise App Stores, Semantic Indexing, OAuth in the Enterprise, Proactive Agents). Actually, App Stores and OAuth doesn't happen in big enterprises, however, small companies have adopted this SaaS model in full force. I'll chalk the prediction failure to not being able to predict how slow enterprises actually change! Remain two predictions that of Semantic Indexing and Proactive Agents have unfortunately not progressed as I had originally projected. I may have overly estimated the AI technology at that time. Deep Learning had not been invented back then.

My Deep Learning predictions will not be at the same conceptual level as my previous predictions. I'm not going to predict enterprise adoption but I rather am going to focus on research trends and predictions. Without a doubt, Deep Learning will drive AI adoption into the enterprise. For those still living underneath a rock, it is a fact that Deep Learning is the primary driver and the most important approach to AI. However, what is not so obvious is what kind of new capabilities will arise in 2017 that will lead to exponential adoption.

So here come my fearless predictions for 2017.

1. **Hardware will accelerate doubling Moore's law (i.e. 2x in 2017).**

This, of course, is entirely obvious if you track developments at Nvidia and Intel. Nvidia will dominate the space throughout the entire 2017 simply because they have the richest Deep Learning ecosystem. Nobody in their right mind will jump to another platform until there is enough of an ecosystem developed for DL. Intel Xeon Phi solutions are dead on arrival with respect to DL. At best they may catch up in performance with Nvidia by mid-2017 when the Nervana derived chips come to market.

Intel's FPGA solutions may see adoption by cloud providers simply because of economics. Power consumption is the number one variable that needs to be reduced. Intel's Nervana based chip will likely clock in at 30 teraflops by mid-2017. That's my guesstimate, but given that Nvidia is already at 20 teraflops today, I wouldn't bet on Intel having a major impact until 2018. The only big ace that Intel may have is in 3D XPoint technology. This will help improve the entire hardware stack but not necessarily the core accelerator capabilities considering that GPUs use HBM2 that's stacked on top of the chip for performance reasons.

Amazon has announced its FPGA based cloud instance. This is based on Xilinx UltraScale+ technology and is offering 6,800 DSP slices and 64 GB of memory on a single instance. That's impressive capability however, the offering may be I/O bound by not offering the HBM version of UltraScale+. The lower memory bandwidth solution as compared with Nvidia, Intel, and even AMD may give developers pause as to whether to invest in a more complicated development process (i.e. VHDL, Verilog etc).

In late breaking news, AMD has revealed its new AMD Instinct line of Deep Learning accelerators. The specifications of these are extremely competitive versus Nvidia hardware. This offering is scheduled to be available early 2017. This is probably should be enough time for AMDs ROCm software to mature.

2. Convolution Networks (CNN) will Dominate

CNNs will be the prevalent bread-and-butter model for DL systems. RNNs and LSTMs with its recurrent configuration and embedded memory nodes are going to be used less simply because they would not be competitive to a CNN based solution. Just like GOTO disappeared in the world of programming, I expect the same for RNNs/LSTMs. Actually, parallel architectures trump sequential architectures in performance.

Differentiable Memory networks will be more Common. This is just a natural consequence of architecture where memory will be refactored out of the core nodes and just reside as a separate component from the computational components. I don't see the need for forget, input and output gates for LSTM that can be replaced by auxiliary differentiable memory.

We already see conversation about refactoring the LSTM to decouple memory (see Augmented Memory RNN).

3. Designers will rely more on Meta-Learning

When I began my Deep Learning journey, I had thought that optimization algorithms, particularly ones that were second-order would lead to massive improvements. Today, the writing is on the wall, DL can now learn the optimization algorithm for you. It is the end of the line for anybody contemplating a better version of SGD. The better version of SGD is the one that is learned by a machine and is the one that is specific to the problem at hand. Meta-learning is able to adaptively optimize its learning based on its domain. Further related to this is whether alternative algorithms to backpropagation will begin to emerge in practice. There is a real possibility that hand tweaked SGD algorithm may be in its last legs in 2017.

4. Reinforcement Learning will only become more creative

Observations about reality will always remain imperfect. There are plenty of problems where SGD is not applicable. This just makes it essential that any practical deployment of DL systems will require some form of RL. In addition to this, we will see RL used in many places in DL training. Meta-Learning, for example, is greatly enabled by RL. In fact, we've seen RL used to find different kinds of neural network architectures. This is like Hyper-parameter optimization on steroids. If you happen to be in the Gaussian Process business then your lunch has just been eaten.

5. Adversarial and Cooperative Learning will be King

In the old days, we had monolithic DL systems with single analytic objective functions. In the new world, I expect to see systems with two or more networks cooperation or competing to arrive at an optimal solution that likely will not be in analytic form. See "Game Theory reveals the

<u>future of Deep Learning</u>". There will be a lot of research in 2017 in trying to manage <u>non-equilibrium</u> contexts. We already see this now where researchers are trying to find ways to handle the non-equilibrium situation with GANs.

6. Predictive Learning or Unsupervised Learning will not progress much

"<u>Predictive Learning</u>" is the new buzzword that Yann LeCun in pitching in replacement to the more common term "Unsupervised Learning". It is unclear whether this new terminology will gain adoption. The question though of whether Unsupervised or Predictive Learning will make great strides in 2017. My current sense is that it simply will not because there seems to be a massive conceptual disconnect as to how exactly it should could work.

If you read my previous post about "<u>5 Capabilities of Deep Learning Intelligence</u>", you get the feeling that Predictive Learning is some completely unknown capability that needs to be shoehorned into the model that I propose. Predictive Learning is like the cosmologists Dark Matter. We know it is there, but we just don't know how to see it. My hunch is that it has something to do with high entropy or otherwise randomness.

7. Transfer Learning leads to Industrialization

Andrew Ng thinks this is important, I think so too!

8. More Applications will use Deep Learning as a component

We saw this already in 2016 where we see Deep Learning used as a function evaluation component in a much larger search algorithm. AlphaGo employed Deep Learning in its value and policy evaluations. Google's Gmail auto-reply system used DL in combination with beam searching. I expect to see a lot more of these hybrid algorithms rather than new end-to-end trained DL systems. End-to-end Deep Learning is a fascinating area of research, but for now hybrid systems are going to be more effective in application domains.

9. Design Patterns will be increasingly Adopted

Deep Learning is just one of those complex fields that need a conceptual structure. Despite all the advanced mathematics involved, there's a lot of hand waving and fuzzy concepts that can best be captured not by formal rigor but rather with a method that has been proven to be effective in other complex domains like software development. I predict practitioners will finally "get it" with regards to Deep Learning and Design Patterns. This will be further motivated by the fact that Deep Learning architectures are becoming more modular rather than monolithic.

10. Engineering will outpace Theory

The background of researchers and the mathematical tools that they employ are a breeding ground for a kind of bias in their research approach. Deep Learning systems and Unsupervised Learning systems are likely these new kinds of things that we have never encountered before. Therefore, there is no evidence that our traditional analytic tools are going to be any help in unraveling the mystery as to how DL actually works. There are plenty of dynamical systems in physics that have remain perplexed about for decades, I see the same situation with regard to dynamical learning systems.

This situation, however, will not prevent the engineering of even more advanced applications despite our lack of understanding of the fundamentals. Deep Learning is almost like biotechnology or genetic engineering. We have created simulated learning machines, we don't know precisely how they work, however that's not preventing anyone from innovating.

https://medium.com/intuitionmachine/10-deep-learning-trends-and-predictions-for-2017-f28ca0666669

Chapter-5: Differencebetween Artificial Intelligence (AI), Machine Learning, and Deep Learning?

5.1 What are the Difference between Artificial Intelligence (AI), Machine Learning, and Deep Learning?

By <u>Glenn Evan Touger,</u> Jun 13, 2017; Uncategorized

It seems as if these three terms are appearing everywhere these days, from news stories to press releases and even TV shows and advertising. For many of us, when we hear artificial intelligence (or AI), we think of either it is Commander Data from Star Trek (the utopian version) or Cylons from Battlestar Galactica (the dystopian version). But what does AI really mean? And how is it different from machine learning (ML) and deep learning (DL)?

Here at Prowess, we've been taking on more and more projects that touch on these technologies. In this post, I'll pass on some of what we've learned about what the terms mean, how the technologies are changing our lives, and what hardware and software developments are enabling AI technologies to take off.

Artificial Intelligence

AI is an umbrella term that dates from the 1950s. Essentially, it refers to computer software that can reason and adapt based on sets of rules and data. The original goals for AI were to mimic human intelligence. Computers, from the outset, have excelled at performing complex calculations quickly; but until recently, they couldn't always identify a dog from a fox or your brother from a stranger. Even now, computers frequently struggle to perform some tasks that humans do almost subconsciously. So why are some tasks so difficult for computers to perform?

As humans, our brains are collecting and processing information constantly. We take in data from all our senses and store it away as experiences that we can draw from to make inferences about new situations. In other words, we can respond to new information and situations by making reasoned assumptions based on past experiences and knowledge.

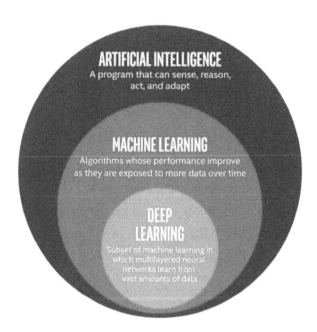

Figure1: Artificial Intelligence is an umbrella term, encompassing machine learning and deep learning [1]

AI, in its basic form, is not nearly as sophisticated. For computers to make useful decisions, they need us to provide them with two things:

- Lots and lots of relevant data
- Specific rules on how to examine that data

The rules involved in AI are usually binary questions that the computer program asks in sequence until it can provide a relevant answer. (For example, identify a dog breed by comparing it to other varieties, one pair at a time. Or playing checkers by measuring the outcome of available moves, one at a time.) If the program repeatedly fails to determine an answer, the programmers have to create more rules that are specific to the problem at hand. In this form, AI is not very adaptable, but it can still be useful because modern processors are capable of working through massive sets of rules and data in a short time. The IBM Watson computer is a good example of a basic AI system.

Machine Learning

The next stage in the development of AI is to use machine learning (ML). ML relies on neural networks– computer systems modeled on the human brain and nervous system—which can classify information into categories based on elements that those categories contain (for example, photos of dogs or heavy metal songs). ML uses probability to make decisions or predictions about data with a reasonable degree of certainty. In addition, it is capable of refining itself when given feedback on whether it is right or wrong. ML can modify how it analyzes data (or what data is relevant) in order to improve its chances of making a correct decision in the future. ML works relatively well for shape detection, like identifying types of objects or letters for transliteration.

The neural networks used for ML were developed in the 1980s but, because they are computationally intensive, they have only been viable on a large scale since the advent of GPUs in 2015, in conjunction with high-performing CPUs.

Deep Learning

Deep learning (DL) is essentially a subset of ML that extends ML capabilities across multilayered neural networks to go beyond just categorizing data. DL can actually learn—self-train, essentially—from massive amounts of data. With DL, it's possible to combine the unique ability of computers to process massive amounts of information quickly, with the human-like ability to take in, categorize, learn, and adapt. Together, these skills allow modern DL programs to perform advanced tasks, such as identifying cancerous tissue in MRI scans. DL also makes it possible to develop driverless cars and designer medications that are tailored to an individual's genome.

ML and DL are Transforming Computing for Businesses and Consumers

Both ML and DL capabilities have been seeping into our daily lives over the last several years, with the rate of change accelerating recently. It seems as if AI, ML, and DL topics are appearing everywhere lately, from technology news stories to company marketing materials and websites. The technologies are undisputedly altering the applications and services landscapes for both enterprises and consumers.

For example, enterprise businesses can use ML and DL to mine much deeper into the data offered by social media, the Internet of Things (IoT), and traditional sources of customer and product data. By combining servers built on modern GPUs and CPUs with accelerated storage and networking hardware, companies can rapidly analyze massive quantities of data in near real time. ML and DL software can identify trends, issues, or opportunities for new products and services by learning over time which data is relevant and important for generating useful insights.

Consumers are benefiting from years of research and investment by Google, Amazon, Apple, Microsoft, and other big players. The personal assistants from these companies are battling for dominance in voice-activated control of online searches and control of apps, devices, and services. As a result, we can sit comfortably on our couches and use voice controls to check our emails and the weather, to start playing music, to purchase groceries, and to turn off the lights. We can also get much more accurate recommendations for music, books, news, and products based on our tastes and interests.

AI is also integrated with virtual reality. Google recently announced new technology that lets you point your phone camera at an object to automatically identify it or take an appropriate action based on the target. For example, you could point the camera at a flower to find out its name, or point at a concert poster for an option to purchase tickets.

AI Use Is Vast and Expanding

AI advancements are continuously fueled by new computer technologies. One of the most recent advancements comes from Google in the form of Tensor Processing Units (TPUs). TPUs are contributing to the widespread adoption of AI because they accelerate the training and running of ML models and they can be easily programmed using TensorFlow, a popular open-source machine learning framework.

As compute times continue to drop, AI adoption rates will likely rise proportionally. We could very well be at the beginning of a golden age for medical advancements alone, based on advanced ML and DL capabilities. But we'll likely see major breakthroughs across many fields, as businesses take advantage of all that AI can offer. Who knows, someday advanced neural networks might even lead to a human-like cyborg.

Intel has a series of web pages and videos on AI, if you're interested in learning more, or if you want to explore AI programming opportunities. And as always, follow Prowess on our blog, Twitter, and LinkedIn for insights on the latest technologies.

[1] Image source: Intel. "How to Get Started as a Developer in AI"? October 2016. https://software.intel.com/en-us/articles/how-to-get-started-as-a-developer-in-ai.

https://www.prowesscorp.com/whats-the-difference-between-artificial-intelligence-ai-machine-learning-and-deep-learning/

5.2   What Is the Difference Between Deep Learning, Machine Learning and AI?

Bernard Marr, **CONTRIBUTOR** (Opinions expressed by Forbes Contributors are their own).

Over the past few years, the term "deep learning" has firmly worked its way into business language when the conversation is about Artificial Intelligence (AI), Big Data and analytics. And with good reason – it is an approach to AI which is showing great promise when it comes to developing the autonomous, self-teaching systems which are revolutionizing many industries.

Deep Learning is used by Google in its voice and image recognition algorithms, by Netflix and Amazon to decide what you want to watch or buy next, and by researchers at MIT to predict the future. The ever-growing industry which has established itself to sell these tools is always keen to talk about how revolutionary this all is. But what exactly is it? And is it just another fad being used to push "old fashioned" AI on us, under a sexy new label?

In my last article I wrote about the difference between AI andMachine Learning (ML). While ML is often described as a sub-discipline of AI, it's better to think of it as the current state-of-the-art – it's the field of AI which today is showing the most promise at providing tools that industry and society can use to drive change.

In turn, it's probably most helpful to think of Deep Learning as the cutting-edge of the cutting-edge. ML takes some of the core ideas of AI and focuses them on solving real-world problems with neural networks designed to mimic our own decision-making. Deep Learning focuses even more narrowly on a subset of ML tools and techniques, and applies them to solving just about any problem which requires "thought" – human or artificial.

How does it work?

Essentially Deep Learning involves feeding a computer system a lot of data, which it can use to make decisions about other data. This data is fed through neural networks, as is the case in machine learning. These networks–logical constructions which ask a series of binary true/false questions, or extract a numerical value, of every bit of data which pass through them, and classify it according to the answers received.

Because Deep Learning work is focused on developing these networks, they become what are known as Deep Neural Networks – logic networks of the complexity needed to deal with classifying datasets as large as, say, Google's image library, or Twitter's fire hose of tweets.

With datasets as comprehensive as these, and logical networks sophisticated enough to handle their classification, it becomes trivial for a computer to take an image and state with a high probability of accuracy what it represents to humans.

Shutter stock

Pictures present a great example of how this works, because they contain a lot of different elements and it isn't easy for us to grasp how a computer, with its one-track, calculation-focused mind, can learn to interpret them in the same way as us. But Deep Learning can be applied to any form of data – machine signals, audio, video, speech, and written words – to produce conclusions that seem as if they have been arrived at by humans – very, very fast ones. Let's look at a practical example.

Bernard Marr is a best-selling author & keynote speaker on business, technology and big data. His new book is Data Strategy. To read his future posts simply join his network here.

https://www.forbes.com/sites/bernardmarr/2016/12/08/what-is-the-difference-between-deep-learning-machine-learning-and-ai/#6c9f79c426cf

5.3   Know the Difference between AI, Machine Learning, and Deep Learning

By ZayanGuedim**; June 24, 2017**

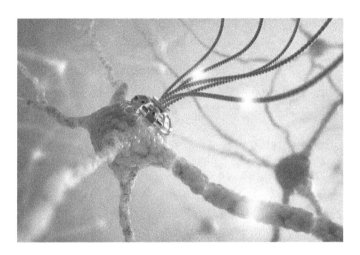

Kts design, shutterstock.com

AI is defined by many terms that crop up everywhere and are often used interchangeably. Read through to better know the difference between AI, Machine Learning, and Deep Learning.

Artificial Intelligence is, locally, a computer algorithm tasked with solving input problems based on accessible data and operational parameters, with respect to the amount of computational power available to the algorithm. More generally, AI is the name given to machine intelligence.

With the vast field of AI are specific concepts like machinelearning and deep learning.

AI, Machine Learning and Deep Learning are close but not the same.

In the same way, as Russian Matryoshka dolls where the small doll is nested inside the bigger one, each of the three segments (Deep Learning,

ML and AI) is a subset of the other. Advances in these three technologies are already revolutionizing many aspects of modern life, and although very much related, they are not the same.

In this post, we'll begin with the biggest doll "AI" and work our way down to the smallest.

Know the Difference Between AI, Machine Learning, and Deep Learning:

1. Artificial Intelligence

As a branch of computer science, AI is an area of research aiming to reproduce the various cognitive capacities of human sentience, especially the ability to solve complex problems, in machines. Admittedly, that's one broad definition of AI, which is a broad and fertile domain itself, open to other scientific and technological disciplines.

AI may refer to NPCs (non-player characters) in video games, image recognition systems, voice and speech recognition platforms, autonomous vehicles, predictive algorithms and other specialized computer programs.

All these forms of AI have one thing in common: they are based on pre-defined input, in other words, programmed beforehand to carry out a specific task. That leads us to the next level, machines that learn by themselves.

2. Machine Learning

A subset of AI, Machine Learning focuses on learning abilities, or how to make machines learn on their own. Without the need to hand-code instructions, ML systems get access to large datasets, apply their knowledge, train and learn from mistakes to complete a specific task.

For example, IBM's Deep Blue–which beat chess master Garry Kasparov in 1997–is not strictly a Machine Learning system because it wasn't able to cross-reference past moves and matches.

However, the Google AlphaGo that beat world champion **Lee Sedol** at the game of Go is a machine learning platform that recalled hundreds of previous plays to inform its tactics.

ML systems sift through data, learn patterns and predict outcomes, that why Machine Learning tools are at the top of interests for data-driven businesses.

3. Deep Learning

As a subfield of Machine Learning, and a sub-subset of AI, Deep Learning is automatic learning technology based on deep neural networks. When you know the difference between AI and terms that further define it, you are practicing the very concept applied to these systems.

A DL algorithm is made of layers of artificial nodes or "neurons", forming sort of a virtual computer where each layer performs simple calculations that serve as input to the following layer. That translates to huge gains in time and efficiency of the whole system. Like with machine learning, these systems are also free of **catastrophic forgetting**, in that they are able to recall data from past computations and apply them to present solutions.

Expensive and requiring huge storage and processing resources to train, DL systems are being developed by major companies, such as Amazon, Facebook, Google, IBM, and Microsoft, and will almost certainly be given the power to make influential decisions in the near future.

https://edgylabs.com/know-the-difference-between-ai-machine-learning-deep-learning/

5.4   Difference between Machine Learning, Data Science, AI, Deep Learning, and Statistics

By <u>Electronics media</u>**; February 18, 2017**

In this article, I clarify the various roles of the data scientist, and how data science compares and overlaps with related fields such as machine learning, deep learning, AI, statistics, IoT, operations research, and applied mathematics. As data science is a broad discipline, I start by describing the different types of data scientists that one may encounter in any business setting: you might even discover that you are a data scientist yourself, without knowing it. As in any scientific discipline, data scientists may borrow techniques from related disciplines, though we have developed our own arsenal, especially techniques and algorithms to handle very large unstructured data sets in automated ways, even without human interactions, to perform transactions in real-time or to make predictions.

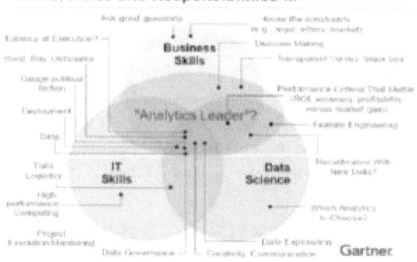

Different Types of Data Scientists: To get started and gain some historical perspective, you can read my article about 9 types of data scientists, published in 2014, or my article where I compare data science with 16 analytic disciplines, also published in 2014.

The following articles, published during the same time period, are still useful:

- Data Scientist versus Data Architect
- Data Scientist versus Data Engineer
- Data Scientist versus Statistician
- Data Scientist versus Business Analyst

More recently (August 2016) Ajit Jaokar discussed Type A (Analytics) versus Type B (Builder) data scientist:

The Type A Data Scientist can code well enough to work with data but is not necessarily an expert. The Type A data scientist may be an expert in experimental design, forecasting, modeling, statistical inference, or other things typically taught in statistics departments. Generally speaking though, the work product of a data scientist is not "p-values and confidence intervals" as academic statistics sometimes seems to suggest (and as it sometimes is for traditional statisticians working in the pharmaceutical industry, for example). At Google, Type A Data Scientists are known variously as Statistician, Quantitative Analyst, Decision Support Engineering Analyst, or Data Scientist, and probably a few more.

Type B Data Scientist: The B is for Building. Type B Data Scientists share some statistical background with Type A, but they are also very strong coders and may be trained software engineers. The Type B Data Scientist is mainly interested in using data "in production." They build models which interact with users, often serving recommendations (products, people you may know, ads, movies, search results).

I also wrote about the ABCD's of business processes optimization where D stands for data science, C for computer science, B for business science, and A for analytics science. Data science may or may not involve coding or mathematical practice, as you can read in my article on low-level versus high-level data science. In a startup, data scientists generally wear several hats, such as executive, data miner, data engineer or architect, researcher, statistician, modeler (as in predictive modeling) or developer.

While the data scientist is generally portrayed as a coder experienced in R, Python, SQL, Hadoop and statistics, this is just the tip of the iceberg, made popular by data camps focusing on teaching some elements of data science. But just like a lab technician can call herself a physicist, the real physicist is much more than that, and her domains of expertise are varied: astronomy, mathematical physics, nuclear physics (which is borderline chemistry), mechanics, electrical engineering, signal processing (also a sub-field of data science) and many more. The same can be said about data scientists: fields are as varied as bioinformatics, information technology, simulations and quality control, computational finance, epidemiology, industrial engineering, and even number theory.

In my case, over the last 10 years, I specialized in machine-to-machine and device-to-device communications, developing systems to automatically process large data sets, to perform automated transactions: for instance, purchasing Internet traffic or automatically generating content. It implies developing algorithms that work with unstructured data, and it is at the intersection of AI (artificial intelligence,) IoT (Internet of things,) and data science. This is referred to as deep data science. It is relatively math-free, and it involves relatively little coding (mostly API's), but it is quite data-intensive (including building data systems) and based on brand new statistical technology designed specifically for this context.

Prior to that, I worked on credit card fraud detection in real time. Earlier in my career (circa 1990) I worked on image remote sensing technology, among other things to identify patterns (or shapes or features, for instance lakes) in satellite images and to perform image segmentation: at that time, my research was labeled as computational statistics, but the people doing the exact same thing in the computer science department next door in my home university, called their research artificial intelligence. Today, it would be called data science or artificial intelligence, the sub-domains being signal processing, computer vision or IoT.

Also, data scientists can be found anywhere in the lifecycle of data science projects, at the data gathering stage, or the data exploratory stage, all the way up to statistical modeling and maintaining existing systems.

2. Machine Learning versus Deep Learning

Before digging deeper into the link between data science and machine learning, let's briefly discuss machine learning and deep learning. Machine learning is a set of algorithms that train on a data set to make predictions or take actions in order to optimize some systems. For instance, supervised classification algorithms are used to classify potential clients into good or bad prospects, for loan purposes, based on historical data. The techniques involved, for a given task (e.g. supervised clustering), are varied: naive Bayes, SVM, neural nets, ensembles, association rules, decision trees, logistic regression, or a combination of many.

All of this is a subset of data science. When these algorithms are automated, as in automated piloting or driver-less cars, it is called AI, and more specifically, deep learning. Click here for another article comparing machine learning with deep learning. If the data collected comes from sensors and if it is transmitted via the Internet, then it is machine learning or data science or deep learning applied to IoT.

Some people have a different definition for deep learning. They consider deep learning as neural networks (a machine learning technique) with a deeper layer. The question was asked on Quora recently, and below is a more detailed explanation (source: Quora)

AI (Artificial intelligence) is a subfield of computer science, that was created in the 1960s, and it was (is) concerned with solving tasks that are easy for humans, but hard for computers. In particular, a so-called Strong AI would be a system that can do anything a human can (perhaps without purely physical things). This is fairly generic, and includes all kinds of tasks, such as planning, moving around in the world, recognizing objects and sounds, speaking, translating, performing social or business transactions, creative work (making art or poetry), etc.

NLP (Natural language processing) is simply the part of AI that has to do with language (usually written).

Machine learning is concerned with one aspect of this: given some AI problem that can be described in discrete terms (e.g. out of a particular set of actions, which one is the right one), and given a lot of information about the world, figure out what is the "correct" action, without having the programmer program it in. Typically some outside process is needed to judge whether the action was correct or not. In mathematical terms, it's a function: you feed in some input, and you want it to produce the right output, so the whole problem is simply to build a model of this mathematical function in some automatic way. To draw a distinction with AI, if I can write a very clever program that has human-like behavior, it can be AI, but unless its parameters are automatically learned from data, it's not machine learning.

Deep learning is one kind of machine learning that's very popular now. It involves a particular kind of mathematical model that can be thought of as a composition of simple blocks (function composition) of a certain type, and where some of these blocks can be adjusted to better predict the final outcome.

What is the difference between machine learning and statistics?

This article tries to answer the question. The author writes that statistics is machine learning with confidence intervals for the quantities being predicted or estimated. I tend to disagree, as I have built engineer-friendly confidence intervals that don't require any mathematical or statistical knowledge.

3. Data Science versus Machine Learning

Machine learning and statistics are part of data science. The word *learning* in machine learning means that the algorithms depend on some data, used as a training set, to fine-tune some model or algorithm parameters. This encompasses many techniques such as regression, naive Bayes or supervised clustering. But not all techniques fit in this category. For instance, unsupervised clustering – a statistical and data science technique – aims at detecting clusters and cluster structures without any a-prior knowledge or training set to help the classification algorithm. A human being is needed to label the clusters found. Some techniques are hybrid, such as semi-supervised classification. Some pattern detection or density estimation techniques fit in this category.

Data science is much more than machine learning though. Data, in data science, may or may not come from a *machine* or mechanical process (survey data could be manually collected, clinical trials involve a specific type of small data) and it might have nothing to do with *learning* as I have just discussed. But the main difference is the fact that data science covers the whole spectrum of data processing, not just the algorithmic or statistical aspects. In particular, data science also covers

- data integration
- distributed architecture
- automating machine learning
- data visualization
- dashboards and BI
- data engineering
- deployment in production mode
- automated, data-driven decisions

Article Written by: Vincent Granville

For more information visit: http://www.datasciencecentral.com/profiles/blogs/difference-between-machine-learning-data-science-ai-deep-learning

https://www.electronicsmedia.info/2017/02/18/difference-machine-learning-data-science-ai-deep-learning-statistics/

ABOUT THE AUTHOR

Award winning Key Note Speaker at International Level, Professor Ajit Kumar Roy is an acclaimed researcher and consultant. Prof. Roy obtained his M.Sc. degree in Statistics and joined Agricultural Research Service (ARS) of Indian Council of Agricultural Research (ICAR) as a Scientist (Statistics) in 1976. In recent past was engaged as National Consultant (Impact Assessment), for East &North-Eastern States of India at National Agricultural Innovation Project (World Bank funded) of ICAR. Prior to that, he had served as a Consultant (Statistics) at Central Agricultural University, Agartala. Earlier had served at CIFA, ICAR, as Principal Scientist and was involved in applied research in the areas of ICT, Statistics, Bioinformatics Analytics, and Economics. At International level, he served as a Computer Specialist at SAARC Agricultural Information Centre (SAIC), Dhaka, Bangladesh for over 3 years. The author with over 45 years of research and teaching experience in Statistical Analysis, Analytics, and information & Knowledge management edited eighteen books and several conference proceedings. Besides, published over 100 articles in refereed journals. His recent best-sellers are Facts and Figures of Demonetization in India-Reactions, Views and comments; Big Data and Data Science Initiative in India- Upcoming Job Opportunities: 'Applied Big Data Analytics'; 'Impact of Big Data Analytics on Business, Economy, Health Care and Society'; 'Data Science - A Career Option for 21st Century';' Self-Learning of Bioinformatics Online'; 'Applied Bioinformatics, Statistics and Economics in Fisheries Research' and 'Applied Computational Biology and Statistics in Biotechnology and Bioinformatics'; Emerging Technologies of the 21st Century.

He is a Member, Organizing Committee Board for the 6th International Conference on 'Biometrics and Biostatistics' to be held during, November 13-14, 2017 Atlanta, Georgia, USA. Editorial Board Member, Jacobs Journal of Biostatistics, Jacobs Publishers, 900 Great Hills, Trail # 150 w, Austin, Texas. Now he is a Visiting Professor, question setter and examiner of four Indian Universities.

www.ingramcontent.com/pod-product-compliance
Lightning Source LLC
LaVergne TN
LVHW022302060326

832902LV00020B/3238